100 CLASSIC HIKES IN
NORTHERN CALIFORNIA

100 CLASSIC HIKES IN
NORTHERN CALIFORNIA

Sierra Nevada / Cascade Mountains / Klamath Mountains / Coast Range and North Coast / San Francisco Bay Area

John R. Soares and Marc J. Soares

THIRD EDITION

THE MOUNTAINEERS BOOKS

To our father, John Severin Soares,
who introduced us to the beauty of nature
and shared with us his love of outdoor adventure

THE MOUNTAINEERS BOOKS
is the nonprofit publishing arm of The Mountaineers Club, an organization founded in 1906 and dedicated to the exploration, preservation, and enjoyment of outdoor and wilderness areas.

1001 SW Klickitat Way, Suite 201, Seattle, WA 98134

© 2008 by John R. Soares and Marc J. Soares

First edition published in 1994 as *100 Hikes in Northern California*. Second edition: first printing 2000, second printing 2004, third printing 2007. Third edition: first printing 2008.

Published simultaneously in Great Britain by Cordee, 3a DeMontfort Street, Leicester, England, LE1 7HD

Manufactured in China

Copy Editor: Heath Lynn Silberfeld / enough said
Series cover and book design: The Mountaineers Books
Layout: Elizabeth Cromwell/Books in Flight
Maps: Moore Creative Design
Photographs by Marc J. Soares unless otherwise noted. Additional photographs by John R. Soares.

Cover photograph: Desolation Wilderness vista
Frontispiece: Mirror Lake in the Trinity Alps

Library of Congress Cataloging-in-Publication Data
Soares, John R.
  100 classic hikes in Northern California / by John R. Soares and Marc J. Soares.—3rd ed.
    p. cm.
  Includes bibliographical references and index.
  ISBN-13: 978-1-59485-062-2
  ISBN-10: 1-59485-062-3
  1. Hiking—California, Northern—Guidebooks. 2. Backpacking—California, Northern—Guidebooks. 3. California, Northern—Guidebooks. I. Soares, Marc J. II. Title. III. Title: One hundred classic hikes in Northern California.
GV199.42.C2S63 2008
917.94—dc22
                    2007036984

CONTENTS

COAST RANGE AND NORTH COAST

SAN FRANCISCO BAY AREA

KEY TO MAP SYMBOLS

Symbol	Meaning	Symbol	Meaning
(5)	Interstate highway	P	Parking
(101)	U.S. highway	▟	Ranger station
(89)	State highway or improved road	▪	Building
——	Road	▲	Mountain
- - - -	Dirt road	❀	Springs
· · · · ·	Trail	↘	Waterfall
◄— — —	Unhiked trail	=	Bridge
· · · · · ·	Cross-country trail	⋀	Campground
◄	Directional symbol	●	Place of interest
		⊼	Picnic area

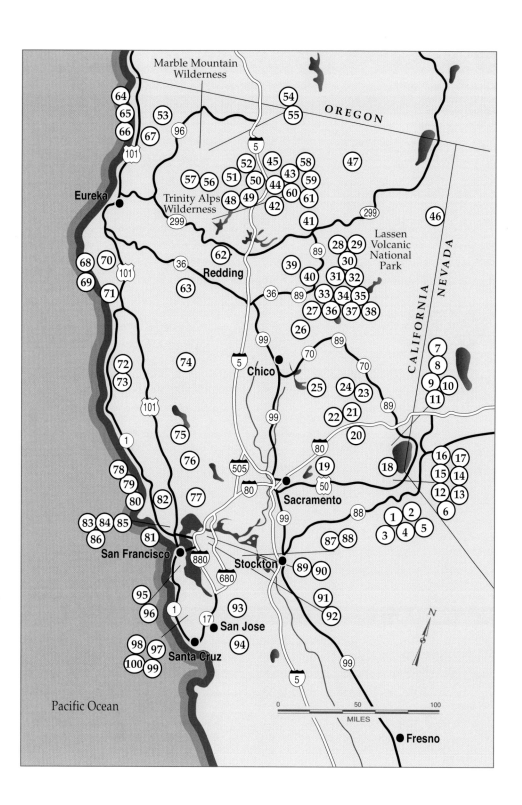

Marble Mountain
Wilderness

OREGON

Eureka

Trinity Alps
Wilderness

Redding

Lassen
Volcanic
National
Park

CALIFORNIA   NEVADA

Chico

Sacramento

San Francisco

Stockton

San Jose

Santa Cruz

Pacific Ocean

Fresno

N

0   50   100
MILES

HIKE NUMBER AND NAME	DISTANCE	DIFFICULTY	HIGHLIGHTS
Sierra Nevada			
1. Granite Lake	4.4	E	mountain views, beautiful lake
2. Winnemucca Lake and Round Top	6.3	S	lakes, flowers, peak climb, vista
3. Emigrant Lake	9.0	E	meadows, lake, craggy peaks
4. Lake Margaret	5.0	E	creek, lake, granite mountains
5. Dardanelles and Round Lakes	8.0	M	streams, meadows, flowers, lakes
6. Tamarack and Ralston Lakes	9.2	E	tall peaks, gorgeous lakes
7. Sylvia and Lyons Lakes	10.0	EM	creek, lakes, Sierra views
8. Grouse, Hemlock, and Smith Lakes	5.6	M	inviting lakes, mountain vistas
9. Twin and Island Lakes	6.2	EM	lakes, Crystal Range views
10. Tyler and Gertrude Lakes	8.0	MS	pristine lakes, stony spires
11. Maud, Lois, and Zitella Lakes	24.7	MS	Desolation Wilderness trek
12. Lake Aloha, Lake of the Woods, and Ropi Lake	13.9	S	stunning lakes, high peaks
13. Half Moon Lake	12.0	M	exquisite glacial cirque, peaks
14. Mount Tallac	11.0	S	360-degree Tahoe/Sierra vista
15. Dicks Lake, Gilmore Lake, Lake Aloha, and Middle Velma Lake	30.0	M	classic Desolation backpacking
16. Eagle Lake and the Velma Lakes	9.2	S	gorgeous lakes and mountains
17. Emerald Bay	10.6	EM	vistas, Lake Tahoe shore
18. Crag Lake and Rubicon Lake	16.2	M	creeks, lakes, mountains
19. North Fork of the American River	5.0	S	river, rolling hills
20. Loch Leven Lakes	7.2	M	easy access, pretty lakes
21. Sand Ridge and the Five Lakes Basin	12.0	M	views, lakes, relative solitude
22. Crooked Lakes Trail to Penner Lake	6.0	E	many lakes, good swimming
23. Mount Elwell	8.2	MS	many lakes, broad vistas
24. Smith Lake to Wades Lake	13.8	M	inviting lakes, relative solitude
25. Feather Falls	8.8	M	creeks, 640-foot waterfall
26. Deer Creek	4.6	M	steep canyon, creek, waterfall
27. Mill Creek	29.6	M	beautiful canyon, spring backpacking
Cascade Mountains			
28. Caribou Wilderness	11.5	EM	forests, lakes, solitude
29. Mount Harkness	6.4	M	far vistas, lake swim
30. Brokeoff Mountain	7.2	S	awesome views from high peak
31. Mill Creek Falls and Ridge Lakes	5.6	MS	50-foot waterfall, alpine lakes
32. Lassen Peak	5.0	MS	signature summit, spectacular vista
33. Crumbaugh Lake and Bumpass Hell	6.0	M	fumaroles, mudpots, boiling lakes
34. Kings Creek Falls and Sifford Lakes	5.3	M	gorgeous waterfall, secluded lakes

KEY: E=easy, M=moderate, S=strenuous, EM=easy to moderate, MS=moderate to strenuous, ES=easy to strenuous

HIKE NUMBER AND NAME	DISTANCE	DIFFICULTY	HIGHLIGHTS
35. Twin Lakes, Horseshoe Lake, and Grassy Swale	15.2	EM	forests, lakes, creeks, views
36. Terrace, Shadow, and Cliff Lakes	8.4	M	waterfall, meadows, lakes
37. Chaos Crags and Manzanita Creek	10.6	M	volcanic features, lake, creek, meadow
38. Cinder Cone, Snag Lake, and Butte Lake	14.0	MS	cinder cone, big lakes, meadows
39. Magee Peak and Thousand Lakes Wilderness	12.6	MS	solitude, deep lakes, far views
40. Subway Cave and Hat Creek	9.1	M	lava tube, rushing cold creek
41. Burney Falls	4.9	E	stunning waterfall, cool stream canyon
42. McCloud River's Three Waterfalls	3.8	E	cool river canyon with three large waterfalls
43. Mount Shasta Summit	12.0	S	top-of-the-world view, challenging climb
44. Panther Meadows, South Gate Meadows, and Gray Butte	8.6	M	lush meadows, spectacular views
45. Black Butte	5.2	M	young volcano, Mount Shasta view
46. Patterson Lake and Squaw Peak	18.0	M	quiet forests, large lake, Nevada, Oregon views
47. Whitney Butte	7.0	E	cinder cone, high desert, open views
Klamath Mountains			
48. Sulphur Creek and Burstarse Falls	6.8	M	secluded waterfall, steep granitic spires
49. Castle Dome	5.8	S	granite wonderland, far views
50. Castle Lake to Heart Lake and Mount Bradley Ridge	5.0	M	mountain lakes, wide vistas
51. Seven Lakes Basin	6.0	M	lake swim, Trinity Alps view
52. Mount Eddy and the Deadfall Lakes	10.0	MS	peak climb, lakes, views
53. Bear Lake	6.0	M	solitude, swimming, rare trees
54. Paradise Lake	15.2	MS	creeks, lake, steep peaks
55. Sky High Lakes and Summit Lake	18.0	MS	lakes, swimming, views
56. Big Bear Lake	10.0	M	easy access to alpine lake
57. Caribou, Emerald, and Sapphire Lakes	30.6	S	Trinity Alps trek: lakes, peaks
58. Horseshoe and Ward Lakes	21.4	MS	roaring creek, alpine lakes
59. Granite Lake and Seven Up Gap	15.6	MS	deep lake, far views
60. Four Lakes Loop	23.9	MS	meadows, lakes, wildflowers, views
61. Canyon Creek Lakes and Boulder Creek Lakes	23.9	S	inviting lakes, steep peaks
62. Mill Creek/Tower House Historical District	5.6	E	mining history, creek, swimming
63. North Yolla Bolly Trails	16.1	MS	meadows, lakes, peaks, views
Coast Range and North Coast			
64. Hidden Beach and False Klamath Rock	8.0	EM	dramatic coast, secluded beach
65. Ossagon Rocks and Gold Bluffs Beach	7.0	E	beach stroll and exploration

HIKE NUMBER AND NAME	DISTANCE	DIFFICULTY	HIGHLIGHTS
66. Fern Canyon and Gold Bluffs Beach	6.3	M	ferns, redwoods, beachcombing
67. Redwood Creek to Tall Trees Grove	18.0	EM	creek, skyscraper redwoods
68. Punta Gorda Lighthouse	6.0	E	ocean, beach, tide pools, sea lions
69. Lost Coast: Bear Harbor to Usal Camp	33.0	S	seclusion, redwoods, mountains, ocean
70. Bull Creek Flats	9.4	E	tall redwoods, creek, river
71. Tan Oak Springs/Durphy Creek Loop	4.4	EM	redwoods, spring, stream
72. Ecological Staircase Nature Trail	5.4	E	beach, seastacks, pygmy forest
73. Fern Canyon Trail to Pygmy Forest	7.9	E	redwoods, ferns, pygmy forest
74. Snow Mountain	8.0	M	two summits, broad vistas
75. Anderson Marsh	5.0	E	open woodlands, flowers, marsh, birds
76. Mount Saint Helena	10.0	M	wide trail, wine country views
77. Bald Mountain	6.4	M	open foothills, spring wildflowers
San Francisco Bay Area			
78. Tomales Point	9.4	E	ocean vistas, tule elk
79. Home Bay, Drakes Estero, and Sunset Beach	7.8	EM	estuary, shorebirds, seals, views
80. Bear Valley and Arch Rock	12.0	E	meadows, flowers, creek, ocean views
81. Pelican Lake and Wildcat Beach	10.2	M	lakes, flowers, ocean views
82. Bolinas Ridge	10.2	EM	bald hills, oaks, bay views
83. Mount Tamalpais: Pantoll Ranger Station to Stinson Beach	7.5	M	forest, ocean views, beach
84. Mount Tamalpais: The Summit to Pantoll Ranger Station	9.0	M	Bay Area vista, forests
85. Muir Woods	6.0	EM	towering redwoods, shaded creek
86. Tennessee Valley Beach	4.0	E	wildflowers, lagoon, beach, ocean
87. Mount Diablo Loop	7.1	M	far vistas, spring flowers, oaks
88. Mount Diablo's Back and Mitchell Canyons	8.6	MS	spring flowers, oaks, open hillsides
89. Briones Regional Park Trails	8.4	EM	rolling hills, broad vistas
90. Wildcat Canyon Regional Park Trails	11.5	M	creek, pond, views
91. Las Trampas Regional Wilderness	15.5	M	grasslands, forests, views
92. Redwood Regional Park Trails	8.4	EM	ridge walk, views, redwoods
93. Grant Park's Peak 2987	9.0	M	oak woodlands, mountain vistas
94. Henry W. Coe State Park: Coit Lake	26.0	MS	wildflowers, hills, creeks, lakes
95. North Peak Montara Mountain	6.0	S	magnificent ocean and mountain views
96. Purisima Creek and Harkins Ridge	7.0	M	redwoods, mountain and ocean views
97. Castle Rock and Goat Rock	5.8	M	big rocks, ocean views
98. Butano State Park Trails	6.2	ES	quiet redwood groves, ocean view
99. Silver Falls and Skyline to the Sea Trail	10.2	M	redwoods, creeks, waterfalls
100. Berry Creek Falls and Skyline to the Sea Trail	16.3	ES	redwoods, waterfalls, ocean views

KEY: E=easy, M=moderate, S=strenuous, EM=easy to moderate, MS=moderate to strenuous, ES=easy to strenuous

ACKNOWLEDGMENTS

The thorough revision of this edition would not have been achieved without the expert knowledge of the many employees of the parks and national forests who read through the hikes and reviewed the maps to make the information as accurate as possible. Thus we extend immense gratitude to Marilyn Muse-Meyer and Susanne Johnson of Eldorado National Forest; Don Lane of the Lake Tahoe Basin Management Unit; Brian Barton of Emerald Bay State Park; Phil Sexton and Dean Lutz of Tahoe National Forest; Judy Schaber and Gary Rogers of Plumas National Forest; Barbara Jackson and Jan Sorochtey of Lassen National Forest; Nancy Bailey and Karen Haner of Lassen Volcanic National Park; Andrew Urlie of McArthur–Burney Falls Memorial State Park; Don Lee, Steve Gut, Judy Hanevold, and Barbara Paolinetti of Shasta-Trinity National Forest; Brett Mizeur of Castle Crags State Park; Katie Eskra at Lava Beds National Monument; Phil McNeal, Deems Burton, and Veronica Selvage of Klamath National Forest; Steve Thede of Whiskeytown-Shasta-Trinity National Recreation Area; Jeff Denny and Debbie Savage of Redwood National and State Parks; Keven Harder of Sinkyone Wilderness State Park; Emily Peterson of Humboldt Redwoods State Park; Valerie Marshall of Jug Handle State Reserve and Van Damme State Park; Tom Nixon of Anderson Marsh State Park; Sandy Jones of Bothe–Napa Valley State Park; Robyn Ishimatsu of Sugarloaf Ridge State Park; Bill Michaels of Point Reyes National Seashore; Glen Ryburn of Mount Tamalpais State Park; Mia Monroe of Muir Woods National Monument; Jeremy Olson of Mount Diablo State Park; Jim Townsend of East Bay Regional Park District; Cameron Bowers and Randy Neufeld of Henry W. Coe State Park; Theresa Nance of Joseph D. Grant County Park; Paul Keel of Half Moon Bay State Beaches; Elaina Cuzick of the Midpeninsula Regional Open Space District; Jason Rule of Castle Rock State Park; Michael Grant of Butano State Park; and Kevin Williams of Big Basin Redwoods State Park.

We give special thanks to our brother, Eric Soares, commander of the Tsunami Rangers and sea kayaker extraordinaire, for hiking companionship, sage advice, and outdoors enthusiasm; and to our mother, Mozelle Fitzhugh Berta, who gave us her total support and love throughout this project and was wise enough to know that children need freedom to explore and discover.

The following wonderful people hiked the trails with us, making our trips even more enjoyable: Marc's wife, Patricia Soares, his daughter, Dionne Soares (who contributed several photos), and his son, Jake Soares; our sister, Camille Soares; and good friends Stephanie Hoffman, Rick Ramos, Noelle Boucherle, Jim Kakuk, Craig Heath, and Sue Loring.

Other family members and friends provided both good hospitality and plenty of encouragement and advice. For this we gratefully thank Les Berta, Bob Soares, Phyllis Soares, Nancy Soares, Derek Moss, Gary Matson, and Becky Ramos.

PREFACE TO THE THIRD EDITION

This third edition contains a number of improvements that will enhance your hiking experiences in Northern California. For starters, trail supervisors supplied us with the most up-to-date information on driving directions, trail routes and conditions, permit requirements, and pertinent regulations. And at the beginning of the book you'll find the "Trails at a Glance" table—it summarizes the key aspects of every hike and helps you quickly choose where you want to go. In addition, the introduction has been thoroughly revised and includes the current consensus on wilderness safety and ethics. We have also added elevation profiles for nearly all hikes; these allow you to easily estimate what sort of effort you'll need to supply in negotiating the ascents and descents of the trail. We also have included website addresses in Appendix 1 for each hike. These websites typically include much information on the human and natural history of the area, along with regulations and tips, and often also a downloadable brochure and/or map. In addition, you can find additional information on hiking in Northern California at *www.soaresoutdoors.com.*

INTRODUCTION

Secluded ocean beaches where powerful waves pulse against rock, sand, and cliff. Steep Sierra peaks stretching high above rock-ringed alpine lakes. The still, silent shade of ancient redwood forests. Hillsides carpeted with an explosion of spring wildflowers. In *100 Classic Hikes in Northern California* we offer you this and much more as we take you along trails that allow you to experience the infinite variety of nature.

The first region takes you to the foothills, lakes, and summits of the Sierra Nevada from Mokelumne Wilderness north. The second region stretches over the Cascade Mountains, with most trails traveling on or near volcanoes and areas of past volcanic activity. The third region details hikes high in the remote Klamath Mountains of far Northern California, where you'll find the most solitude. The fourth region describes hikes on and near the Pacific Coast and in the bordering Coast Range. The fifth region covers the San Francisco Bay Area, where the surprisingly numerous trails offer both solitude and beautiful scenery. Whether you want to hike in spring, summer, fall, or winter, whether you want a strenuous seven-day backpacking trip or an easy day hike, you'll find just what you desire in the following pages.

HOW TO USE THIS BOOK

The beginning of each hike description lists information in summary form that gives you a basic feel for the hike. Within the main body of the text you'll find directions to the trailhead; specific data regarding distances, trail junctions, and major sights; and a discussion of trailside natural history.

Length. This is the total round-trip distance for the hike (in miles), unless otherwise specified. Note that if you are short on time or energy, you needn't do the entire hike to enjoy beautiful surroundings. Read the main body of the text for distances to good turnaround points such as lakes, meadows, and areas with scenic views.

Hiking time. This is a subjective indicator that allows the average hiker ample time for resting, viewing scenery, and eating.

High point. This gives the elevation (in feet) of the highest point encountered on the hike.

Total elevation gain. This is the total number of feet you'll climb in getting to the main destination high point for hikes on which you return the way you came. For loop hikes it gives the total number of feet climbed during the entire hike.

Difficulty. Total elevation gain, length, necessary physical exertion, and required agility determine whether a hike is rated easy, moderate, or strenuous; however, this can vary due to local or seasonal changes. A big storm can make a steep trail very slippery and turn an easy boulder-hop across a small stream into a tricky, waist-high wade through a swift-moving current. Most people, including younger children, can do hikes with an easy rating. Moderate and strenuous hikes require careful assessment of your abilities and preparedness. Keep in mind that some hikes rated moderate or strenuous may be easy for the first two or more miles to a good turnaround point; read the hike description to find out.

Season. This gives the approximate time of year in which the trail is easily hikable. All trails below 2,000 feet elevation, including all those on or near the coast and in mountain foothills, offer year-round hiking, although they may be hot and dry during the summer. Others in the 2,000- to 4,000-foot range are snow-free for most of the winter, but before leaving to hike, check current conditions by phoning the relevant government agency (see "Information," elsewhere in this introduction, and Appendix 1). For high-elevation hikes, the season listed covers the estimated period between the time most of the trailside snow melts and the time the first major fall snowstorm hits. These times can vary, depending on the amount of precipitation in a given winter and when that first fall storm arrives, so call the agency listed in "Information" first. If you desire solitude, hike on weekdays or off-season. Also,

Corn lily

note that most state, county, and regional parks close from roughly dusk to dawn; prominently displayed signs at each park entrance and at trailheads usually give the exact times. In some cases, the access roads are locked during closed hours, which means your short moonlight stroll may turn into an overnight stay.

Water. This indicates the trailside availability of water, usually from lakes and streams, although some sources can dry up in late summer and early fall, especially in drought years. Be sure you understand how to purify water properly so you don't get giardiasis or other waterborne diseases (see "Safety"). However, for all but overnight backpacking trips, bring all the water you need from home. Of course, always stash some iodine tablets or other means of purification in your pack, just in case.

Maps. The maps in this book are for reference only. Although they are adequate for many hikes, you shouldn't rely solely on them. Get the listed United States Geological Survey (USGS) and United States Forest Service (USFS) topographic maps for more details on terrain, creeks, and so forth. These usually are sold at engineering supply stores and outdoor supply stores. Note that many USGS maps were made a while ago and may not show some of the trails described in this book; they may also show trails that no longer exist. You can purchase USGS topo maps at *www.store.usgs.gov* and at many outdoor stores. Several software packages contain USGS and other maps. The USFS maps are much more up-to-date. The USFS also sells general maps for each national forest that show all the roads and many of the trails. Visit *www.fs.fed.us/maps* to order any national forest map. These help you navigate when driving to trailheads but often are inadequate for trail guidance. Most national, state, regional, and county parks offer brochures with trail maps at the parks themselves, often for a small fee. These are usually excellent guides to an area, and they often explain natural and human history and discuss other hiking options, along with park rules.

Information. Here you will find the name of the government agency with jurisdiction over the trail. Look in Appendix 1 for the address, phone number, and website URL. Call or visit these people (in person or online) to find out about trail access and conditions and to obtain maps and wilderness permits. Wilderness permits are required for most hikes in USFS wilderness areas and for overnight trips in Lassen Volcanic National Park. Some popular areas may impose a limit on the number of permits issued; it's always wise to call ahead before going. **Note:** Some of the information in this book may have changed since the book went to press, such as trail access and the need for a wilderness permit; phone ahead to be sure that the hike is still permitted.

Elevation profiles. This feature is new to this third edition. Each elevation profile provides an approximate guide to that particular hike's ups and downs. Be sure to look carefully at the elevation numbers on the vertical axis and the mileage numbers on the horizontal axis so you have a good feel for interpreting the profile. Elevation profiles are not included for those few hikes that have only small elevation changes over large distances.

Driving directions. You'll find these in the second paragraph of each hike's text. They take you from the nearest highway or town to the trailhead. All trailheads in this book usually are accessible by all types of vehicles, including two-wheel-drive passenger cars, unless you go out of season when the road is very wet or covered with snow. Also keep in mind that odometer accuracy varies, so look for described turnoffs and the like before you reach the mileage listed in the hike description. Please be aware that you will be sharing some of those narrow national forest roads with behemoth logging trucks: look out for them, and go slow around blind corners.

Trailhead theft. Don't leave valuables in your car, and always lock the doors and close the windows tightly. Human rip-off artists aren't your only concern. Bears often visit trailhead parking areas and rip off a door or window in search of a tasty snack. Because bears follow their noses, don't leave any food or garbage in your car for them to smell.

Fees. Expect to pay entrance fees and/or permit fees at Lassen Volcanic National Park, all state parks, and many other areas.

Dogs. Many dog owners love their pets and want to take them along on hikes. As a general rule, national and state parks do not allow dogs on trails. Dogs are allowed on most trails in national forests and in some county parks. Always call ahead or check the park website to find out about the latest rules regarding dogs. You must have control of your dog at all times: leashes may be mandatory, and voice control is the minimum necessary requirement. Be sure your pet does not harass wildlife or other hikers, and always yield the right-of-way to equestrians and other hikers. Bring plastic bags to clean up after your pet.

WHAT TO TAKE

The Ten Essentials. On all hikes, always take extra clothing, extra food, sunglasses, a knife (for first aid or emergency kindling), firestarter (for wet wood), a first-aid kit, matches (in a waterproof container), flashlight (with an extra bulb and batteries), maps, and a compass. In addition, take water, a water purifier, toilet paper, and a watch. Also include an emergency signaling device, such as a whistle, mirror, or piece of brightly colored plastic or cloth. (See Appendix 3 for a complete list of supplies for both day hikes and backpacking trips.) The classic list of the Ten Essentials has evolved from a list of individual items to a list of functional systems:

1. Navigation (map and compass)
2. Sun protection (sunglasses and sunscreen)
3. Insulation (extra clothing)
4. Illumination (headlamp or flashlight)
5. First-aid supplies
6. Fire (firestarter and matches/lighter)

Steller's jay

7. Repair kit and tools (including knife)
8. Nutrition (extra food)
9. Hydration (extra water)
10. Emergency shelter

Clothing. Pack extra layers of clothes in your daypack; temperatures can drop suddenly, winds can kick up, or an unexpected storm can suddenly move in over a ridge top. At a minimum, bring pants, a sweatshirt, a knit cap, and a poncho. For many hikes you'll find that a good pair of running shoes will do just fine; however, lightweight hiking boots can be just as comfortable while providing greater ankle support, more foot protection, and better traction. For protection from the sun, wear a wide-brimmed hat, good sunglasses, and a strong sunblock.

SAFETY

Most of this book's journeys travel through areas where the hiker faces potential dangers. The following information helps you minimize the risks, but it is no substitute for reading books and taking classes devoted solely to wilderness safety, travel, and first aid. (See Appendix 2 for books on these subjects.)

Know your limitations. Don't exceed your or your group's physical conditioning, agility, and preparedness. It's better to be prudent than dead.

Traveling alone. If you decide to hike alone, inform a responsible person of your route and the time you expect to return. Once you're home again, call and confirm your safe arrival. Remember, when going alone, there is no room for error; always be alert!

Weather. Check the weather forecast before you hike. In many areas you can call the National Weather Service or check on cable TV for a weather channel, which often broadcasts up-to-the-minute forecasts several times an hour. Always bring a poncho or space blanket. Both are lightweight and will keep you fairly dry and out of the wind if you're caught in a storm or have to spend an unexpected night in the wilderness. When backpacking, you should have a good tent, a sleeping pad, and a sleeping bag that's rated for temperatures below what you expect. Also, although thunderstorms and

lightning can occur any time of the year, they are most prevalent in summer and at higher elevations. If you see tall thunderheads gathering in the vicinity, stay away from exposed ridges and peaks and wait out the show among the shorter trees in the nearest forest.

Hypothermia. This sometimes fatal physical condition occurs when body temperature drops drastically, usually through some combination of wind, wetness, cold, and fatigue. Persons suffering from hypothermia usually exhibit coordination loss, shivering, and inarticulate speech. Forethought offers the best way to avoid hypothermia: Bring warm clothes, including a windbreaker; stay dry; and avoid hikes that stretch your physical limits and those of your party. If you or an accompanying hiker shows signs of hypothermia, immediately seek shelter away from rain and wind, change into dry clothes, build a fire, and eat food that contains carbohydrates (preferably grains, breads, or candy), which are quickly converted to heat energy.

Water. The days of drinking directly from lakes and streams are over, primarily because of *Giardia lamblia,* a microorganism that can cause intense intestinal distress and has spread to much of Northern California's waters. The best way to avoid infection by Giardia (or anything else) is to boil all water for at least twenty minutes. Chemical purifiers, usually iodine compounds, are the second-best option, but treated water tastes terrible. You also can use a water-filtering device, hoping that it's not defective and that it actually meets the manufacturer's claims. Outdoor stores sell both chemical compounds and filtering devices. You'll find information about water availability at the beginning of each hike description. Keep in mind that you should always purify outdoor water. For day hikes, pack your own water from the faucet at home.

Ticks. These creatures occasionally carry Lyme disease, which they can pass to you when they drill a hole through your skin and drink your blood. Ticks inhabit brushy areas and tall grasses, where they come in contact with unsuspecting animals like you. To decrease the probability of a tick encounter, wear pants and a long-sleeved shirt and thoroughly check your skin and scalp after hiking through tick territory. If a tick does

You'll often share the backcountry with people on horses. (Photo by John R. Soares)

attach itself, you can attempt a careful removal with a tick removal kit, or visit a doctor. Always visit a doctor if you feel any symptoms after a tick bite.

Rattlesnakes. This dangerous reptile's trademark is a jointed rattle at the tail end, but it usually bites only if cornered or touched. Found below 6,000 feet elevation and active in warmer months, it frequents dry, rocky areas, brushy spots, and occasionally the sides of trails. Check both sides of the trail when you hike, and be especially careful of where you put your hands and feet when hiking off-trail. If you are bitten by a rattlesnake, stay calm and relaxed. Get to a hospital as soon as possible (preferably within twelve hours) for an antivenin shot.

Black bears. These creatures generally avoid humans and usually turn tail and run away at high speed when they see you. To lessen the chance of an unhappy encounter with a bear around the campsite, use a rope to suspend all food, garbage, and scented products (such as deodorant and toothpaste) from a tree at night (at least ten feet from the ground, ten feet from the trunk, and five feet from the branch). The tree should be both downwind and as far from camp as practical. Avoid using scented products whenever possible. Also, don't leave food scraps lying around the campsite, and be sure that no food or food smell is on your body or clothes or in your tent. Of course, never feed bears (or any other wild animals). The greatest danger occurs when

Dicks Lake in Desolation Wilderness

you get between a mother bear and her cub. If this happens, wave your arms, slowly back away, and speak to the mother in a nonthreatening voice. If a confrontation seems imminent, roll into the fetal position and play dead. Often a bear will leave once it asserts its dominance. Bears can run thirty-five miles per hour, much faster than you, so don't try to outrun a bear.

Mountain lions. You'll probably never see a mountain lion; however, they are definitely around and they will see you. General safety guidelines include keeping children and pets close to you. Also be aware that lions are attracted to four-legged prey such as deer; when you bend over or squat, you look more like food to them. If you do see a mountain lion, first pick up any small children. Then shout and extend your arms in a threatening manner, and also throw rocks. In complete contrast to what you should do in a bear attack, you should fight for your life if attacked by a lion. Note that dogs can attract mountain lions, which is a consideration if you want to take your pooch with you.

Horses. If you encounter these creatures and their riders on the trail, you must give them the right-of-way. Step to the side of the path and talk in a calm voice to the riders. This lets the horses know that you are not some strange beast that may harm them.

Poison oak. This deciduous plant, quite common below 5,000 feet, takes the form of either a vine or a shrub. Its leaves, green in spring and summer and red in fall, usually form clusters of three, although size and shape vary. When in doubt, assume a plant is poison oak. You may develop a red itchy rash after coming into contact with poison oak. If you think you've touched it, wash immediately with soap and cool water, and also wash the clothes you were wearing. Pharmacies stock ointments that help relieve the symptoms.

Ocean. When near this powerful body of water, always watch for rogue waves, especially in winter. These waves, much larger than other waves, can sweep you or members of your party into the cold, turbulent waters. Also, be careful when hiking near ocean cliffs, which are often unstable and can break off and fall to the rocks, sand, and surf below.

WILDERNESS ETHICS

Walking in the wilderness. Resist the temptation to shortcut up and down switchbacks. This destroys trailside plant life and accelerates trail erosion. Always try to minimize the impact of your feet on the land by stepping on rock or firm, dry ground when possible. Be especially careful in meadows, which contain a variety of sensitive plants. Your philosophy should be that of minimum impact, which means you strive to leave no trace of your visit. For detailed information on the leave-no-trace philosophy, visit *www.leavenotrace.org.*

Camping. Minimum-impact philosophy also applies to campsites. Select a site at least a hundred feet away from streams and rivers so that you won't disturb waterside plants or pollute the water. Whenever possible, use an existing site in the forest or on bare rock that's far from any water. Do not create new campsites. Always put a plastic tarp under your tent to keep out rainwater. Never dig ditches.

Fires. The minimum-impact hiker doesn't need a fire. Burning wood removes organic material from the ecosystem, contributes to air pollution, and scares away animal life. Instead of cozying up to a campfire, bring enough clothes to ensure your warmth at night. Those addicted to caffeine can bring caffeine pills as a substitute for morning coffee. If you must have a hot meal, bring a gas stove; however, a wide variety of enjoyable foods don't require cooking. If you insist on having a fire, do so only in or near heavily wooded areas, keep the fire small, and use only downed deadwood in an established campfire ring. When finished, douse the fire thoroughly with water until you're sure it's completely out. Note: You will need a valid fire permit for fires on any national forest property. You can obtain one at most national forest ranger stations, Bureau of Land Management offices, and California Department of Forestry and Fire Protection offices. Permits are valid throughout the state of California but are subject to local fire restrictions. Often, fires are prohibited due to the increased danger of wildfires, especially from midsummer onward and during drought years.

Washing. Detergents and food particles harm aquatic life and can alter water chemistry, so wash yourself and your dishes far from lakes and streams. Carry water off for washing to the woods or bare rock, and use biodegradable soaps available at outdoor stores.

Sanitation. Use established backcountry toilets when available. Otherwise, defecate in a shallow hole six to ten inches deep, preferably in forest duff, where covered feces will decompose quickly. Be sure your spot is at least 200 feet from water and well away from trails and campsites.

You needn't be so careful with urine because it's sterile, but do stay away from water sources and don't pee all over any single plant. Spread it around and let it provide the soil with valuable nitrogen. Don't bury toilet paper; pack it out.

Garbage. Pack it all out, including any you find that's not yours.

Hiker courtesy. Your goal is to be as unobtrusive as possible. Choose subdued colors such as gray, green, and brown for your clothing and equipment. Travel only in small groups. Set up an inconspicuous camp. Talk in a quiet voice.

A NOTE ABOUT SAFETY

Safety is an important concern in all outdoor activities. No guidebook can alert you to every hazard or anticipate the limitations of every reader. Therefore, the descriptions of roads, trails, routes, and natural features in this book are not representations that a particular place or excursion will be safe for your party. When you follow any of the routes described in this book, you assume responsibility for your own safety. Under normal conditions, such excursions require the usual attention to traffic, road and trail conditions, weather, terrain, the capabilities of your party, and other factors. Keeping informed on current conditions and exercising common sense are the keys to a safe, enjoyable outing.

—The Mountaineers Books

SIERRA NEVADA

Red firs at Caples Lake

This is the land of a thousand lakes in an alpine and subalpine setting laced with meadows. City dwellers flock here in summer for uncivilized bliss amid the water, rock, and vegetation, many climbing through mountain passes and summiting peaks that top 10,000 feet. Treks through the glacially carved granite hillocks and spires of Desolation Wilderness seduce the majority of northern Sierra Nevada visitors, but this book also guides you to the lesser-known and more secluded Sierra treasures that wait in Mokelumne Wilderness and a host of other spots, including one hike to the lip of Feather Falls, a 640-foot thundering cascade. Whether you want dense forest, calming lakes, crashing creeks, or unending views of mountain upon mountain, you'll find it in the northern Sierra.

1 GRANITE LAKE

Length: 4.4 miles round-trip
Hiking time: 3 hours or overnight
High point: 8,700 feet
Total elevation gain: 600 feet
Difficulty: easy
Season: mid-July through late October
Water: available from Middle Creek and at Granite Lake (purify first)
Maps: USGS 7.5' Carson Pass, USGS 7.5' Pacific Valley, USFS Mokelumne
   Wilderness
Information: Amador Ranger District, Eldorado National Forest

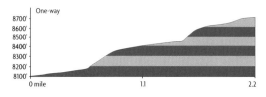

This hike offers an easy way in to some of Mokelumne Wilderness's most beautiful territory. The gentle climb to Granite Lake allows good views of high Sierra peaks, and the lake itself offers swimming, picnicking, and solitude. Day hikers do not need permits. Overnight hikers need to contact the Amador Ranger Station for more information on obtaining a permit (209-295-4251; *www.fs.fed.us/r5/eldorado*). No fires are allowed, so bring your backpacking stove. Groups are limited to a maximum size of twelve for day hikes and eight for overnight trips.

Take Blue Lakes Road, which leaves Highway 88's south side 6.3 miles east of Carson Pass and 2.5 miles west of Highway 89. Ignore a left-forking road at 7 miles signed for Wet Meadows and continue to a paved road junction 11.5 miles from Highway 88. Go right, reach Middle Creek Campground after another 1.5 miles of driving, and continue another 300 yards and park in the lot on the left.

The hike begins on a small metal bridge that leads to a crossing of the dam. The main trail

Lower Blue Lake

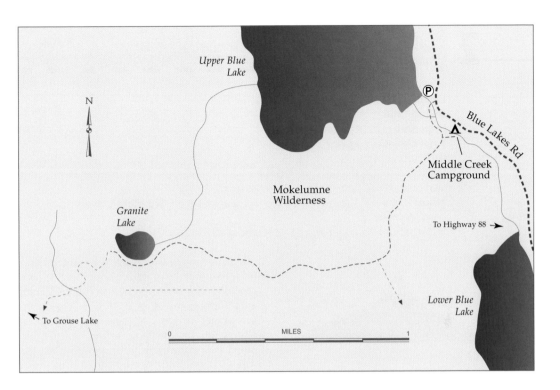

begins a gentle southwest climb away from the creek. First small and then large red fir join the forest cover, eventually followed by western white pine. As you walk past large granite boulders, note that the trail tread consists of coarse granite sands, the product of millions of years of erosion.

At 0.7 mile look through tree gaps for views of dozens of high Sierra peaks stretching to the south, west, and north. An unsigned trail takes off on the left near a wilderness boundary sign at 1 mile. Go straight and zigzag up a ridge as you enjoy a northward view of Upper Blue Lake. You'll eventually reach a small granite-encircled pond that sits just to the right of the trail at 1.5 miles.

The gentle climb to Granite Lake allows views of dozens of high Sierra Peaks.

You then begin an ascent, which is made easier by mountain vistas to the southeast. At 1.9 miles the trail crosses a seasonal stream and then passes by large numbers of lupines. The willow-lined banks of Granite Lake's outlet stream at 2.1 miles signal the nearness of the lake itself, which you reach after a final 0.1-mile uphill stretch.

Low ridges of granite surround the deep body of water, where you can wade from the sandy shore into the deep areas on warm days. If you want to camp, an appropriate site awaits on the small ridge just above the south shore, with the shade of lodgepole pine, whitebark pine, and mountain hemlock nearby. If you want to do more hiking, continue west on the trail in the direction of Grouse Lake, 4 miles away. You can also easily surmount the surrounding ridges and obtain broad vistas of lakes, valleys, and peaks.

2 WINNEMUCCA LAKE AND ROUND TOP

Length: 6.3 miles round-trip
Hiking time: 5 hours or overnight
High point: 10,381 feet
Total elevation gain: 2,200 feet
Difficulty: strenuous
Season: late July through mid-October
Water: available from streams and lakes (purify first)
Maps: USGS 7.5' Carson Pass, USGS 7.5' Caples Lake, USFS Mokelumne
  Wilderness
Information: Amador Ranger District, Eldorado National Forest

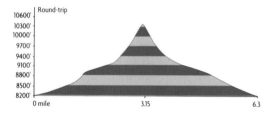

This hike takes you past two gorgeous alpine lakes where you can picnic, swim, and camp, and allows you to climb Round Top, where an extensive Sierra Nevada panorama awaits. Day hikers do not need permits. Overnight hikers need to contact the Amador Ranger Station for more information on obtaining a permit for the designated campsites, which are reserved on a first-come, first serve basis (209-295-4251; *www.fs.fed.us/r5/eldorado*; you can also call the Carson Pass Information Station at 209-258-8606 during the summer season.) No fires are allowed, so bring your backpacking stove. Groups are limited to a maximum size of twelve for day hikes and eight for overnight trips. Dogs must be leashed at all times.

Take the Woods Lake Campground turnoff, which is on Highway 88's south side 3.2 miles east of the Caples Lake Dam and 1.7 miles west of Carson Pass. Follow the paved road 1.5 miles to the campground, bear left, and park in the trailhead parking area (parking fee charged).

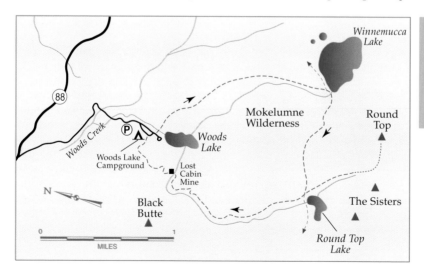

An open hillside covered with sagebrush and wildflowers leads to Round Top's summit.

The trail, signed for Winnemucca Lake, begins on the west side of the road just across the bridge from the parking area. It parallels the road for a very short distance and then crosses the road and follows the creek. Reach an information board and begin a climb through a forest of mountain hemlock, lodgepole pine, and western white pine. At 0.8 mile leave the trees behind and hike across an open hillside covered with sagebrush and a multitude of wildflowers as views of Round Top's summit lure you upward.

The sparkling waters of Winnemucca Lake await at 1.5 miles. Here, under Round Top's steep cliffs, you can swim and sunbathe on warm days and also camp at one of the several sites along the south and west shores.

To continue, head right at a trail fork, cross Winnemucca Lake's outlet, and begin climbing westward. As you gain elevation, look north for good views of Desolation Wilderness. At 2.2 miles the trail passes through a small saddle populated by whitebark pine before dropping 150 yards to Round Top Lake, which is guarded on the south by the high peaks of The Sisters and Round Top. Those seeking campsites will find two on the lake's northwest side.

If you want an easy 4.8-mile hike, head downhill to the trailhead at Woods Lake. If you want to climb Round Top, be sure you have several layers of warm clothing, good boots, sunscreen, sunglasses, a hat, and plenty of food and water. Be aware that there are several steep sections, which can be dangerous when covered with snow, a condition that usually persists well into August.

To begin the ascent, head left at the lake and take a faint trail southeast. It travels along the left side of a gully and climbs 0.5 mile to a saddle between Round Top and the easternmost peak of The Sisters, where you'll have views similar to those from Round Top's summit.

From the saddle, scramble 400 yards along Round Top's steep, boulder-shouldered south side to the double-humped summit, elevation 10,381 feet. You can easily surmount the western hump, but avoid the much steeper and more dangerous east hump. Fantastic views await in all directions: To the south, you'll see range upon range of high Sierra peaks, to the southwest lies

Round Top, paintbrush, mules ears, lupine

the bulk of Mokelumne Wilderness, numerous lakes spread out far below on the north side, and the white peaks of Desolation Wilderness beckon to the far north.

When you've imbibed as much of this magnificence as possible, retrace your steps to Round Top Lake and take the 2.5-mile downhill trail signed for Woods Lake. The path initially travels near the lake's outlet stream, as Black Butte looms ahead, and enters a forest of whitebark pine and mountain hemlock. The trail eventually passes by red fir and western white pine to join a dirt road. Follow the dirt road 0.4 mile to its gated end on the west side of Woods Lake Campground. From here, make your way through the campground to the trailhead parking area.

3 EMIGRANT LAKE

Length: 9 miles round-trip
Hiking time: 5 hours or overnight
High point: 8,600 feet
Total elevation gain: 950 feet
Difficulty: easy
Season: mid-July through late October
Water: available from Caples Lake and Emigrant Lake (purify first)
Maps: USGS 7.5' Caples Lake, USFS Mokelumne Wilderness
Information: Amador Ranger District, Eldorado National Forest

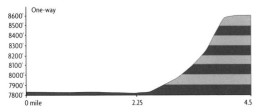

This trail offers an easy day hike or overnight trip that's suitable for all. You'll travel through small, flower-filled meadows and a mixed pine/fir forest to deep Emigrant Lake, where mountain peaks tower high above. Day hikers do not need permits. Overnight hikers need to contact the Amador Ranger Station for more information on obtaining a permit (209-295-4251; *www.fs.fed.us/r5/eldorado;* during the summer season you can also call the Carson Pass Information Station, 209-258-8606.) No fires are allowed, so bring your backpacking stove. Groups are limited to a maximum size of twelve for day hikes and eight for overnight trips.

The trailhead parking area, signed for Caples Lake, is on the south side of Highway 88 by the

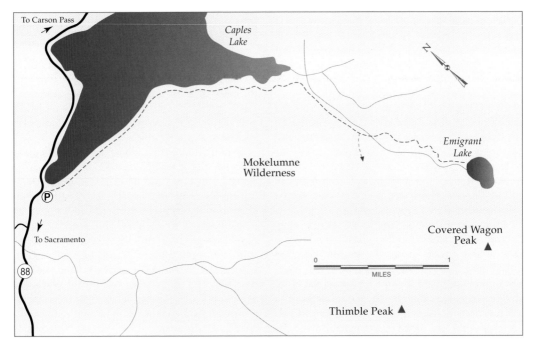

Caples Lake Dam, which is 4.9 miles west of Carson Pass (parking fee).

The signed trail begins near the bathrooms and, after passing a few quaking aspen, contours just above the shore of Caples Lake through a mixed forest of red fir and lodgepole pine. Caples Lake, quite popular for fishing, also offers cool refreshment on hot days.

Open views of Round Top's summit (Hike 2: Winnemucca Lake and Round Top) appear 1 mile from the trailhead. You'll also see the vast expanse of the high ridge north of Highway 88. At 1.2 miles note the sign for Emigrant Road; however, most traces of this historic trail have disappeared.

Continue straight and pass through a small grove of quaking aspen. The trail crosses four seasonal creeks over the next 1.2 miles, each bordered by lush greenery. The path then angles south along Emigrant Creek and away from Caples Lake.

The way now climbs gently through small meadow patches and past granite boulders and outcrops. Mountain hemlocks join the forest as you walk near the willow-lined creek bank and go left at a trail fork at 3.4 miles.

A rock hop across Emigrant Lake's outlet stream awaits at 4 miles, after which you'll have occasional eastward views through the trees of The Sisters' rocky spires as the climb continues. At 4.3 miles the trail levels and parallels a small meadow near the stream, which is bordered by an abundance of red mountain heather.

Finally, 4.5 miles from the trailhead, you reach the deep, granite-ringed waters of glacier-formed Emigrant Lake. A steep, talus-clad cliff rises from the lake's south shore, and to the southwest lies the broad ridge of 9,565-foot Covered Wagon Peak. Farther west towers 9,805-foot Thimble Peak, a volcanic vent that covered much of this area with lava, volcanic ash, and mudflows 4 million to 20 million years ago.

> Let your eyes wander from lake to cliff to peak to sky.

Emigrant Lake offers several good swimming sites in late summer. Those who stay overnight can find campsites, but they must be at least 300 feet from the lake.

Caples Lake

4 LAKE MARGARET

Length: 5 miles round-trip
Hiking time: 3 hours or overnight
High point: 7,725 feet
Total elevation gain: 550 feet
Difficulty: easy
Season: early July through late October
Water: available from streams and Lake Margaret (purify first)
Maps: USGS 7.5′ Caples Lake, USFS Mokelumne Wilderness
Information: Amador Ranger District, Eldorado National Forest

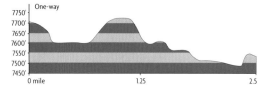

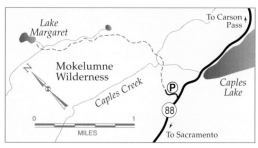

This hike's gentle trail takes you near the lush green banks of Caples Creek and past huge slabs of granite to Lake Margaret, where you can picnic, swim, and enjoy the mountain scenery. It's a good outing for those wanting a lot of nature for only a little effort. Feel free to contact the Amador Ranger Station (209-295-4251; *www.fs.fed.us/r5/eldorado*) for more information about campfire permits and fire restrictions (stove use recommended). During summer, you can also call the Carson Pass Information Station (209-258-8606).

Take the turnoff on the north side of Highway 88 about 0.2 mile west of the Caples Lake Dam

Juniper tree above Lake Margaret

(the trailhead for Hike 3: Emigrant Lake) and 0.5 mile east of the turnoff for the Kirkwood Ski Area. Follow the short road 150 yards to its end.

The signed trail begins at the west end of the parking area, just north of the road. Descend through a lodgepole pine and red fir forest at a moderate pitch, and then cross a seasonal creek at 0.2 mile. The trail heads east briefly; look straight ahead for glimpses of the high mountain ridge just north of Caples Lake.

> Huge slabs of granite stretch high above and far below the surface of Lake Margaret.

The path briefly parallels and then crosses another seasonal creek. A good picnic spot lies just to the left of the trail as you near the banks of Caples Creek at 0.6 mile, where there's green grass and the creek's clear waters are deep enough for wading.

The trail quickly reaches the creek itself and crosses it on a fallen tree. You soon begin a gentle climb through a gully bordered by huge granite hillocks. After the path levels, it skirts a small, lodgepole pine- and willow-ringed pond on the left at 1.2 miles and then crosses some granite.

A much larger pond, surrounded by lodgepole pine and red fir, awaits on the right at 1.6 miles. You soon cross a stream, pass through a large thicket of mountain alder, and then note that western white pine has joined the forest cover.

Quaking aspen, with their tremulous green leaves and bright white bark, begin to border the trail at 2.2 miles; they accompany you for 300 yards to a stream, which you cross on a log. You now begin the final ascent to your destination, following rock ducks (cairns) up the gently sloping granite.

After the brief climb, you reach the deep waters of Lake Margaret. Numerous granite slabs stretch from high above to far below the lake's surface. You'll find many places to swim, either near the shore or out to some of the small granite islands that dot the lake's surface. Campers will find two sites along the east shore and two more near the west shore.

5 DARDANELLES AND ROUND LAKES

Length: 8 miles round-trip
Hiking time: 5 hours or overnight
High point: 8,070 feet
Total elevation gain: 1,400 feet
Difficulty: moderate
Season: late June to mid-October
Water: available from streams and lakes (purify first)
Maps: USGS 7.5′ Echo Lake, USFS Desolation Wilderness
Information: Lake Tahoe Basin Management Unit

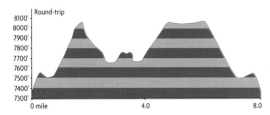

This hike takes you through expansive meadows, across clear streams, and past numerous wild-flowers to visit two magnificent, cliff-bordered lakes that offer good swimming and camping.

From the junction of Highways 50 and 89, drive south on 89 for 5.2 miles to the signed Big Meadow trailhead. Go 150 yards farther and park in the lot on the left.

Cross carefully to the other side of Highway 89 to the trailhead. Start climbing past Jeffrey and ponderosa pine and red and white

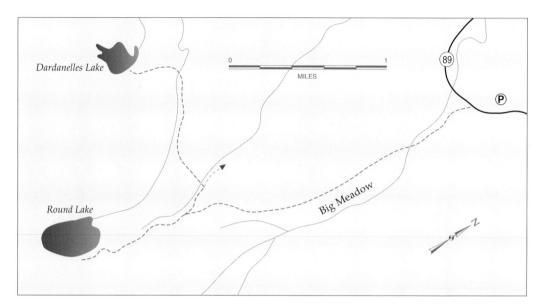

fir. Lodgepole pine and quaking aspen flank a gate at 0.4 mile. Go right 75 yards farther at a signpost and promptly enter Big Meadow. Cross a wooden bridge and follow the path 0.4 mile through the middle of the green expanse. Resume gentle climbing at 0.8 mile through an open, dry forest, which provides ideal conditions for blue lupine, orange Indian paintbrush, and aster. At 1.6 miles the climb steepens as you notice a slender meadow to the right, covered with corn lily, meadow goldenrod, aster, and some yarrow.

Note the trail junction to Round Lake (a side trip described later) at 2 miles. For now, bear right and walk 0.1 mile to a flat, noting the fallen, sliced Jeffrey pine next to the path. Go 50 yards farther and carefully travel up the unsigned,

> Dardanelles Lake offers good summertime swimming.

scant trail to the left, which takes you to a stream 20 yards away. Cross this brook and stroll along the now obvious trail past sage and aspen 0.1 mile to cross a bigger creek. The trail gradually drops, leading you past an enormous Sierra juniper on the left at 2.6 miles. Cross Round Lake's outlet stream at 2.9 miles and reach the east shore of Dardanelles Lake at 3.3 miles.

Highlights of this shallow lake include a 300-foot sheer rock dome on the south shore and

Dardanelles Lake

two small peninsulas. The surprisingly warm lake also offers comfortable swimming by mid-summer. Several campsites lie near the east and north shores. Stroll the shore amid Sierra juniper, western white pine, lodgepole pine, and pine-mat manzanita and find the marsh where Indian pond lily flourishes on the north side.

Retrace your steps for 1.3 miles, and go right on the Round Lake Trail. It stays mostly level through a fir forest, undertaking a brief ascent after 0.3 mile past a maze of big boulders. You reach aptly named Round Lake 0.7 mile from the trail junction. Plan to take the easy, shoreline cross-country stroll past sage, Sierra juniper, and lodgepole and western white pine. Three camp-site retreats near the north shore give good views of the sheer rock dome that towers 500 feet above the water on the east side.

6 TAMARACK AND RALSTON LAKES VIA ECHO LAKES

Length: 9.2 miles round-trip
Hiking time: 5 hours or overnight
High point: 7,880 feet
Total elevation gain: 550 feet
Difficulty: easy
Season: early July to mid-October
Water: available only at the lakes (purify first)
Maps: USGS 7.5' Echo Lake, USFS Desolation Wilderness
Information: Lake Tahoe Basin Management Unit

Take a long, leisurely hillside stroll just above the twin Echo Lakes, and then admire windswept, twisted conifers and High Sierra mountain views on the way to island-dotted Tamarack and Ralston Lakes. Day hikers can get a free

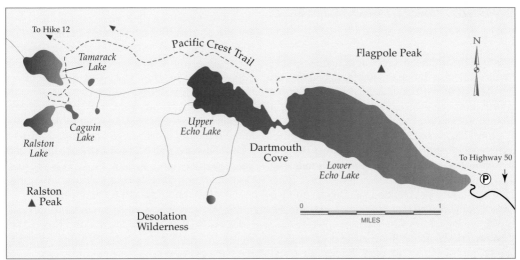

Echo Lake and Sierra juniper

Trail on the far northeast side, and leave most of the hustle and bustle behind. After a brief 100 yards, take a side-trail to the right to a gap that has open views of the southern portion of Lake Tahoe, the valley holding Highway 50, and many, many mountains.

The sandy, level trail keeps you close to sky-blue Echo Lake and whisks you past Sierra juniper, Jeffrey pine, ponderosa pine, and a dry chaparral understory of manzanita and huckleberry oak. You'll see exquisite lakeside summer cottages and notice the jagged rock outcrops hovering above you on the right. Eventually you arrive at a vista point above Dartmouth Cove, which separates Lower Echo Lake from Upper Echo Lake.

> Sierra juniper, Jeffrey pine, and ponderosa pine line the sandy trail.

The trail climbs away from Upper Echo Lake to allow eastward views of the alpine mountains neighboring the twin lakes. Pyramid Peak rises westward above stunted Sierra juniper as you continue up this exposed, rocky trail section. Reach a trailfork at 3.6 miles and go left. The ascending path then ducks into an open forest dotted with orange wavy-leafed paintbrush, white yarrow, and blue lupine.

At 4.1 miles leave the Pacific Crest Trail and go left for the 0.2-mile stroll to Tamarack Lake. A granite wall, laced with communities of fir and western white pine, rises above the lake's far side, topped by the steepest flank of 9,235-foot Ralston Peak. Stands of slender western white pine dominate the shoreline and grow to equal 50-foot heights. The east shoreline offers some campsites.

The on-again, off-again trail skirts the east shoreline, crosses Tamarack Lake's outlet stream, and then passes near the lake's marshy south side. Climb the faint trail 0.2 mile to overlook Ralston Lake, nestled below Ralston Peak. This pristine, deep lake and neighboring Cagwin Lake offer excellent swimming and a few campsites.

Note that you can walk the trails of Hike 12 (Lake Aloha, Lake of the Woods, and Ropi Lake) by traveling 0.5 mile northwest upon rejoining the Pacific Crest Trail.

permit at the trailhead. Overnight hikers need to contact the Lake Tahoe Basin Management Unit (530-543-2694; *www.fs.fed.us/r5/ltbmu*) for more information on overnight quotas, obtaining a permit, and paying overnight camping fees.

From Highway 50 at Echo Pass 9.2 miles southwest of the junction of Highway 50 and 89 in South Lake Tahoe, drive west 0.9 mile and turn right (north) on Johnson Pass Road. Turn left 0.5 mile farther on Echo Lake Road, and then drive 0.9 mile to the large parking lot on the left and above Echo Lake Chalet.

Walk briefly down the road and cross Echo Lake's spillway area to gain the Pacific Crest

7 SYLVIA AND LYONS LAKES

Length: 10 miles round-trip
Hiking time: 6 hours or overnight
High point: 8,380 feet
Total elevation gain: 1,700 feet
Difficulty: easy to Lake Sylvia, moderate to Lyons Lake
Season: early July through mid-October
Water: available from lakes and Lyons Creek (purify first)
Maps: USGS 7.5' Pyramid Peak, USFS Desolation Wilderness
Information: Pacific Ranger District, Eldorado National Forest

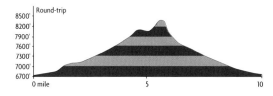

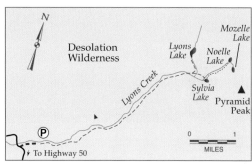

This hike takes you along the waters of Lyons Creek to some of the most beautiful territory in Desolation Wilderness: the Crystal Range and Pyramid Peak, and also Lyons Lake. Day hikers can get a free permit at the trailhead. Overnight hikers need to contact the Pacific Ranger District (530-647-5415; *www.fs.fed.us/r5/eldorado*) for more information on overnight quotas, obtaining a permit, and paying overnight camping fees.

Take the paved road signed for Wrights Lake, which is on the north side of Highway 50 about 46 miles east of Placerville and 17 miles west of the junction of Highways 50 and 89. Follow Wrights Lake Road (Road 11N26) 4 miles and turn right at a dirt road signed for the Lyons Creek Trail for the final 0.4 mile.

The trail travels most of its length near the granite- and mountain-alder-lined banks of Lyons Creek. Lodgepole pine is the primary tree species, and as you continue you'll pass by several meadows and seasonal streams. Numerous wildflowers provide a multihued display in midsummer; look for corn lily, brodiaea, and lupine.

Glimpses of 9,983-foot Pyramid Peak lead you onward. Bear right at a trail junction at 1.5 miles and continue on to the Desolation Wilderness

boundary at 2.8 miles. If you want to cool off on a warm day, look for some small pools in the creek about 100 yards past the boundary. The path then climbs past granite boulders and hillocks to a crossing of Lyons Creek at 4 miles and to a trail junction at 4.1 miles.

Sylvia Lake lies 0.4 mile up the right fork. Several campsites lie between lodgepole pine and mountain hemlock near the west shore. From the lake's edges you can see mighty Pyramid Peak and its accom-

> A short, cross-country hike leads to solitude at Noelle and Mozelle Lakes.

panying granite ridges. Consider the 1-mile cross-country hike northeast along a small creek to granite-encased Noelle and Mozelle Lakes. Here, nestled under Pyramid Peak's shoulder, you're much more likely to find solitude.

A left turn at the trail fork will take you 0.5 mile up a steep granitic ridge to Lyons Lake.

This large, deep, granite-ringed body of water ranks as one of the prettiest anywhere. The Crystal Range's exfoliated granite rises over 1,500 steep feet on the east side, and more moderately sloping granite lies to the north and west. Granite slabs and granite sand beaches surround the entire lake, making for easy access to an invigorating swim in the deep cold water. Look for campsites on the southeast side of the lake, or search near the lake's perimeter for a level granite slab. An easy northwesterly cross-country scramble up the rock of at least 150 vertical feet will reward you with southward views of Round Top (Hike 2: Winnemucca Lake and Round Top) and other peaks in Mokelumne Wilderness.

Glacially carved peaks in Desolation Wilderness

8   GROUSE, HEMLOCK, AND SMITH LAKES

Length: 5.6 miles round-trip
Hiking time: 4 hours or overnight
High point: 8,700 feet
Total elevation gain: 1,750 feet
Difficulty: moderate
Season: early July through mid-October
Water: available at the lakes (purify first)
Maps: USGS 7.5' Pyramid Peak, USFS Desolation Wilderness
Information: Pacific Ranger District, Eldorado National Forest

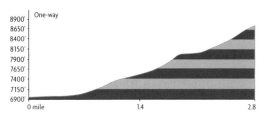

Climb a forested trail to three magnificent lakes. Besides opportunities for swimming, picnicking, and camping, you'll be treated to expansive views of steep-sided granite Sierra peaks that pierce the sky at nearly 10,000 feet. Day hikers can get a free permit at the trailhead. Overnight hikers need to contact the Pacific Ranger District (530-647-5415; *www.fs.fed.us/r5/eldorado*) for more information on overnight quotas, obtaining a permit, and paying overnight camping fees.

On the north side of Highway 50 about 46 miles east of Placerville and 17 miles west of the Highway 50/89 junction, take the paved road signed for Wrights Lake. Follow this road (initially signed 11N26), and go straight where a dirt road turns off to the right for Sylvia and Lyons Lakes (Hike 7: Sylvia and Lyons Lakes) 4 miles from Highway 50; stay straight again at another

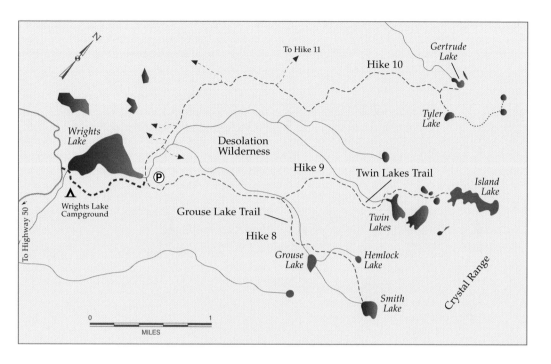

junction 6 miles from Highway 50. Look for a wilderness area parking lot on the right another 1.7 miles farther; you must park here if you will be backpacking. Day hikers follow the main road through the campground (bear right at two road forks) and continue another 1.1 miles to the

Buckwheat and sage

signed trailhead, where there are self-serve day-hike permits.

The path skirts a lush meadow surrounding a marshy area that may be populated by cattle in late summer, and then it begins a gentle climb. You'll hike past lodgepole pine, red fir, and an occasional Jeffrey pine as intermittent views tantalize you with northward vistas of rolling hills of forest

> A forest of mountain hemlock leads to Smith Lake, one of the prettiest lakes in the Sierra Nevada.

and granite. After crossing some granite slabs (look for rock ducks, or cairns), the path encounters a small stream at 0.9 mile and reaches a trail fork at 1.1 miles. Hike 9 to Twin and Island Lakes goes left; you go right, as indicated by the sign for Smith Lake.

Cross more granite and ascend an increasingly steep slope through the forest to reach the grass-lined shore of Grouse Lake at 1.8 miles, a good spot for a rest or perhaps a swim in the shallow waters. Several adequate campsites lie near the lake's east and south sides.

Once past Grouse Lake, the trail crosses a seasonal stream, passes through a wet area, and begins a stiff climb. Look for views down to Wrights Lake at 2.2 miles, just before reaching Hemlock Lake at 2.4 miles. Mountain hemlock trees grow in abundance here, nicely complementing the steep granite rising from the north and east shores. The small lake offers two campsites.

However, the splendor of Smith Lake awaits. Continue up through a forest of mountain hemlock and ascend bare granite slopes that require careful attention to the rock duck guides. Finally, 2.8 miles from the trailhead, you reach Smith Lake, where high walls of exfoliated granite surround the lake's deep, cold waters on three sides, leaving open views to the north. This lake, one of the prettiest in the Sierra Nevada, is well worth the effort. Backpackers should search for a level stretch of granite to sleep on.

9 TWIN AND ISLAND LAKES

Length: 6.2 miles round-trip
Hiking time: 4 hours or overnight
High point: 8,150 feet
Total elevation gain: 1,200 feet
Difficulty: easy to moderate
Season: early July through mid-October
Water: available from streams and lakes (purify first)
Maps: USGS 7.5′ Pyramid Peak, USGS 7.5′ Rockbound Valley, USFS
   Desolation Wilderness
Information: Pacific Ranger District, Eldorado National Forest

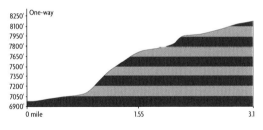

Twin and Island Lakes offer numerous campsites, excellent swimming, and magnificent views of Desolation Wilderness's granitic Crystal Range. Day hikers can get a free permit at the trailhead. Overnight hikers need to contact the Pacific Ranger District (530-647-5415; *www.fs.fed.us /r5/eldorado*) for more information on overnight quotas, obtaining a permit, and paying overnight camping fees.

From the north side of Highway 50 about 46 miles east of Placerville and 17 miles west of the junction of Highways 50 and 89, take signed Wrights Lake Road. This paved road, initially signed 11N26, reaches a dirt road after 4 miles (the trailhead for Hike 7: Sylvia and Lyons Lakes). Go straight here and at another road junction 2 miles farther. After another 1.7 miles, you'll see a wilderness area parking lot on the right. Backpackers must leave their cars here, but day hikers can continue along the main road another 1.1 miles (go right at two road forks) to the trailhead, where you'll find self-serve day hike permits.

The trail initially travels near the border of a lush meadow/marsh, which provides good eating for the cattle that inhabit the vicinity in late summer. You soon leave them behind, however, and enter a forest of red fir and lodgepole pine. The path crosses granite slabs (look for rock ducks, or cairns), meets a small stream, and then hits a trail fork at 1.1 miles. The right-hand trail is discussed in Hike 8: Grouse, Hemlock, and Smith Lakes. You go left.

From here to the shore of Twin Lakes, you'll be walking across a lot of granite. Carefully placed rocks often line the trail, or you'll see rock ducks. Pay attention; it's easy to lose the way. The main distraction is the high, stark granite peaks of the Crystal Range looming straight ahead as you climb eastward toward the lakes. At 2.2 miles the trail skirts some small pools of the Twin Lakes outlet stream and then passes through a wet area.

The deep waters of the first Twin Lake await at 2.5 miles. Take a while to imbibe the grandeur of the surrounding mountains. Then, if it's late enough in summer, dive from granite ledges into the lake's deep waters (be sure to check for submerged rocks first). Look for a couple of campsites at the west end of the lake.

The path crosses a rock dam and then travels along the north shore of the first Twin Lake. You'll eventually catch sight of the other Twin Lake to the east as you climb toward Island Lake. A deep pond on the left at 2.8 miles also offers good swimming; several smaller ponds line the trail farther on.

Aptly named Island Lake lies in a shallow glacial valley 3.1 miles from the trailhead and offers the best views of the Crystal Range. You can swim in its cool waters or hike along its circumscribing granite. However, camping options are limited; look for a few mediocre sites near the west end of the lake.

Sunbathing in the Crystal Range

10   TYLER AND GERTRUDE LAKES

Length: 8 miles round-trip
Hiking time: 6 hours or overnight
High point: 8,200 feet
Total elevation gain: 1,400 feet
Difficulty: moderate to strenuous
Season: late July to mid-October
Water: bring your own
Maps: USGS 7.5' Rockbound Valley, USGS 7.5' Pyramid Peak, USFS
     Desolation Wilderness
Information: Pacific Ranger District, Eldorado National Forest

Enjoy seclusion while admiring rugged and scenic alpine backcountry on this trek to two small lakes that rate among the most pristine in the High Sierra. Choose from several lake

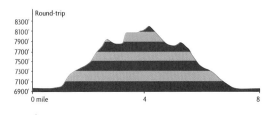

campsites that allow good views of steep rocky ridges. Day hikers can get a free permit at the trailhead. Overnight hikers need to contact the Pacific Ranger District (530-647-5415; *www .fs.fed.us/r5/eldorado*) for more information on overnight quotas, obtaining a permit, and paying overnight camping fees.

Drive Highway 50 to about 46 miles east of Placerville and 17 miles west of the junction of Highways 50 and 89. Take paved Wrights Lake Road (initially signed 11N26), and reach a dirt road after 4 miles (the trailhead for Hike 7: Sylvia and Lyons Lakes). Go straight here and again 2 miles farther. After another 1.7 miles, note the wilderness area parking lot on the right. Backpackers leave vehicles here, but day hikers continue along the main road another 1.1 miles (go right at two road forks) to the trailhead.

From the north side of the trailhead parking lot, cross the creek, and then pass through the meadow as you enjoy eastward views of Mount Price. Walk through an open red fir and Jeffrey pine forest, and stay left at a trail junction at 0.4 mile. Bear right at two other trail forks shortly thereafter, and then go right again on the Rockbound Trail at 1.2 miles.

Take the Tyler Lake Trail by making a right 0.5 mile farther (the left-hand trail is described in Hike 11: Maud, Lois, and Zitella Lakes). Proceed past quaking aspen, huckleberry oak, and lodgepole pine, and then watch for rock ducks (cairns) as you ascend a steep gully. The jagged mountaintops to the east come into view at 2 miles, after which the trail climbs steeply.

The trail levels at a saddle at 2.2 miles. From here, climb past a section of scattered Sierra juniper and Jeffrey pine at 2.6 miles, and then pass a dark bog in a mountain hemlock forest 0.2 mile farther. At 3.3 miles, watch for the sign directing you to the Tyler grave site.

Arrow-shaped Gertrude Lake appears on the left at 3.8 miles. Mountain hemlock and lodgepole pine adorn the shoreline of this shallow and swimmable lake. Two exposed campsites sit atop the rocky ledge above the north shore.

Plan on spending most of your time at the more scenic Tyler Lake. Retrace your steps 75 yards and locate the rock ducks that guide you 0.2 mile to the oval-shaped and deeper body of water, sided by steep granite on the south, east, and north sides. A superb campsite rests near the northwest shore beneath a large western white pine and smaller whitebark pine. Find other campsites partway up the smooth granite slabs that taper to the north shore. An easy 0.5-mile cross-country climb northwest to a bench just west of Peak 9441 lets you visit two large, clear alpine ponds. If you want more hiking, consider the trails of Hike 11 (Maud, Lois, and Zitella Lakes), Hike 9 (Twin and Island Lakes), and Hike 8 (Grouse, Hemlock, and Smith Lakes).

Alpine pond and Peak 9441

11 MAUD, LOIS, AND ZITELLA LAKES

Length: 24.7 miles round-trip
Hiking time: 3 to 5 days
High point: 8,650 feet
Total elevation gain: 5,400 feet
Difficulty: moderate to strenuous
Season: late July to early October
Water: plenty at the lakes (purify first), but bring water to Maud Lake
Maps: USGS 7.5' Rockbound Valley, USGS 7.5' Pyramid Peak, USFS Desolation Wilderness
Information: Pacific Ranger District, Eldorado National Forest

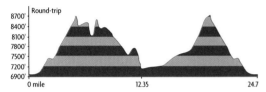

Journey deep into one of Desolation Wilderness's more remote sections and visit numerous high lakes and vista points. Day hikers can get a free permit at the trailhead. Overnight hikers need to contact the Pacific Ranger District (530-647-5415; *www.fs.fed.us/r5/eldorado*) for more information on overnight quotas, obtaining a permit, and paying overnight camping fees.

From the north side of Highway 50 about 46 miles east of Placerville and 17 miles west of the junction of Highways 50 and 89, take signed Wrights Lake Road. This paved road, initially signed 11N26, reaches a dirt road after 4 miles (see Hike 7: Sylvia and Lyons Lakes). Go straight here and at another road junction 2 miles farther. After another 1.9 miles, bear left at a three-way junction, and then go 0.5 mile to the trailhead, 0.2 mile south of Dark Lake.

The trail skirts the west and north shores of Beauty Lake at 0.5 mile, followed by a left turn at a signed trail fork 0.1 mile farther. Teasing views of Mount Price become more prominent when the ridge crests from 0.9 to 1.1 miles. Go left at the trail sign at 1.8 miles, break into open granite boulder country, and bear left again 0.4 mile farther. (The right fork leads to Tyler and Gertrude Lakes—see Hike 10.)

Walk past quaking aspen, white fir, lodgepole pine, and mountain hemlock to your first sighting of Rockbound Pass at 3.1 miles, and then cross Silver Creek 0.2 mile farther. Head straight at an unsigned junction just outside a lodgepole pine and white fir forest at 4.1 miles.

Massive Sierra juniper shrubs appear just before your arrival at shallow and slightly muddy Maud Lake. The numerous campsites here often fill up on late summer weekends, but other overnight spots are readily available in the wide, open basin above the lake.

Switchback 1.1 miles and climb past profuse alpine wildflowers to splendid views east and west atop often windy Rockbound Pass. Hardy whitebark pine survive in this stark environment as wide-growing shrubs, and a lone, weathered mountain hemlock bears the sign of the 8,650-foot pass.

Drop 0.5 mile to Lake Doris, where you can find campsites with views of the sky-blue waters. A couple of sheltered campsites rest in the more forested north area.

> Splendid views await from 8,650-foot-high Rockbound Pass.

A sloping meadow leads gently down from Lake Doris to a trail sign 0.2 mile away, where you bear left on the Blakely Trail at 6 miles. The level tread rounds a bend, heads into a lupine-covered field by a pond, and reaches scenic Lake Lois at 6.7 miles. A few adequate campsites exist around

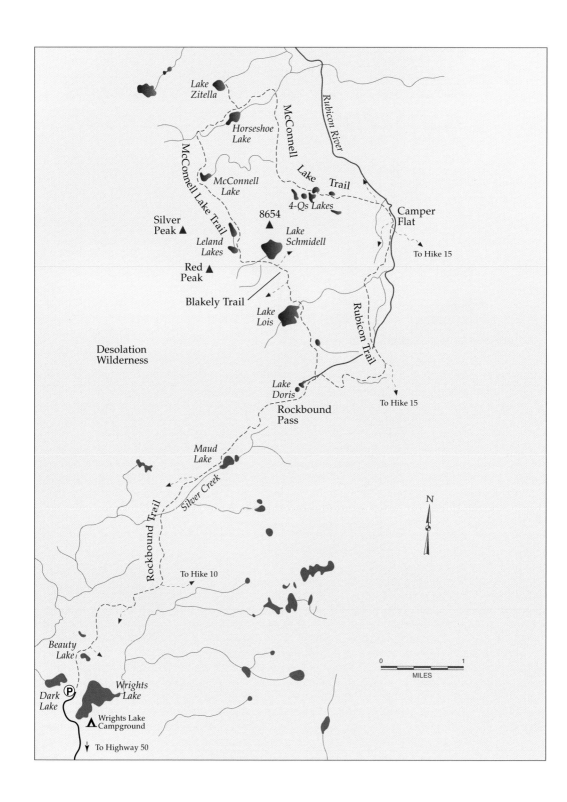

this deep and clear lake, which is bounded by chunks and walls of metamorphic rock.

After a brief climbing burst past Lake Lois, the trail levels to a signed junction, where you continue straight at 7.3 miles. The path then offers magnificent northerly views, including an inaugural sighting of Lake Schmidell. Plunge into a western white pine and mountain hemlock forest for 0.3 mile, and then go left onto the McConnell Lake Trail. A brief scamper to the right leads down to roundish Lake Schmidell, which offers plenty of campsites and views of steep cliffs to the west and north.

Back on the McConnell Lake Trail, cross one of the lake's inlet creeks and begin a climb with numerous vantage points for viewing Lake Schmidell. Reach a mountain-hemlock-covered saddle at 8.4 miles, a good perch for eagle's-eye views of Leland Lakes. The trail winds by the east shoreline of both Leland Lakes, revealing an array of good campsites. Eastward, gently sloping rock mounds culminate in Peak 8654. The west walls are decidedly steeper, climaxed by 8,930-foot Silver Peak due west and 9,307-foot Red Peak to the southwest.

Leave Leland Lakes behind at 9.6 miles and gently descend for 1 mile in open forest. Pay close attention to the rock ducks (cairns) that guide you the final 0.2 mile to the west side of shallow, marshy McConnell Lake. Following the countless rock ducks from this lake on the mile-long journey to Horseshoe Lake is tricky, so be alert. A small island highlights this grassy lake at 11.4 miles, where two campsites nestle underneath the pines on the northwest side.

Just beyond Horseshoe Lake, turn left at the signed trail junction for Lake Zitella. Rock ducks lead you 0.4 mile to this beautiful spot, where you can admire tiny islands decorating the surface. A campsite awaits on a ledge on the lake's south side, and you'll discover a couple of hidden sites in the woods on the north side.

If you prefer the more scenic return, retrace your steps to the trailhead. For a more diversified round-trip, return to the signed junction near Horseshoe Lake, head left (northeast), and drop 0.5 mile through open forest to a flat at 13.4 miles. The trail goes south upon crossing Horseshoe Lake's outlet and remains mostly flat to the shallow 4-Qs Lakes at 15.2 miles.

Granite spire above Lake Zitella

Bear right 0.5 mile farther onto the signed Rubicon Trail, proceed into denser forest, cross the sometimes dry Lake Schmidell outlet, and hike through Camper Flat, where you'll find good campsites and the opportunity to connect with the trails of Hike 15 (Dicks Lake, Gilmore Lake, Lake Aloha, and Middle Velma Lake). Stay left at a junction at 16.2 miles (unless you choose to climb 1.4 miles west to Lake Schmidell), and go right 0.1 mile farther.

The following mile stays level and just above the Rubicon River. At 17.4 miles bear right onto the Rockbound Trail, and then climb steadily for 1.3 miles to Lake Doris. From here, it's a 6-mile hoof through Rockbound Pass on previously trod trail to the trailhead.

12 LAKE ALOHA, LAKE OF THE WOODS, AND ROPI LAKE

Length: 13.9 miles round-trip
Hiking time: 2 to 3 days
High point: 8,400 feet
Total elevation gain: 2,800 feet
Difficulty: strenuous
Season: early July to late September
Water: available from lakes and streams (purify first)
Maps: USGS 7.5' Echo Lake, USGS 7.5' Pyramid Peak, USGS 7.5' Emerald
    Bay, USFS Desolation Wilderness
Information: Lake Tahoe Basin Management Unit

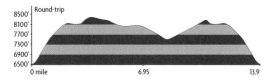

This hike offers extensive views of high Sierra peaks as it takes you to five beautiful lakes. You must obtain a permit for this hike. Day hikers can get a free permit at the trailhead. Overnight hikers need to contact the Lake Tahoe Basin Management Unit (530-543-2694; *www.fs.fed.us/r5/ltbmu*) for more information on overnight quotas, obtaining a permit, and paying overnight camping fees.

From the Lake Tahoe Visitor Center on Highway 89 (3.1 miles northwest of the junction of Highways 89 and 50), drive east 0.1 mile and turn right (south) on Fallen Leaf Road. Go 4.6 miles to the former Fallen Leaf Lodge. Watch closely for the signed trailhead on the left, 0.1 mile past the lodge.

The initial 3.2 miles of this hike travel a rugged, unmaintained trail—watch your step. For the first 1.9 miles, the trail (17E10) often crosses Lily Lake's inlet streams as it steeply ascends rocky switchbacks that necessitate the use of occasional handholds. The next 0.5 mile, level or slightly downhill, passes sulfur flower and sage with great views to the left of rocky Angora Peak. At 2.4 miles head straight at a trail intersection.

At 2.8 miles you reach the highest elevation of this journey, 8,400 feet, which features a panorama of nearby high Sierra lakes and mountains, including Echo Lakes to the east and an open display of Desolation Wilderness scenery to the south and west. The next 0.4 mile reveals many odd-shaped Sierra juniper growing in exposed spots, with the steep Sierra slopes beyond. Tamarack Lake, Ralston Lake, and Ralston Peak lie to the south, and the upper 500 feet of Pyramid Peak rises to the west.

Reach the Pacific Crest Trail at 3.2 miles. A left turn leads to Tamarack, Ralston, and Echo Lakes (see Hike 6: Tamarack and Ralston Lakes via Echo Lakes). Go right and gently climb for 0.3 mile along a plateau sporting scattered sage, native fescue grasses, red fir, and tall western white pine to scenic Haypress Meadows. Bear right 0.1 mile farther at a signed trail intersection. Go right at 3.8 miles, left 100 yards farther, and then look right for a view of a green pond and Lake Margery.

> **Dozens of granite islets punctuate the surface of Lake Aloha.**

At 4.1 miles the path leads through a meadow highlighted by blue lupine and red mountain heather. Bear right at a trail fork 0.1 mile farther, followed shortly by your first full view of Pyramid Peak.

Reach a trail fork near the middle of Lake Aloha's east shoreline at 5.3 miles (a right turn leads to Heather and Susie Lakes; see Hike 15: Dicks Lake, Gilmore Lake, Lake Aloha, and Middle Velma Lake). Go left for a scenic shoreline stroll. Note the western white pine and mountain

Pyramid Peak and Lake Aloha

hemlock thriving on the countless granite rock islands that highlight shallow Lake Aloha. Also note campsites a short distance from the lake.

Bear right at 5.8 miles and then left 100 yards farther at an unsigned junction. Follow the faint trail as it skirts the northeast flank of Peak 8383. At 5.9 miles a crest affords a view of aptly named Lake of the Woods, which rivals Lake Aloha in

popularity because of the numerous campsites. The path drops to the north shore and two campsites before it heads east.

At 6.2 miles note the return trail on the left at the northeast corner of Lake of the Woods and proceed straight. At 6.7 miles the trail departs Lake of the Woods and heads south 0.3 mile onto a flat. You soon cross Lake of the Woods's outlet

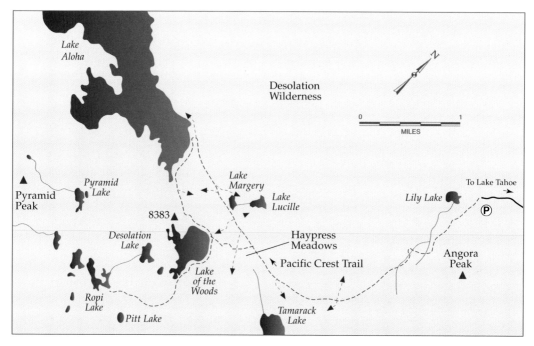

stream. Head due west, just south of a steep cliff. At 7.6 miles arrive at rocky Ropi Lake, which has several places to camp. This uniquely shaped, snag-covered lake invites a circumnavigating trek highlighted by views of Pyramid Peak. Consider easy cross-country walks to Toem Lake (west) and Avalanche Lake (south).

To return to the trailhead, retrace your steps to the junction at the northeast tip of Lake of the Woods. Turn right here and climb for 0.5 mile, and then go straight at a trail intersection. Hike down into Haypress Meadows, and then head right 0.2 mile farther at the signed trail junction onto previously trekked trails.

13 HALF MOON LAKE

Length: 12 miles round-trip
Hiking time: 8 hours or overnight
High point: 8,200 feet
Total elevation gain: 2,000 feet
Difficulty: moderate
Season: mid-July through early October
Water: available from Glen Alpine Creek, Half Moon Lake, and Gilmore
 Lake's outlet stream (purify first)
Maps: USGS 7.5' Emerald Bay, USGS 7.5' Rockbound Valley, USGS 7.5' Echo
 Lake, USFS Desolation Wilderness
Information: Lake Tahoe Basin Management Unit

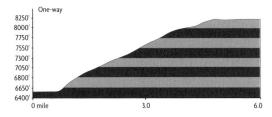

The huge glacial cirque that holds Half Moon and Alta Morris Lakes rates among the most gorgeous areas in the northern Sierra. Swim, sun, and admire steep peaks and high ridges. You must obtain a permit for this hike. Day hikers can get a free permit at the trailhead. Overnight hikers need to contact the Lake Tahoe Basin Management Unit (530-543-2694; *www.fs.fed.us/r5/ltbmu*) for more information on overnight quotas, obtaining a permit, and paying overnight camping fees.

From the junction of Highways 50 and 89, drive 3 miles northwest on Highway 89. Turn left on Fallen Leaf Road. Go 4.6 miles to Fallen Leaf Lodge and continue past it to the fire station. Turn left just past the station and follow the road to its dead-end to find the trailhead.

The hike begins on the gravel road beyond the locked National Forest Service gate. Skirt several summer cottages at 0.6 mile, and then pass one of Glen Alpine Creek's many scenic falls, flanked by Cathedral Peak to the north and Angora Peak to the south. Step into a shaded forest at 1.8 miles at a reunion with Glen Alpine Creek. Bear right 0.1 mile farther at a signed trail junction. (The left trail travels 0.7 mile to Grass Lake, which offers good swimming and camping.)

Sections of strenuous climbing pass scattered ferns, sage, red-flowered mountain spiraea, and huckleberry oak and then Sierra juniper, Jeffrey pine, pinemat manzanita, and ceanothus. Bear right at a signed trail junction at 3.6 miles. Note a spectacular display of Indian pond lilies dotting a black pond 0.2 mile farther on the left. A few more footsteps connect you with Hike

A large glacial cirque cradles Half Moon Lake.

15 (Dicks Lake, Gilmore Lake, Lake Aloha, and Middle Velma Lake) at a four-way trail intersection: The left fork heads for Susie and Heather Lakes and Lake Aloha; the right fork goes to Gilmore Lake. You proceed straight. At 4.2 miles come to a rocky flat where Sierra junipers frame a view of Susie Lake, surrounded by numerous high peaks.

Continue up into a large glacial cirque, accompanied by mountain hemlock, juvenile lodgepole pine, and several ponds, to the lightly visited yet

Dicks Peak

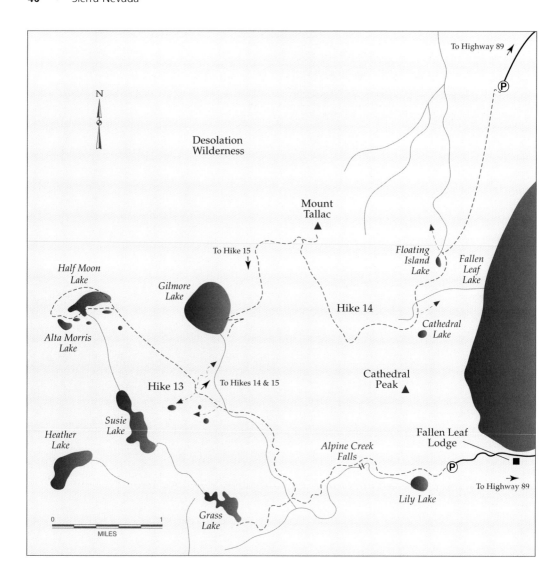

very beautiful Half Moon Lake, where the deep waters reflect the steep visages of nearby Jacks and Dicks Peaks.

The scenic north shoreline trail escorts you past a mix of lodgepole and western white pine, sage, abundant corn lily, and sulfur flower. At 6 miles, cross an alder-choked inlet stream and a colorful meadow to Alta Morris Lake, where you'll spot a large campsite on the Dicks Peak side. Continue cross-country along Half Moon Lake's south side and past several campsites to regain the trail back to the parking area.

14 MOUNT TALLAC

Length: 11 miles round-trip
Hiking time: 7 hours
High point: 9,735 feet
Total elevation gain: 3,400 feet
Difficulty: strenuous
Season: early July through mid-October
Water: available at Floating Island and Cathedral Lakes (purify first), little to
    none along the last 2.7 steep miles
Maps: USGS 7.5' Emerald Bay, USFS Desolation Wilderness
Information: Lake Tahoe Basin Management Unit

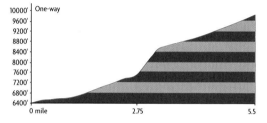

This hike challenges even the most physically fit, but the reward of a panoramic view over Lake Tahoe, Desolation Wilderness, and the rest of the northern Sierra Nevada makes the exertion worthwhile. Be sure to bring warm clothing and protection from the sun. Also check the weather; you don't want to get caught in a thunderstorm on Mount Tallac's exposed ridges and summit. Hardy backpackers can climb Mount Tallac and head down to Gilmore Lake and the trails of Hike 15 (Dicks Lake, Gilmore Lake, Lake Aloha, and Middle Velma Lake). You must obtain a permit for this hike. Day hikers can get a free permit at the trailhead. Overnight hikers need to contact the Lake Tahoe Basin Management Unit (530-543-2694; *www.fs.fed.us/r5/ltbmu*) for more information on overnight quotas, obtaining a permit, and paying overnight camping fees.

From the junction of Highways 89 and 50 in South Lake Tahoe, go northwest on Highway 89. After 3.9 miles take the road on the left that's signed for Mount Tallac. The paved road continues 1.5 miles to dead-end at the trailhead.

Fallen Leaf Lake and Mount Tallac

Travel through both chaparral and forest, gradually ascending to a ridge overlooking Fallen Leaf Lake. Enjoy excellent views of Lake Tahoe and the mountains that surround it. Reach Floating Island Lake at 1.9 miles. Here you'll find a few campsites and good swimming in shallow waters.

Follow the trail nearest the lakeshore, and then climb through a mixed red fir–lodgepole pine forest, with occasional views of Mount Tallac. Look for a small, rocky knob ringed by western juniper just east of the trail at 2.4 miles; from its top are excellent views of Fallen Leaf Lake, Lake Tahoe, and the steep Sierra peaks to the east. Back on the trail, cross Cathedral Creek, go right at a trail fork, and reach Cathedral Lake, guarded by steep-walled Cathedral Peak. The lake's waters offer good swimming in late summer.

So far your path has climbed very gently; now it becomes very steep, testing your leg strength and aerobic conditioning. As you leave Cathedral Lake, look for views of Fallen Leaf Lake, Lake Tahoe, and the surrounding mountains. Lodgepole pine, mountain hemlock, and stunted Jeffrey pine dot the landscape, and numerous wildflowers help you forget your pounding heart. At 3.5 miles the trail begins switchbacking west up a glacially carved bowl. Go left at the trail junction to reach the ridge at 4 miles. From here, your eyes take in nearly the whole of Desolation Wilderness, with westward views of Pyramid Peak, the Crystal Range, and numerous lakes.

Savor this fantastic scenery as you climb northwest just below the ridge's crest. A stone cairn at 5.2 miles marks a trail junction. A 1.5-mile downhill walk brings you to Gilmore Lake (see Hike 15: Dicks Lake, Gilmore Lake, Lake Aloha, and Middle Velma Lake). Head uphill for the final rocky 0.3 mile to your lofty goal.

Plan to spend a lot of time perched on metamorphic Mount Tallac's 9,735-foot summit. You'll have fantastic views over all of the northern Sierra Nevada and some of Nevada's basin and range topography.

15 DICKS LAKE, GILMORE LAKE, LAKE ALOHA, AND MIDDLE VELMA LAKE

Length: 30 miles round-trip
Hiking time: 4 days
High point: 9,300 feet
Total elevation gain: 4,700 feet
Difficulty: moderate
Season: late July to early October
Water: available from lakes and streams (purify first)
Maps: USGS 7.5′ Emerald Bay, USGS 7.5′ Rockbound Valley, USFS Desolation Wilderness
Information: Lake Tahoe Basin Management Unit

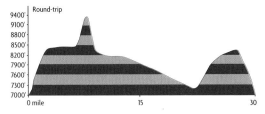

Camp near clear mountain lakes, hike past beautiful wildflower displays, and gaze at expansive vistas of high Sierra peaks on this journey through the heart of Desolation Wilderness. You must obtain a permit for this hike. Day hikers can get a free permit at the trailhead. Overnight hikers need to contact the Lake Tahoe Basin Management Unit (530-543-2694; *www.fs.fed.us/r5/ltbmu*) for more information on overnight quotas, obtaining a permit, and paying overnight camping fees.

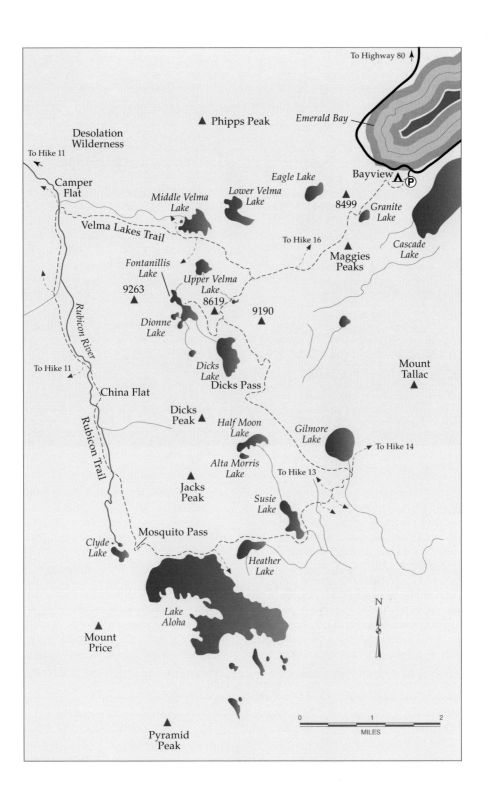

To Highway 80

Phipps Peak

Emerald Bay

Desolation
Wilderness

To Hike 11

Camper
Flat

Middle Velma
Lake

Lower Velma
Lake

Eagle Lake

Bayview

8499

Granite
Lake

Velma Lakes Trail

To Hike 16

Maggies
Peaks

Cascade
Lake

Fontanillis
Lake

Upper Velma
Lake

Rubicon River

9263

8619

9190

Dionne
Lake

Dicks
Lake

Mount
Tallac

To Hike 11

China Flat

Dicks Pass

Rubicon Trail

Dicks
Peak

Half Moon
Lake

Gilmore
Lake

To Hike 14

Alta Morris
Lake

To Hike 13

Jacks
Peak

Susie
Lake

Clyde
Lake

Mosquito Pass

Heather
Lake

N

Lake
Aloha

Mount
Price

0   1   2
MILES

Pyramid
Peak

Dicks Pass

From the intersection of Highways 89 and 28, drive south on Highway 89 for 20 miles to Bayview Campground. From the intersection of Highways 89 and 50, take Highway 89 north for 9 miles to the campground. Park in the dirt parking area next to Bayview Campground. (No overnight parking in the campground itself.) The trailhead is at the back end of the campground.

Begin climbing steadily through a mixed conifer forest past tobacco brush to a vista point at 0.6 mile of Emerald Bay and the stark, steep, south-facing slopes of Peak 9195. The deep waters of gray-green Granite Lake appear at 1.1 miles. Look for several white fir- and lodgepole pine-shaded campsites near the alder-clogged outlet stream.

Continuous views of Granite Lake, Emerald Bay, and Lake Tahoe accompany the steep climb to the boulder-strewn pass that splits the twin

Maggies Peaks at 1.9 miles. From here you can admire white firs framing Lake Tahoe to the east. Eagle Lake shimmers to the northwest, and there are impressive views of Peak 9263 to the west.

Stroll level trail as statuesque Sierra juniper and shapely western white pine foreground numerous views, especially that of Mount Tallac's jagged walls to the south. Go left at a trail fork 1.2 miles past the gap as you briefly join the trails of Hike 16 (Eagle Lake and the Velma Lakes). Turn left again 0.7 mile farther. At 4.5 miles note an attractive, unnamed, grass-lined lake stashed at the bottom of granitic Peak 9190. Look for dwarf western white pine decorating the lake's numerous rock islands.

The trail then switchbacks past mountain spiraea and red mountain heather while showing off the Velma Lakes to the north. From a gap at

5 miles, look back for the best vista yet of scenic Lake Tahoe, and then scurry westward up Peak 8619 for great views of Fontanillis Lake.

Regain the gap, find the trail fork, and bear right for a quick descent down to Dicks and Fontanillis Lakes, two of the most beautiful bodies of water in Desolation Wilderness. The high-usage campsites at Dicks Lake lie on the outskirts of a small meadow on the north shore. More exposed sites sit on a granite outcrop overlooking the lake above the east shoreline.

Although the east shore of Fontanillis Lake sports many campsites, more secluded spots rest amid granitic rock outcrops above the lake's southwest section. You can dip into the chilly, gray-blue waters from an array of boulders on the southeast shore. Farther west, a separate unnamed lake sits invitingly above Fontanillis Lake; a slim creek connects the two.

Back at the gap, note the prominent wildflowers nestled in the rocks on the climb to Dicks Pass. Yellow ivesia and sulphur flower are soon replaced by aster, orange Indian paintbrush, and red mountain heather. After numerous switchbacks—the last portion through an open forest of mountain hemlock and whitebark pine—you reach view-filled Dicks Pass at 7.2 miles.

From this 9,280-foot vantage point, Dicks and Fontanillis Lakes gleam to the north, Dicks Peak towers to the west, and farther south sit Jacks Peak, Pyramid Peak, and the distant southern Sierra. For better views walk to each of the four corners of this football-size field and marvel at Half Moon and Susie Lakes and Lake Aloha to the south. The south-facing slope of Dicks Pass features an inspiring array of wildflowers; look for ivesia, sulphur flower, sunflower, paintbrush, bitter brush, and big sage.

Continue for an open 1.6 miles past sloping wildflower gardens highlighted by blue lupine. Most of the way you'll also enjoy views toward the south of lakes and mountains. Go left at a trail fork to scenic Gilmore Lake, which takes on the same deep blue hue of Lake Tahoe. Look for numerous campsites in the flower-covered meadow above the south shore. Note that you can climb Mount Tallac (Hike 14), which towers to the east, by taking the trail from the lake's southeast shore.

From the trail fork just south of Gilmore Lake, go left down the wildflower-bordered trail and note Pyramid Peak jutting to the southwest during the 0.4-mile stretch to an intersection with the trail to Half Moon and Alta Morris Lakes (see Hike 13: Half Moon Lake). Go straight, turn right 0.3 mile farther, and reach deep-gray Susie Lake. From this attractive lake's rock-lined shore, you can look north to the lofty heights of Dicks Peak and Dicks Pass. You'll find good campsites near the east shore by the outlets. Heather Lake, 0.5 mile past Susie Lake, shares similar scenic qualities and also has east-shore campsites. Look nearby for a 20-foot waterfall.

> This route through the heart of Desolation Wilderness offers several views of Lake Tahoe.

Reach a trail fork 0.4 mile past Heather Lake and go right. (The trails of Hike 12: Lake Aloha, Lake of the Woods, and Ropi Lake lie 1.5 miles to the left.) Now walk 0.7 mile along the shore of island-rich Lake Aloha, the largest lake in Desolation Wilderness, and then climb up to Mosquito Pass for inspiring southward views. From the pass turn left down to Clyde Lake, which hosts suitable campsites between the lake and two small bodies of water just to the north.

Back on the main trail, head north on the Rubicon Trail. Meadow camping among lodgepole pine awaits after 2.5 miles at China Flat. Reach a trail fork 0.4 mile farther. The trails of Hike 11 (Maud, Lois, and Zitella Lakes) lie to the left; however, go right and walk near the Rubicon River for 2.7 miles to Camper Flat, another popular meadow loaded with campsites. (You can also connect with Hike 11 trails here.)

From Camper Flat, go right onto the Velma Lakes Trail for a 1.8-mile gradual climb to the Velma Lakes (described in Hike 16: Eagle Lake and the Velma Lakes). Go right at a trail fork just before Middle Velma Lake and go left at another fork 0.3 mile farther. From here it's another mile to reach previously encountered paths and the route back to the trailhead.

16 EAGLE LAKE AND THE VELMA LAKES

Length: 9.2 miles round-trip
Hiking time: 6 hours or overnight
High point: 8,300 feet
Total elevation gain: 2,100 feet
Difficulty: strenuous
Season: late June to early October
Water: available only from the lakes (purify first); have at least a quart on hand
Maps: USGS 7.5' Rockbound Valley, USGS 7.5' Emerald Bay, USFS Desolation Wilderness
Information: Lake Tahoe Basin Management Unit

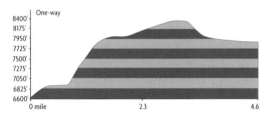

This popular trip gives great views of Lake Tahoe and several Sierra peaks as it travels to many of Desolation Wilderness's most beautiful lakes, where swimming and camping opportunities abound. You must obtain a permit for this hike. Day hikers can get a free permit at the trailhead. Overnight hikers need to contact the Lake Tahoe Basin Management Unit (530-543-2694; *www.fs.fed.us/r5/ltbmu*) for more information on overnight quotas, obtaining a permit, and paying overnight camping fees.

From the junction of Highways 89 and 28, drive south on Highway 89 for 19 miles to Emerald Bay. From the junction of Highways 89 and 50, drive north on Highway 89 for 10 miles to Emerald Bay. Park (parking fee required) at either the Vikingsholm parking lot or the Eagle Falls trailhead.

Red fir shades the continuous climb past alder, thimbleberry, and a waterfall to a rocky clearing at 0.4 mile, which features an exquisite view of deep-blue Lake Tahoe. At 0.5 mile huge granitic outcrops and twisted, gnarled Sierra juniper hint at the more stark alpine

conditions to come. After another steep 0.4 mile, reach the Eagle Lake turnoff. This very popular lake, encased by rigid rock cliffs, has designated campsites and offers good swimming and

Lake Tahoe from above Middle Velma Lake

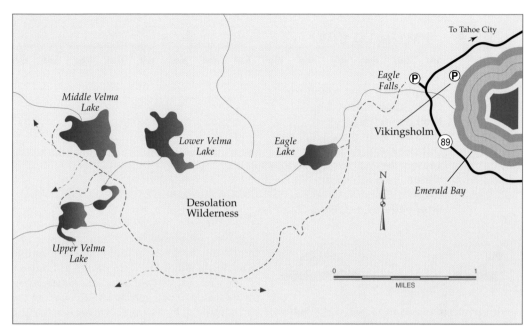

picnicking. Explore the lake's lightly forested shoreline, and then return to the main trail and observe the lake from afar as you bear south for the Velma Lakes.

Climb steadily to 1.3 miles, where the view of Eagle Lake vanishes. Enter a forest of mountain hemlock, western white pine, and red fir. The path grows faint from 1.5 to 1.7 miles, so follow the rock ducks (cairns) closely.

At 2.2 miles reach a crest where lodgepole pine predominates, signaling an end to most of the strenuous climbing. At 2.5 miles start a modest ascent amid mountain hemlock and red fir alongside a seasonal stream. When you reach another crest at 2.8 miles, head right at the signed trail junction and enjoy a long stretch of nearly level strolling past pinemat manzanita, red fir, western white pine, and Jeffrey pine, highlighted by an inspiring panorama of Lake Tahoe and scenic Sierra peaks.

Keep right at another trail junction at 3.5 miles, and then view Middle Velma Lake ahead as you begin a gradual descent. At 4.2 miles the path skirts a grass-lined lake on the left. Cross the outlet stream of Upper Velma Lake 0.1 mile farther,

proceed past a small open field featuring lupine and aster, and head right at a signed trail junction (the left fork goes to Upper Velma Lake).

At 4.6 miles continue right at another trail junction, enter a hemlock forest, and reach picturesque Middle Velma Lake 0.2 mile farther. Although peak views diminish, campsites abound here for the many backpackers, and numerous rock islands make good swimming destinations. Scout the many side trails that lead to the other Velma Lakes nearby for more campsites and slightly more seclusion. Although not as picturesque as Middle Velma Lake, Upper Velma Lake has just as many campsites and a little more seclusion. You can extend your trip by doing all or part of Hike 15 (Dicks Lake, Gilmore Lake, Lake Aloha, and Middle Velma Lake).

> Scenic Middle Velma Lake and the less-crowded Upper Velma Lake have many campsites for those desiring an overnight stay.

17 EMERALD BAY

Length: 10.6 miles round-trip
Hiking time: 6 hours
High point: 6,600 feet
Total elevation gain: 1,200 feet
Difficulty: easy to moderate
Season: late May through early October
Water: bring your own
Maps: USGS 7.5' Emerald Bay, USFS Desolation Wilderness
Information: Emerald Bay State Park

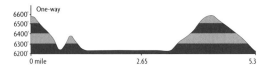

Get great views of Mount Tallac, Lake Tahoe, and Emerald Bay's Fannette Island on this scenic shoreline excursion.

From the junction of Highways 28 and 89, drive Highway 89 south for 19 miles to Emerald Bay. From the Highway 50 junction with Highway 89, travel north on Highway 89 for 9 miles to Emerald Bay. Park (parking fee required) at either the Vikingsholm parking lot on the east side or the Eagle Falls trailhead on the west side. (For a vehicle shuttle, park at the end of the trail by driving 2.5 miles north of the trailhead, turning right into D. L. Bliss State Park—parking fee required—and continuing another 2.3 miles.)

Pick up the trail off the east side of Highway 89. It drops 0.7 mile to Vikingsholm Castle,

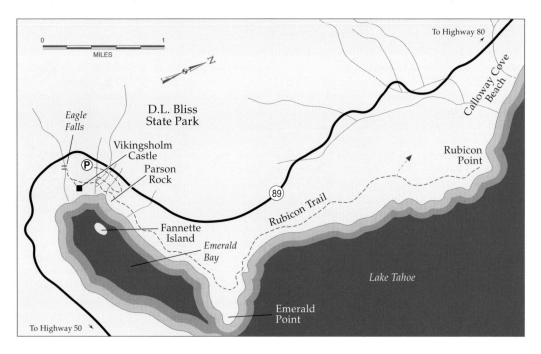

View from Maggies Peaks above Emerald Bay

the exquisite castle. Continue 0.2 mile farther to impressive Eagle Falls.

After your castle and falls visit, head north on Vikingsholm Beach 0.1 mile until you gain the Rubicon Trail proper. The sandy tread leads past beachside views of Emerald Bay and decorative Fannette Island. At 1.3 miles choose between two side trails that escort you to Parson Rock for open scenery of Emerald Bay, Lake Tahoe, and surrounding Sierra mountains.

Travel through forest, and then pass the boaters' campground at 2.1 miles. Good views of beach, bay, and mountain continue as you near Emerald Point at 2.6 miles.

The trail continues close to the shoreline and into an open forest featuring sugar pine. Keep right at 3.2 miles at a signed trail junction. The path ascends 100 feet at 3.6 miles, providing a prime view atop boulders of Lake Tahoe between white fir. The path gradually descends to a seasonal creek and then starts a longer climb at 4.2 miles. Keep right at 4.4 miles when you spot an old dirt road. Bear right at another trail junction at 5 miles. Reach Rubicon Point at 5.3 miles. Take the spur trail here and climb the rocks for good views of Lake Tahoe.

> **Exquisite Vikingsholm Castle is an early highlight of this hike.**

The final 100 yards bring you to Calloway Cove Beach in D. L. Bliss State Park, another good spot to picnic and beachcomb.

past ponderosa pine, Jeffrey pine, incense cedar, and quaking aspen. At 0.6 mile you'll find three sturdy, hand-carved wooden chairs and a signed junction. Bear right here and walk the 0.1 mile to

18 CRAG LAKE AND RUBICON LAKE

Length: 16.2 miles round-trip
Hiking time: 2 days
High point: 8,300 feet
Total elevation gain: 2,200 feet
Difficulty: moderate
Season: early July through early October
Water: available from Meeks Creek most of the way (purify first)
Maps: USGS 7.5' Rockbound Valley, USGS 7.5' Homewood, USFS Desolation Wilderness
Information: Lake Tahoe Basin Management Unit

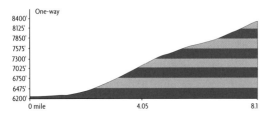

This backpack trip features both peaceful, easy walking near delightful Meeks Creek and visits to six high Sierra lakes. You must obtain a permit for this hike. Day hikers can get a free permit at the trailhead. Overnight hikers need to contact the Lake Tahoe Basin Management Unit (530-543-2694; *www.fs.fed.us/r5/ltbmu*) for more information on overnight quotas, obtaining a permit, and paying overnight camping fees.

On Highway 89 drive 0.1 mile southwest of Lake Tahoe's Meeks Bay Resort (11 miles south of Tahoe City and 16 miles from the interchange of Highways 89 and 50) and park at the signed trailhead. Day hikers can fill out self-issue wilderness permits here.

Walk around the locked gate and then stroll along the level dirt road to the signed trail junction at 1.3 miles, where you bear right on the Meeks Creek Trail. Watch closely for an eye-catching handful of rare red snow plants (protected by law) that decorate the dry chaparral hillside. At 1.7 miles climb to a view of Lake Tahoe.

> Gorgeous lakes follow one after the other.

White yarrow and red wavy-leafed paintbrush border Meeks Creek at trailside at 2 miles. At 2.3 miles you pass through a field lined with mysterious dead, white-limbed trees. The steady sound of Meeks Creek accompanies a 0.5-mile trek into a wide basin where huckleberry oak prospers in the sunny sections and thimbleberry

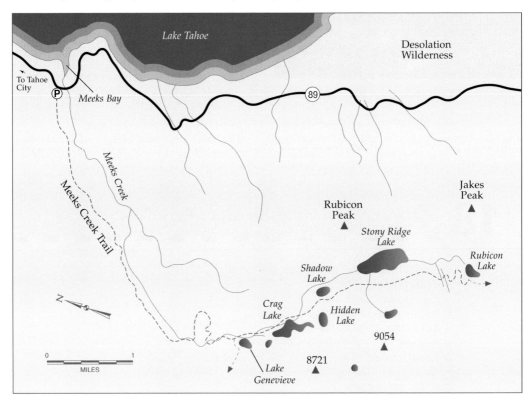

Sierra waterfall

thrives beneath the shade of western white pine and Jeffrey pine. Cross the wooden bridge over Meeks Creek at 3.3 miles. Swing away from Meeks Creek and into a white- and red-fir forest. Continue walking past pinemat manzanita to the welcome return of Meeks Creek at 4.2 miles.

A campsite awaits at 4.7 miles near the north shore of Lake Genevieve, where the shallow lake's waters reflect Peak 9054. Keep left at the signed trail junction just past two campsites near the lake's east shore.

Another campsite awaits 0.3 mile farther at Crag Lake next to the dam's spillway. Peak 9054 also hovers above this lake, which features a peninsula on the south side. The trail skirts the east shore past several campsites nestled under red fir and western white pine.

The path briefly climbs to pond lily-covered Shadow Lake, promptly followed by another mysterious stand of bare, rotting tree trunks at 6 miles. At 6.6 miles the main trail reaches the west shoreline of Stony Ridge Lake, which features two good trailside campsites. To the east Rubicon Peak towers above the lake, along with siblings Peak 9269 and Jakes Peak. Native fescue grasses abound, as do Sierra juniper and western white pine. Look for camping sites on the south side.

Climb gently through forest and meadow, cross a stream, and begin negotiating a series of steep switchbacks at 7.8 miles. Reach gorgeous Rubicon Lake at 8.1 miles, where you'll enjoy refreshing swimming and mountain views.

19 NORTH FORK OF THE AMERICAN RIVER

Length: 5-mile loop
Hiking time: 3 hours
High point: 1,600 feet
Total elevation gain: 1,000 feet
Difficulty: strenuous
Season: year-round
Water: bring your own
Maps: USGS 7.5' Auburn, Auburn State Recreation Area topo map
Information: Auburn State Recreation Area

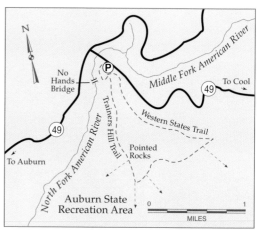

The North Fork of the American River is touted for whitewater rafting and gold mining. It's rough and scenic, with boulder banks, raging rapids, and deep-blue pools. This ruggedly secluded hike lets you get intimate with this famous fork, and then it heads into rolling foothills, highlighted by photogenic views of the river and some bizarre rock outcrops called Pointed Rocks.

From Auburn on Interstate 80, take Highway 49 East for 3.3 miles to the junction with Old Foresthill Road. Stay right, promptly cross the North Fork of the American River bridge, and park immediately on the right a few yards past the gate.

A dirt service road (no vehicles allowed) leads 200 yards to the historic No Hands Bridge, which overlooks the stark river canyon. After checking out the views, double back to the bridge entry and get on the unsigned dirt path (Trainers Hill Trail), which promptly reaches two Y-junctions (go right each time).

Climbing ensues (0.2 mile) on a wide phone-service dirt road past whiteleaf manzanita and two species of ceanothus to a view down to the river. Continue through a young, scattered forest dotted with ponderosa pine, knobcone pine, gray pine, interior live oak, and occasional Douglas fir.

Pointed Rocks shows off its plentiful native wildflowers in spring.

Moss-covered, odd-shaped blue oak specimens mingle with pines (1.1 miles) as steep climbing continues.

Reach the ridge top 0.4 mile farther, where toyon and coffeeberry in blue oak woodland form an isolated Western-movielike landscape. Stay on the wide trail as it winds gracefully along a gentle, grassy grade.

Stay straight at a trail fork (2.1 miles) to reach several clusters of the mostly chair-size, lichen-coated boulders collectively called Pointed Rocks. Native wildflowers abound here in March and April.

Continue ahead. At 2.3 miles you'll reach the Western States Trail, which follows the ridge awhile before descending into a more shaded canyon. Views past ponderosa pine and Douglas fir are mostly of the distant Sierras almost all the way back to the trailhead.

North Fork of the American River

20 LOCH LEVEN LAKES

Length: 7.2 miles round-trip
Hiking time: 5 hours or overnight
High point: 6,875 feet
Total elevation gain: 1,350 feet
Difficulty: moderate
Season: mid-June to late October
Water: available from streams and lakes (purify first)
Maps: USGS 7.5′ Cisco Grove, USGS 7.5′ Soda Springs
Information: Big Bend Visitor Center, Tahoe National Forest

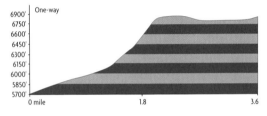

This hike takes you to three granite-ringed lakes and serves equally well as a good day hike or an easy overnight backpacking trip. An added bonus is its easy access from Interstate 80; however, this easy access means the trail is very popular. Weekdays and before or after the main summer hiking season are the best times to hike.

The trailhead and parking area lie a short way east of the Big Bend Visitor Center on Hampshire Rocks Road, which is off I-80 about 75 miles northeast of Sacramento. Going east on I-80, take the Big Bend exit (exit 166), turn left (east) on Hampshire Rocks Road, and go about a half mile. Going west on I-80, take the Big Bend/Rainbow Road exit (exit 168), bear left (west) on Hampshire Rocks Road, and go 1.5 miles.

The signed trail begins on the south side of the road. Jeffrey and lodgepole pine and some western

> Granite slabs surround the island-dotted lakes, inviting you to stretch out, rest your bones, and enjoy the views.

juniper provide intermittent shade as you make your way uphill past outcroppings of granite. Pass a pond at 0.6 mile, continue along a hillside covered by white-flowered red cherry bushes, and at 1.1 miles reach a bridge across an alder-lined creek.

You'll cross railroad tracks at 1.3 miles. Continue the uphill push as western white pine and the occasional quaking aspen join the forest cover. Be sure to look north for good views of forested mountains and the South Yuba River. At 2.2 miles the trail levels and passes through a red fir forest before starting the descent to the lakes at 2.5 miles.

Lower Loch Leven Lake

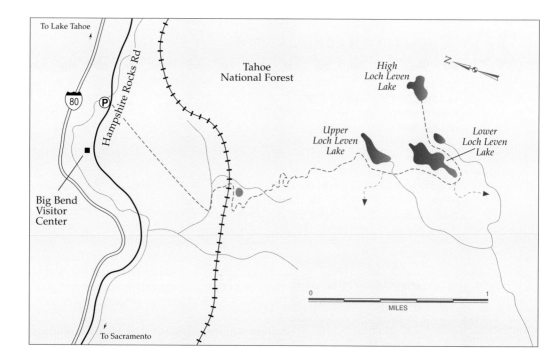

Upper Loch Leven Lake, surrounded by granite and pine, awaits at 2.7 miles. You'll find numerous campsites near the water, along with several good swimming spots. A trail fork lies at the lake's south end. (A right would take you 0.4 mile to less crowded Salmon Lake.) Head left 150 yards to Lower Loch Leven Lake, which is prettier than its upper cousin. The path, bounded by purple lupine and huckleberry oak, travels by the lake's shore, where you'll find several campsites.

Bear left at another trail junction at 3.1 miles. Follow the occasionally faint path for the last 0.5 mile as you enjoy good views of Snow Mountain to the south. High Loch Leven Lake is both the least visited and most beautiful of the Loch Leven Lakes. Granite slabs surround most of the island-dotted waters, and red fir, lodgepole pine, and western white pine provide shoreline shade for the south-side campsites. Spend most of your time here.

21 SAND RIDGE AND THE FIVE LAKES BASIN

Length: 12 miles round-trip
Hiking time: 7 hours or overnight
High point: 7,400 feet
Total elevation gain: 1,400 feet
Difficulty: moderate
Season: late June through October
Water: available from lakes and streams (purify first)
Maps: USGS 7.5' Graniteville, USGS 7.5' English Mtn
Information: Yuba River Ranger District, Tahoe National Forest

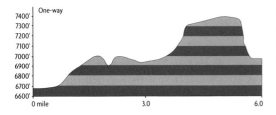

A series of beautiful lakes lines the trail on this hike, and most have campsites and deep sections suitable for a summer swim. You'll also enjoy a 360-degree view over much of the northern Sierra from the spine of Sand Ridge.

From the junction of Highway 20 and Interstate 80, drive 4 miles west on Highway 20. Turn right (north) onto Bowman Lake Road (Forest Road 18). Go 8.4 miles on this paved road, and turn right at a sign for Carr Lake, your destination. Stay on the main, somewhat rough dirt road and bear right at all road junctions for the last 2.7 miles to the trailhead at Carr Lake Campground.

> **Sand Ridge Trail hikers see the Black Buttes, Fall Creek Mountain, the Sierra Buttes, and the Sacramento Valley.**

Follow the road, which becomes the Round Lake Trail after crossing a creek. The path borders the shores of Feely Lake, popular for fishing, and offers good views of Fall Creek Mountain. After 0.5 mile begin a gentle climb past red fir and western white pine. Reach an unnamed lake on the left at 1 mile with several campsites on its east edge and immediately reach a trail junction. Go right (the left-hand trail is covered in Hike 22: Crooked Lakes Trail to Penner Lake) and ascend above the granite-lined shores of Island Lake, the prettiest lake in the region. At least two campsites lie among lodgepole pine near the water's edge down to the left. If others have already claimed these, try one of the several sites along the lake's west shore.

Arrive at a crest at 1.2 miles with good views of Island Lake and the serrated Sierra Buttes to the north. The trail then descends 0.2 mile to a creek that runs from Round Lake to Long Lake. On the creek's far side, take a footpath to the right for the short streamside stroll past mountain heather to Round Lake. Granite and metamorphic rock stretch

steeply upward on the lake's southeast side, and red fir and lodgepole pine clothe the rest of the lake's shore. Camp at one of the sites near the northwest shore if you find Island Lake too crowded.

Back on the main trail, at 1.5 miles you'll see a faint path traveling through a shallow gully on the left. It leads to Long Lake, which has two campsites on its east shore and, like Round Lake, sees few visitors. One hundred yards past the Long Lake turnoff, you'll see another spur trail to Round Lake on the right. Stay left and climb gently to a spur trail on the right heading down to Milk Lake at 2.1 miles. This shallow lake has a good campsite underneath a two-trunked fir tree near the water's edge. Note that this is your last sure source of water for the next 2.7 miles.

At 2.2 miles you reach a trail junction. Go left and travel under the shade of the red fir forest.

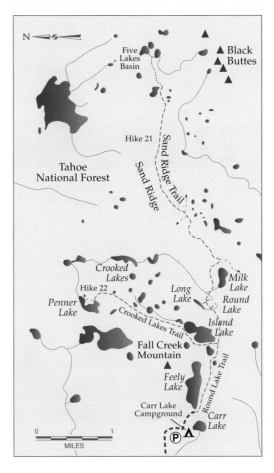

Island Lake

You now walk along the open ridge covered with a multicolored floral display including mule ear, phlox, and purple lupine. Western white pine, red fir, and an occasional mountain hemlock grow here and there in the exposed landscape but rarely hinder views of the imposing peaks of the Black Buttes to the southeast, Stoddard Lake and the Sacramento Valley to the southwest, Fall Creek Mountain to the west, the Sierra Buttes and numerous other mountains to the north, and English Mountain to the northeast.

The trail eventually descends from the ridge and reaches a shallow but swimmable lake at 4.8 miles. A faint trail runs near the south shore, where you'll find several campsites.

From the lake's east side, you'll see the Five Lakes Basin, the hike's final destination, another 0.5 mile east and 250 feet below. Choose your own cross-country route over the gently sloping granite slabs. Most of the lakes offer several campsites and good swimming. Consider adding Hike 22 (Crooked Lakes Trail to Penner Lake) to your itinerary on the way back to the trailhead.

A trail fork awaits at 2.8 miles. Go right and 100 yards farther go left for the Sand Ridge Trail, where your path initially passes through a grove of young lodgepole pine.

The Sand Ridge Trail gains most of its elevation over 0.3 mile and then levels out at 3.5 miles.

22 CROOKED LAKES TRAIL TO PENNER LAKE

Length: 6 miles round-trip
Hiking time: 3 hours
High point: 7,035 feet
Total elevation gain: 600 feet
Difficulty: easy
Season: mid-June through October
Water: available from trailside lakes (purify first)
Maps: USGS 7.5' Graniteville, USGS 7.5' English Mtn
Information: Yuba River Ranger District, Tahoe National Forest

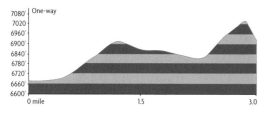

Hike 22, Crooked Lakes to Penner Lake

Gentle climbing and numerous campsites make this hike an excellent family backpacking trip. The Crooked Lakes Trail leads you past a bounty of large and small bodies of water, where you'll have ample opportunity to picnic, swim, and fish.

From its junction with Interstate 80, drive

Highway 20 west 4 miles, and turn right (north) onto Bowman Lake Road (Forest Road 18). Follow this paved road 8.4 miles and turn right at a sign for Carr Lake, your destination. Stay on the main road and bear right at all road junctions as you drive the last 2.7 miles of a somewhat rough dirt road to the trailhead at Carr Lake Campground.

Take the campground road east, where it crosses a creek before turning into the trail. The path initially travels along the shores of Feely Lake, a favorite spot for fishing, and offers good views of Fall Creek Mountain to the north. Begin a gentle ascent at 0.5 mile and then level off by a small, shallow pond.

Turn left at 1 mile onto the Crooked Lakes Trail just after encountering an unnamed lake (Hike 21: Sand Ridge and the Five Lakes Basin, travels to the right). You now pass between the unnamed lake on the left and the much larger and deeper Island Lake on the right. Granite-encased Island Lake, with its clear waters and small islands, rivals your final destination, Penner Lake, for swimmability and the most scenic beauty of the hike. Several campsites line the west shore of Island Lake and the east shore of the lake on the left.

Leave Island Lake behind at 1.5 miles and travel through a red fir forest. Look for a small waterfall on Island Lake's alder-lined outlet creek at 1.8 miles. The first of the Crooked Lakes lies to the right at 2 miles, but press past its shallow, marshy waters to the better lakes to come.

As the path descends at 2.3 miles, take a small side trail on the right just before reaching a small lake. Follow it across the creek to the best of the Crooked Lakes, a large, deep lake rimmed by granite. You'll find a good campsite right where the trail ends, and from the lake's shore you'll have open views of the Black Buttes to the east.

Back on the Crooked Lakes Trail, climb steadily for the next 0.5 mile over rocky tread and past pinemat manzanita and huckleberry oak. At 2.8 miles crest a ridge and see the rocky shores of expansive Penner Lake below. Follow the trail the final 0.2 mile down to the lake,

where you'll find excellent swimming spots but few campsites.

Be sure to enjoy the open views of the surrounding mountains as you hike back to the trailhead. Consider adding part of Hike 21 (Sand Ridge and the Five Lakes Basin) to your journey.

Penner Lake

23 MOUNT ELWELL

Length: 8.2 miles round-trip
Hiking time: 5 hours
High point: 7,818 feet
Total elevation gain: 1,600 feet
Difficulty: moderate to strenuous
Season: mid-June through October
Water: available from lakes and streams, except for the last 1.5 miles (purify
   first)
Map: USGS 7.5' Gold Lake
Information: Beckwourth Ranger District, Plumas National Forest

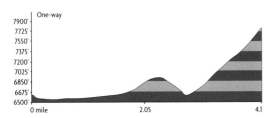

This trip takes you past numerous rock-encircled high Sierra lakes to the top of Mount Elwell, a peak that offers panoramic views of the Lakes Basin and northern Sierra Nevada. Note that camping outside of official campgrounds is prohibited in this area.

The dirt road to the trailhead lies on the west

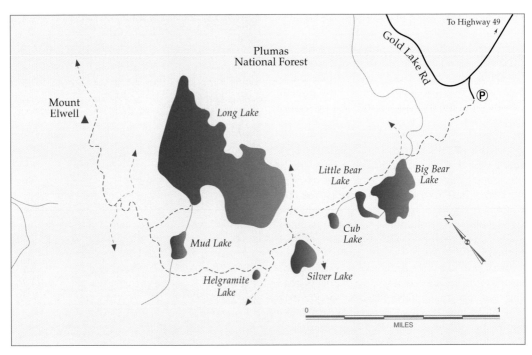

side of Gold Lake Road, 8 miles northwest of Highway 49 and 8 miles southeast of Highway 89, and is just south of the Sierra-Plumas county line. You'll see a sign for the Round Lake Trail. Go 200 feet and park.

Go right at 0.2 mile onto a trail and then descend gently past two small ponds. Reach Big Bear Lake at 0.7 mile. The large lake's deep waters, surrounding forest, and rocky crest tie it with the upcoming Long Lake for the most picturesque body of water in the Lakes Basin.

Go left at the trail fork just beyond Big Bear Lake's outlet and walk under the shade of red fir, lodgepole pine, and Jeffrey pine. At 1.1 miles you'll encounter Little Bear Lake. The trail then climbs to a rendezvous with Cub Lake at 1.3 miles and to a trail junction at 1.5 miles. Turn left and enjoy the magnificent view of your destination: the summit of Mount Elwell towering above the broad expanse of Long Lake.

Silver Lake, another deep and beautiful lake nearly on par with Big Bear Lake, awaits at 1.7 miles. Go right at a trail junction at the lake's shore and right again at 2.2 miles. After passing small and shallow Helgramite Lake, the trail descends to Mud Lake, crossing its inlet creek at 2.7 miles. Note that this is your last sure source of water.

At 2.9 miles you'll see an unsigned spur trail that travels 0.3 mile down to the shore of Long Lake, an excellent side trip. The main path now climbs in earnest up an open, moist slope before encountering a double trail junction at 3.3 miles. Go left and immediately right following signs for Mount Elwell.

> Numerous lakes lie sprinkled below the rocky 7,818-foot summit of Mount Elwell.

The path ascends steeply for the last 0.8 mile, initially past pink, purple, white, and blue phlox and large blue lupine and later past pinemat manzanita and bush chinquapin. Stately red fir clad in coats of green lichen provide occasional shade.

After the vigorous workout, you finally reach

Mules ears and red firs

the rocky summit of Mount Elwell, elevation 7,818 feet. To the immediate south lies the Lakes Basin, with Long Lake directly below. Farther south the sharp-edged Sierra Buttes puncture the sky, and to the southeast rise the vast, high ridges of the Tahoe Sierra region. Rock, Jamison, and Wades Lakes inhabit the valley just to the west (see Hike 24: Smith Lake to Wades Lake). To the north and farther west forested mountains stretch to the skyline.

24 SMITH LAKE TO WADES LAKE

Length: 13.8 miles round-trip
Hiking time: 2 days
High point: 6,600 feet
Total elevation gain: 1,600 feet
Difficulty: moderate
Season: mid-June through October
Water: available from numerous creeks and lakes (purify first)
Map: USGS 7.5' Sierra City
Information: Beckwourth Ranger District, Plumas National Forest

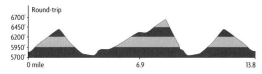

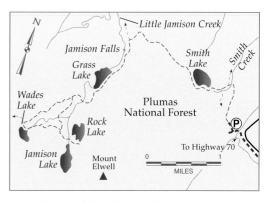

This hike takes you past the cascading waters of clear mountain streams as you travel through pine and fir forests. You'll also visit five of the Sierra's northernmost glacial lakes and enjoy fine alpine views of rocky ridges.

Turn onto Gray Eagle Lodge Road, which is on the west side of Gold Lake Road 11 miles north of Highway 49 and 5 miles southwest of Highway 89. Drive 0.6 mile, bear right at a fork, and go another 0.2 mile to the trailhead.

The path climbs gently north, first through open chaparral and then under forest shade. Just after crossing Smith Creek at 0.6 mile, bear left at a trail fork. As you continue to follow Smith Creek upstream, stay right at another trail junction.

Reach Smith Lake at 1 mile. With its two good campsites along the south shore, this lake makes a good destination for those getting a late afternoon start. Note that camping (except in camp-grounds) is forbidden in the Lakes Basin except at this hike's five lakes.

> The Sierra Nevada's glacial history is evident in the rock striations found at Jamison and Rock Lakes.

The trail ascends west of Smith Lake and then gradually descends through red fir forest to a trail fork at 3.7 miles.

Turn left and head uphill, paralleling Little Jamison Creek. At 3.9 miles your ears will guide you to 40-foot-high Jamison Falls to the right of the trail.

Campsites abound on all sides of Grass Lake at 4.2 miles. Western serviceberry surrounds much of the lake, as do Jeffrey pine, lodgepole pine, and red fir. You'll have views of the rocky ridges to the north and west, and you can also search the lake's surface for ducks and beavers.

Large numbers of quaking aspen populate the moist area along the trail just south of Grass Lake as you climb to cross Little Jamison Creek at 5 miles. Hike under the shade of red fir, incense cedar, and Jeffrey pine, and go left at trail junctions at 5.4 miles and 6.2 miles.

Jamison Lake, at 6.4 miles, has two campsites, one near the northeast shore, the other near the northwest shore. Rock Lake, 0.2 mile farther, offers more picturesque surroundings. The rock-rimmed lake, much deeper than Jamison, allows

much better swimming opportunities and also has several campsites at its south end. At both lakes you'll see rock striations and other evidence of the glaciers that carved the wide valley through these mountains and scooped out the lakes.

To reach Wades Lake, return to the trail fork 0.2 mile below Jamison Lake and turn left. For the first 0.5 mile, the path climbs west over a rocky ridge and can be a bit difficult to follow. Begin climbing south next to the lake's outlet stream at 0.7 mile. You'll reach Wades Lake 0.9 mile from the last trail fork. Rimmed by willow, mountain alder, lodgepole pine, and red fir, this lake offers the best mountain ridge views of all the lakes on this hike. You'll find two good campsites along the south shore.

Take the trail that begins by a sign giving Wades Lake's elevation and follow it downhill, initially through an open meadow. Bear right at a trail junction 0.25 mile from the lake, and then enjoy increasingly open views of Mount Elwell towering over Rock and Jamison Lakes to the east and Grass Lake and the distant mountains to the north and northeast. You'll reach a trail junction 0.9 mile from Wades Lake, which is the same one encountered at mile 5.4. Head left to return to the trailhead.

Paintbrush, mules ears, and lupine

25   FEATHER FALLS

Length: 8.8 miles round-trip
Hiking time: 5 hours
High point: 2,500 feet
Total elevation gain: 1,100 feet
Difficulty: moderate
Season: year-round
Water: available from Frey Creek and Fall River (purify first)
Maps: USGS 7.5' Forbestown, USGS 7.5' Brush Creek
Information: Feather River Ranger District, Plumas National Forest

This hike offers a smorgasbord of natural delights. You'll walk through tall stands of incense cedar and ponderosa pine, along streams shaded by bigleaf maple and dogwood, and past a multitude of spring and early summer wildflowers to Feather Falls, where the clear

Feather Falls (Photo by John R. Soares)

waters of the Fall River drop 640 feet into a granitic gorge.

Take Highway 70 to Oroville, exit onto Oro Dam Boulevard, head northeast, and turn right after 1.5 miles onto Olive Highway. Go 6 miles and turn right onto Forbestown Road. Go another 6 miles and turn left onto Lumpkin Road. Follow Lumpkin Road 10 miles and turn left at a Feather Falls sign for the final 1.6 miles to the trailhead.

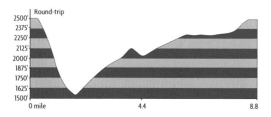

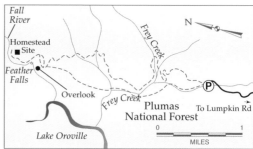

For the first 200 yards, the path travels past dozens of madrone trees, easily recognizable by their large, shiny green leaves and peeling red bark. Bear left at a trail fork, noting that you'll return by the right fork. Near the 0.5-mile marker, look for the scarce California nutmeg tree, which has long, sharp needles.

Reach the cool canyon shade of Frey Creek at 1.1 miles. As you gradually descend near the gurgling water, look for a swimming hole at the bottom of a two-stage waterfall to the left at 1.4 miles.

Views through the trees of the middle fork of the Feather River and its steep canyon walls appear at 1.5 miles; look for the smooth granite head of Bald Rock Dome looming above the river's west bank. From here, you descend for 1 shady mile and then begin a moderate climb to a trail fork at 3.2 miles. Stay left and follow the safety railings to another trail fork. Go left again to reach the overlook.

From the overlook you have a magnificent view of Feather Falls, where the aptly named Fall River drops 640 vertical feet past sheer granite cliffs to the canyon far below before joining the middle fork of the Feather River and Lake Oroville.

After imbibing this broad view of the sixth-highest waterfall in the United States, go back to the last trail fork, turn

> **Feather Falls' 640-foot drop makes it the sixth highest waterfall in the United States.**

left, and walk 0.2 mile to where a small trail leads to granite boulders at the lip of the falls. Those not afraid of heights can lean against a chain-link fence and watch the water plummet all the way to the bottom of the canyon.

This side trail continues another mile upstream along the Fall River. Summer swimmers will find good swimming holes, and overnighters will find several campsites. Near the end of the trail, you'll see some old fruit trees and an old water ditch, which are all that remain of an old homestead.

The return portion of the loop is 1.2 miles longer than the route to the falls, but it has very little elevation change. This upper portion leaves from near the overlook and offers excellent views of Frey Creek and Bald Rock Dome. It connects to the bottom portion of the loop near the trailhead.

26 DEER CREEK

Length: 4.6 miles round-trip
Hiking time: 3 hours
High point: 3,225 feet
Total elevation gain: 650 feet
Difficulty: moderate
Season: year-round, occasional winter snow
Water: available from Deer Creek and tributaries (purify first)
Map: USGS 7.5′ Onion Butte
Information: Almanor Ranger District, Lassen National Forest

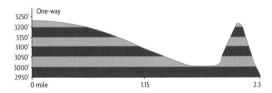

Steep canyon walls, shady forest, and crashing waterfalls large and small highlight this hike along Deer Creek. You can walk this enticing trail nearly any time of year because it's usually below the snowline in winter. The route can also serve as excellent preparation for summer backpacking, with campsites spread liberally near the path. It also leaves right from Highway 32, so there's no dirt road driving.

Take Highway 32 off Highway 99 in Chico and head 40 miles north to the first bridge across Deer Creek. (The bridge is terra cotta-colored.) Park in the area on the right 100 feet beyond. The parking area is also 1.6 miles southwest of Potato Patch Campground if you're coming down from Highway 36. **Note:** Highway 32 has many curves and is not recommended for motor homes and vehicles with trailers.

Lower Deer Creek Falls

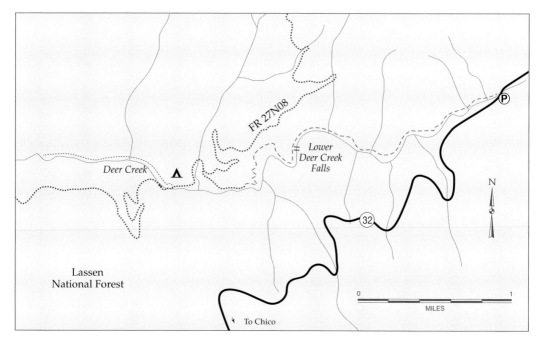

Walk to the northwest side of the bridge on the opposite side of the road. The trail begins near a "Deer Creek Trail" sign. Enter a forest of Douglas fir, ponderosa pine, incense cedar, and canyon live oak, the major shade species you'll encounter on the hike. You'll soon reach a small stream that empties into Deer Creek, the first of several over the next 2 miles or so. Just beyond, a rock outcrop serves as an excellent vantage point for viewing alder-lined Deer Creek.

A small cave nestles in the mountainside at 0.4 mile. Just beyond, look for the rare California nutmeg tree; it has sharp, dark green needles. Travel past several suitable tent sites and a series of small waterfalls, and then climb to run level in the shade of canyon live oaks.

At 1.6 miles you reach the largest and most impressive cataract: Lower Deer Creek Falls. Two parallel trails lead to the bottom of the falls, where the 15-foot thunder creates a fine mist that caresses your face.

Once you leave the falls, continue downstream on the main path. You'll reach more camping areas and amble through California laurel groves thick with the peppery smell of bay leaves. Gain more views of the 1,000-foot-high walls of Deer Creek canyon before descending steeply to the end of the trail (and some campsites) near the creek at 2.3 miles.

If you want to explore farther, continue downstream on the dirt road that begins at the trail's end to Forest Road 27N08, where you go left and drop 0.3 mile to a primitive campground on the north side of Deer Creek by a bridge. Go through the campground and find a trail you can follow across small streams for a mile or so. If you want to arrange a car shuttle, have someone take Forest Road 27N08 from Highway 32 (3.6 miles southwest of the parking area, 36.4 miles north of Highway 99, and signed for Deer Creek) and drive 6 miles to the bridge.

27 | MILL CREEK

Length: 29.6 miles round-trip
Hiking time: 3 to 4 days
High point: 4,550 feet
Total elevation gain: 3,000 feet
Difficulty: moderate
Season: mid-April through November
Water: available from Mill Creek and other streams (purify first)
Maps: USGS 7.5' Mineral, USGS 7.5' Onion Butte, USGS 7.5' Barkley Mountain
Information: Almanor Ranger District, Lassen National Forest

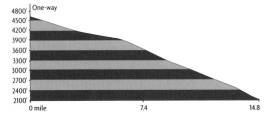

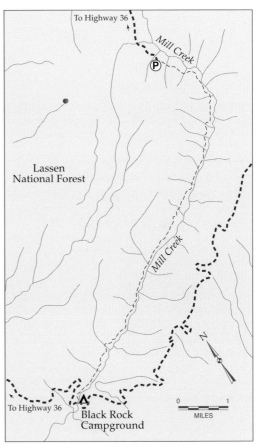

The Mill Creek Trail offers backpackers an ideal spring trip. While trails at higher elevations still lie under several feet of snow, you can enjoy views of a 1,000-foot-high canyon rim, a bounty of wildflowers, and fresh green leaves on deciduous trees. In autumn, when the first snows cloak distant peaks, those same deciduous tree leaves turn to vibrant shades of pink, orange, and yellow. **Note:** A stream crossing encountered just past the trailhead can be difficult to cross during periods of high water flow. In addition, downed trees occasionally block the trail.

Drive to the intersection of Highways 36 and 172, which is located 9 miles east of Mineral and 9 miles northwest of the junction of Highways 32 and 36. Go 3 miles down Highway 172 to the town of Mill Creek. Turn left 0.3 mile past Mill Creek Resort onto an unsigned dirt road. Go straight at an intersection 2.8 miles farther, and continue another 1.5 miles to the trailhead.

It is possible to do this hike one-way with a car shuttle. To reach Black Rock Campground, take Highway 36 to the town of Paynes Creek. Then take Paynes Creek Road and turn right 0.3 mile farther onto Plum Creek Road. After 8 miles, turn right onto Ponderosa Way. Travel this dirt road for 20 miles to the trail, following signs for Black Rock and Mill Creek at all intersections. **Note:** The road is occasionally rough (though still passable for two-wheel-drive vehicles), and crossing Antelope Creek may be difficult during periods of high water flow.

The journey begins at the far end of the parking area. Douglas fir dominate the forest here and along most of the length of the Mill Creek Trail. These stately trees, along with a few incense cedar and large-coned sugar pine, provide ample shade as you gently descend 4 miles to a bluff that allows the first views of the rapids and waterfalls of Mill Creek.

The trail undulates uphill as you pass by numerous dogwood trees (with large, white, six-petaled "flowers" in spring) and cross several streams. After slowly descending back to Mill Creek, you'll find the first good campsite at 6.3 miles. Spacious, well-shaded, and situated by the water, this makes a good first-day stopping point.

The path again climbs, and at 7.3 miles you'll encounter the rare California nutmeg tree. It sports dark green, stiff, sharp needles; a gentle squeeze of a branch is all that is necessary to identify it. You'll notice dozens of others farther along the trail.

At 8.3 miles the trail begins traveling along a dry, exposed, south-facing slope punctured by volcanic rocks. Chaparral shrubs such as buckbrush and whiteleaf and greenleaf manzanita dot the hillside, and white popcorn flowers, purple brodiaea, and numerous other wildflowers grow amid the grasses. This is also where you'll see the first open views of the steep, rock-studded mountain slope on the other side of Mill Creek.

> Dogwood blooms add color to Mill Creek Trail in spring, while deciduous trees glow with fire hues in autumn.

An increasing number of ponderosa pine and numerous canyon live oak and black oak line the trail as you again descend to another rendezvous

Mill Creek below Black Rock
(Photo by John R. Soares)

with Mill Creek at 9.9 miles. An obvious campsite lies just to the left, and as the trail travels near the creek for the next 1.7 miles, you'll find several other flat areas suitable for camping.

At 10 miles the trail passes through a flat area populated with ponderosa pine, climbs to a lush spring, and descends to a large, wet meadow at 13.2 miles, where you can find a camping spot near the creek. After crossing through the meadow, hike 1 more mile to Black Rock Campground.

CASCADE MOUNTAINS

Cinder Cone and mountain mahogany shrub, Lassen Volcanic National Park

Dozens of waterfalls grace the Cascade Mountains, along with verdant meadows, vibrant wildflowers, high mountain lakes, and vast expanses of pine and fir forests interspersed with groves of quaking aspen. The collision of the Pacific Ocean floor with continental North America fired the formation of the Cascade volcanoes. Lassen Volcanic National Park is justly famous for its bubbling hot springs, smoking fumaroles, steaming lakes, and percolating ponds. Lassen Peak and Mount Shasta dominate the region; numerous trails take you along the slopes and to the summits of these giants. Views from Lassen and Shasta and many lower vantage points encompass the Sacramento Valley, the rugged Klamath Mountains, and the high-desert expanse in the Cascades rainshadow to the east.

28 CARIBOU WILDERNESS

Length: 11.5 miles round-trip
Hiking time: 8 hours or 2 days
High point: 7,150 feet
Total elevation gain: 950 feet
Difficulty: easy to moderate
Season: mid-June through late October; many mosquitoes through late July
Water: available from lakes (purify first)
Maps: USGS 7.5′ Harvey Mountain, USGS 7.5′ Red Cinder, USGS 7.5′ Bogard Buttes
Information: Almanor Ranger District, Lassen National Forest

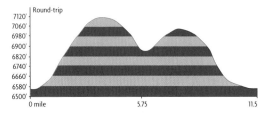

No, you won't find any caribou here, but you will find plenty of deer, squirrels, birds, and other wildlife, along with an impressive array of glacial lakes, all harbored in a seldom-visited wilderness area that abuts the east edge of Lassen Volcanic National Park.

Take Road A21 4.5 miles southwest from its junction with Highway 44 (14 miles north of Westwood). Go west on Silver Lake Road (also called Mooney Road) for 6 miles, and head right on Road M10. Follow trailhead signs for the final mile.

Sign in at the trail register and then walk above Caribou Lake's dam. Note the red fir and Jeffrey and lodgepole pines. They're the major tree species you'll see on the hike, along with a few western white pines.

Keep to the right at 0.4 mile, bisect two ponds, and turn left at 0.7 mile. (You'll return on the right-hand fork.) Contour around a shallow lake and begin a climb that ends at 1.7 miles at a trail fork.

Go left for now and reach Emerald Lake at 1.9 miles. This is one of the crown jewels of Caribou Wilderness, with sparkling green water and an excellent campsite.

Travel east through chaparral, eventually heading west to an escarpment at 2.7 miles. Sit at the edge and enjoy the views of treetops and forested mountains stretching in all directions.

Continue another 0.2 mile to Rim Lake, where you'll find an even better panorama. If you fancy a dip, head for the deeper waters along the southwest shore. Backpackers will find several level areas to pitch a tent.

> Emerald Lake's sparkling green waters make it a crown jewel of the Caribou Wilderness.

Silver Lake in the Caribou Wilderness

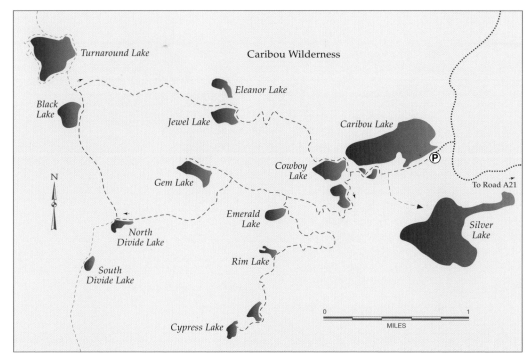

Continue southwest to two lakes. The first, at 3.5 miles, is shallow and forefronts a steep cliff; Cypress Lake lies another 0.2 mile farther; both have campsites.

Head back to the trail junction below Emerald Lake; go left. Continue to a trail fork, where a 300-yard walk to the right brings you to Gem Lake, with deep swimming waters but no campsites.

On the main trail travel 1 mile to North Divide Lake and a trail fork. (A 0.3-mile saunter to the left leads to South Divide Lake, which has better campsites than North Divide Lake.) Go right (north) 0.8 mile to grass-lined Black Lake, which has several campsites on its north and south sides.

Go right at the trail fork north of Black Lake. Climb and descend gently east for 1.5 miles to Jewel Lake, host of several north shore campsites and deep waters for swimming. Descend 1.1 miles to Cowboy Lake and soon reach a trail junction. Head left for the last 0.7 mile to the trailhead.

29 MOUNT HARKNESS

Length: 6.4 miles round-trip
Hiking time: 4 hours or 2 days
High point: 8,046 feet
Total elevation gain: 1,750 feet
Difficulty: moderate
Season: early July through mid-October
Water: none; bring at least 2 quarts per person for the day hike
Maps: USGS 7.5′ Mount Harkness, park brochure
Information: Lassen Volcanic National Park

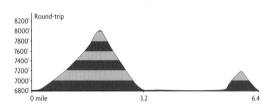

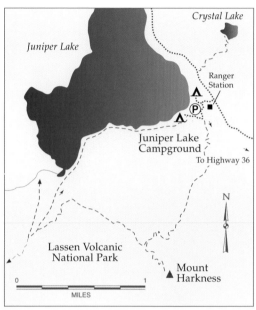

Of the major peaks in Lassen Volcanic National Park, Mount Harkness is the easiest climb, but it has a full complement of views that rival those of its sibling summits. Most people do Harkness as a day hike, but if you're set on backpacking you'll find the occasional level patch among trees. If you do an overnighter, bring all your water. Overnight trips require a permit. Get one at the park or via email (530-595-4444; *www.nps .gov/lavo*). Once you have finished your climb of Mount Harkness, you can make the side trip to Crystal Lake.

On Highway 36 in Chester, go 100 feet east of the North Fork Feather River bridge and head north on Feather River Drive. Bear right at 0.7 mile, roll on pavement another 5.5 miles, and transfer to dirt surface that's too rough for trailers. Turn into Juniper Lake Campground 12 miles from Highway 36 and park in the lot on the right. The trail begins by site 5.

Warm up on the level portion of the path's beginning before climbing steeply south with the company of red firs and western white pines, soon joined by mountain hemlocks. After the 1-mile mark you'll pass a few level areas, obtain the first good view of the park, and then leave the forest for continuous long-range views fronted by blue lupines and goldenbush.

Swing left at 1.6 miles at a trail fork as you continue up past basalt flows, evidence of the numerous eruptions that formed Mount Harkness, a shield volcano. Eventually ascend a series of switchbacks up the cinder cone that crowns Harkness's summit.

At close range on the summit, you'll note the cinder cone's 100-foot-deep caldera and a few stunted trees that barely survive the rough winters. But your eyes will quickly be drawn to the distant vistas. Topping the list are Brokeoff Mountain, Lassen Peak, and Chaos Crags to the west. Mount Shasta gleams in the far north, with Hat Mountain, Magee Peak, Prospect Peak, and West Prospect Peak claiming the nearer ground. The cinder cones and other volcanoes of Caribou Wilderness lie east, with Lake Almanor and the Sierra Nevada to the south.

When ready, descend to the trail fork and go left through a forest that has a few level spots for backpackers. Head right at another trail fork 1.7 miles from the summit and continue another 1.8 miles to the campground, the last section just above Juniper Lake's south shore.

Cap off the day by making the steep 0.4-mile ascent to Crystal Lake. (The path leaves the road 0.3 mile north of the campground.) You can swim in the clear waters and enjoy views of Mount Harkness and Lassen Peak, along with other notable summits. A few western junipers call the slope above the southwest shore home; they're the namesakes for Juniper Lake.

Opposite: Lassen Peak from Mount Harkness (Photo by John R. Soares)

30 BROKEOFF MOUNTAIN

Length: 7.2 miles round-trip
Hiking time: 5 hours
High point: 9,235 feet
Total elevation gain: 2,600 feet
Difficulty: strenuous
Season: mid-July through October
Water: available only the first 2 miles (purify first)
Maps: USGS 7.5' Lassen Peak, park brochure
Information: Lassen Volcanic National Park

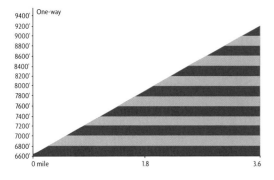

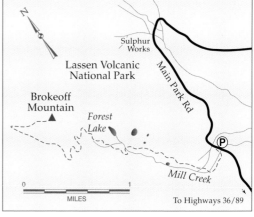

This hike offers two rewards. First, you'll travel through several plant habitats with a variety of multicolored wildflowers. Second, you'll gain an excellent view of Lassen Volcanic National Park and Northern California that rivals that of nearby Lassen Peak (Hike 32), but you'll share it with far fewer people. However, read the warning in Hike 32, which also applies to this journey.

Find the trailhead 0.25 mile south of the entrance station on the main park road, which is 4.8 miles from the intersection of Highways 36 and 89 and 29.2 miles from the intersection of Highways 44 and 89.

The path begins near a willow- and alder-lined creek. After climbing through a mixed

> Brokeoff Mountain is a remnant of ancient Brokeoff Volcano, a volcano that once rose to more than 11,000 feet before its catastrophic demise.

forest of lodgepole and western white pine, it reaches a marshy pond at 0.8 mile. Towering red fir begin to dominate the forest as you ascend past several small meadows. For a pleasant side trip, at 1.3 miles follow the creek north 250 yards to the shallow waters of Forest Lake.

The trail then offers increasingly open views as it heads up Brokeoff's south ridge. The final 1.1 miles, a mild ascent to the summit, pass through a weather-tortured subalpine zone, where a few stunted red fir eke out an existence among whitebark pine and mountain hemlock.

The summit of Brokeoff Mountain offers unobstructed views. To the immediate northeast, a ridge punctuated by Mount Diller, Pilot Pinnacle, and Eagle Peak stretches to Lassen Peak's flanks and beyond to Chaos Crags. Long-distance views encompass the Warner Mountains in the

View of Lassen Peak from the summit of Brokeoff Mountain

far northeast, Lake Almanor to the east, the Sierra Nevada marching southward, the Coast Range and Klamath Mountains to the west and northwest, and the snow-clad slopes of mighty Mount Shasta gleaming to the north.

Brokeoff Mountain, along with nearby Mount Diller, is a remnant of ancient Brokeoff Volcano (also known as Mount Tehama), which once soared to an elevation of 11,000 to 11,500 feet and boasted a 5-mile diameter. A combination of numerous eruptions from its sides and the action of ice-age glaciers slowly destroyed the mighty volcano. Sulphur Works, part of Brokeoff Volcano's vent, lies 2,400 feet below and 1 mile east of Brokeoff's summit. After you finish this hike, visit this small hydrothermally active area (located 1.5 miles north of the Brokeoff Mountain trailhead on the main park road).

31 MILL CREEK FALLS AND RIDGE LAKES

Length: 5.6 miles round-trip
Hiking time: 4 hours
High point: 8,000 feet
Total elevation gain: 1,350 feet
Difficulty: moderate to strenuous
Season: late June through late October
Water: bring your own
Maps: USGS 7.5' Lassen Peak, park brochure
Information: Lassen Volcanic National Park

A mile of pavement on the main park road separates the trail to Mill Creek Falls from the trail to Ridge Lakes, but more than the short distance differentiates them. The walk to Mill Creek Falls travels gently through forest to the spectacular cataract where Mill Creek, a major Cascade stream that drains into the Sacramento River, has its origin. The path to Ridge Lakes climbs 1,000 feet over 1.2 miles, but it takes you to two lakes and gives open views over vast swaths of Northern California topography. A permit is required for overnight trips to the Ridge Lakes. Get one at the park or via email (530-595-4444; *www.nps.gov/lavo*). Backpacking is not permitted on the trail to Mill Creek Falls.

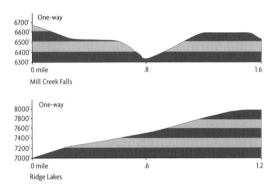

For Mill Creek Falls, go to Lassen Volcanic National Park's Southwest Campground, which lies on the east side of the main park road about 6 miles north of the junction of Highways 36 and 89 and 28 miles southeast of the junction of Highways 44 and 89. Begin the hike at site 19.

Drop gently 0.3 mile past red firs and lodgepole pines to a wooden bridge across West Sulphur Creek, a mineral-laden stream that drains Sulphur Works. The path rises and falls moderately through a western white pine and red and white fir forest. Stay alert for intermittent views of Brokeoff Mountain, Mount Diller, Mount Conard, and Diamond Peak.

The increasing cacophony of thundering water announces your approach to the vista point for Mill Creek Falls at 1.6 miles. East Sulphur Creek

Mill Creek Falls (Photo by John R. Soares)

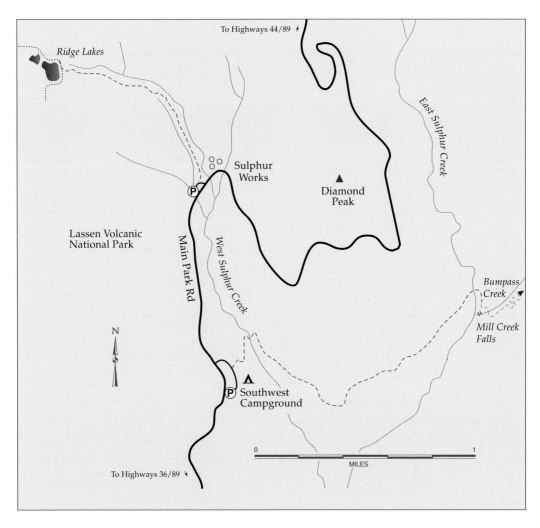

and the stream that passes through Bumpass Hell join forces at the top of the falls to merge and plunge 75 feet into a pool. The water has created brown-red stains on the bordering cliffs that contrast beautifully with patches of green moss.

> **Sulphur Works provides an up-close history lesson in vulcanology.**

To reach the Ridge Lakes trailhead, drive 1 mile north of Southwest Campground and park at Sulphur Works. Informational signs explain the geological processes that created the fuma-roles, mudpots, and steam vents that you can explore up close via a boardwalk.

The trail begins from the parking lot's north side. Top a crest and then go up, up, and up, alternating between red fir–western white pine forest and open areas strewn with ferns and flowers. Glimpse Brokeoff Mountain to the left and look behind for open vistas of the southern Cascades and the northern Sierra Nevada.

Mountain hemlocks join the forest just before you reach the Ridge Lakes nestled in a glacial cirque. The best swimming in the chilly waters is in the deepest part of the southern lake. (Note that the two lakes don't separate until late summer.)

Two easy cross-country routes begin at the lakes. You can head to the southwest side of the lakes and make a short ascent through myriad lupines to a gap, or you can scramble up a gully on the northwest side. A 300-foot-elevation climb to the ridge rewards you amply with views of the Sacramento Valley, the Coast Range, the Klamath Mountains, and Mount Shasta.

32 LASSEN PEAK

Length: 5 miles round-trip
Hiking time: 4 hours
High point: 10,453 feet
Total elevation gain: 2,000 feet
Difficulty: moderate to strenuous
Season: mid-July through October
Water: none; bring plenty
Maps: USGS 7.5' Lassen Peak, park brochure
Information: Lassen Volcanic National Park

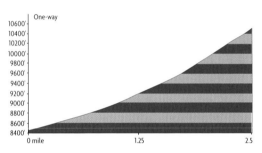

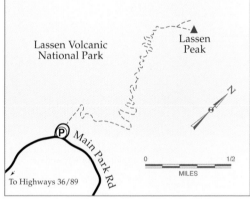

Along with its cousin Mount Shasta, Lassen Peak dominates the skyline of inland Northern California. Climb this massive volcano, which last erupted in 1921, and enjoy panoramic views ranging over a hundred miles in every direction.

Conditions on the summit often differ dramatically from those at the trailhead. Prepare for high winds and snow-reflected sunlight by bringing layers of warm clothes, a hat, sunglasses, and sunblock. Also, don't begin the climb in threatening weather; you'll find nowhere to hide from lightning strikes.

To reach the trailhead, drive 12 miles north on the main park road from Highway 36 or 22 miles south on Highway 89 from Highway 44.

Begin the steady ascent and enjoy good views. As you climb, the mountain hemlock trees decrease in size and eventually disappear as whitebark pine—which can better tolerate the harsher weather conditions prevalent at higher elevations—increase in number.

Once you reach the summit at 2.5 miles, the topography of Northern California spreads in all directions: To the north, Mount Shasta, second highest of the Cascade volcanoes, reigns in white splendor; the broad Modoc Plateau and steep-sided Warner Mountains lie to the northeast; the mighty Sierra Nevada extends from Lake Almanor south; across the vast extent of the Sacramento Valley, the Coast Range marches

View of Lassen Peak from the east

westward; and north of the Coast Range, the rocky peaks of the Trinity Alps punctuate the Klamath Mountains.

Near Lassen Volcanic National Park, you can see numerous natural features, including examples of the four major volcano types. Plug dome volcanoes, such as Lassen Peak, extrude thick, pasty, dacite lava. Shield volcanoes, such as Prospect Peak 10 miles to the northwest, emit liquid basalt, which can spread for miles. Cinder cones, such as the aptly named Cinder Cone (2 miles southwest of Prospect Peak), eject ash, cinders, and rocks. Stratovolcanoes, such as Mount Shasta, contain layers of andesitic lava, cinders, and ash and are thus called composite volcanoes. Brokeoff Volcano, a former major peak in the park, was also a stratovolcano, with Sulphur Works as its probable central vent. Look south at Pilots Pinnacle, Mount Diller, and Brokeoff Mountain, the remnants of Tehama's west rim.

Be sure to hike around Lassen Peak's summit and see how the volcanic activity from 1914 to 1917 dramatically altered its topography; much of the snow-encrusted, chunky rock on the top was extruded during that time. Eruptions sent an ash cloud 33,000 feet into the air and caused mud and rock to course down the mountain's northeast flank, destroying several square miles of forest now known as the Devastated Area.

> Lassen Peak, a plug dome volcano that last erupted in 1921, reminds us that nature can be both violent and beautiful.

33 CRUMBAUGH LAKE AND BUMPASS HELL

Length: 6 miles round-trip
Hiking time: 4 hours
High point: 8,250 feet
Total elevation gain: 1,500 feet
Difficulty: moderate
Season: late June through October
Water: available from Crumbaugh Lake and seasonal streams (purify first)
Maps: USGS 7.5' Reading Peak, USGS 7.5' Lassen Peak, park brochure
Information: Lassen Volcanic National Park

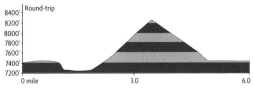

This walk takes you the back way to Bumpass Hell, thus avoiding the crowds that reach this entrancing volcanic landscape from the other end of the trail near Lake Helen. Along the way you'll visit Cold Boiling Lake, which lives up to its name, and Crumbaugh Lake, which offers the opportunity for a quiet picnic with scenic views.

Go to Kings Creek Picnic Area on the main park road, which is 17.5 miles from the intersection

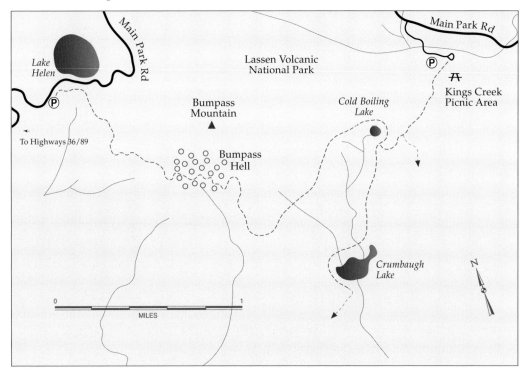

Crumbaugh Lake from east of Bumpass Hell

of Highways 44 and 89 and 16.6 miles from the intersection of Highways 36 and 89. Turn onto the road signed for the picnic area and drive another 0.3 mile to the trailhead parking lot.

The trail begins from the lot's south side. After a brief climb, it stays fairly level through a forest of mountain hemlock, lodgepole pine, and red fir, tree species present for most of the hike.

Stay straight at a trail fork at 0.5 mile. At 0.7 mile, reach Cold Boiling Lake, where gasses bubble up from far below the lake's bottom.

The trail splits at Cold Boiling Lake. For now, take the left-hand path and descend gently. After a pleasant 0.5-mile stroll, you'll reach a trail fork just above Crumbaugh Lake. Take either path to reach the shore, where you can explore or rest and enjoy the southward view of Mount Conard.

When you've had your fill of Crumbaugh Lake, return to Cold Boiling Lake and take the path signed for Bumpass Hell. As you begin the ascent to this hike's final destination, you'll have views of Bumpass Mountain, Cold Boiling Lake, Crumbaugh Lake, Mount Conard, and many other outstanding topographic features of Lassen Volcanic National Park. You'll also cross a small, flower-bordered stream.

The path eventually reaches a saddle, which offers an excellent view of Bumpass Hell, and then descends the final 0.2 mile to the hike's prime destination. Plan to spend a lot of time exploring the steam vents, fumaroles, and mud pots. This hydrothermal activity results from groundwater percolating deep underground to a hot magma chamber, which heats it and forces it back up to the surface at Bumpass Hell. Note that for your own safety you must stay on the boardwalk. Watch young children carefully: the water and steam are boiling hot and quite acidic.

> Steam vents, fumaroles, and mudpots create a surreal scene at Bumpass Hell.

It's a 2.5-mile walk back to Kings Creek Picnic Area. If you want to arrange a car shuttle instead, leave a vehicle at the Bumpass Hell Nature Trail parking lot, which is on the south side of the main park road by Lake Helen, 23.2 miles from the junction of Highways 44 and 89 and 11 miles from the junction of Highways 36 and 89. To reach the parking lot from Bumpass Hell, hike 1.5 miles northwest and enjoy magnificent views of Lassen Peak (Hike 32), Brokeoff Mountain (Hike 30), and many other high summits.

34 KINGS CREEK FALLS AND SIFFORD LAKES

Length: 5.3 miles round-trip
Hiking time: 3 hours
High point: 7,270 feet
Total elevation gain: 650 feet
Difficulty: moderate
Season: late June through October
Water: available from Kings Creek and Sifford Lakes (purify first)
Maps: USGS 7.5' Reading Peak, park brochure
Information: Lassen Volcanic National Park

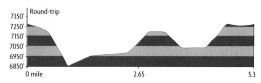

Hike through verdant, flower-filled meadows bordering the cascading waters of Kings Creek to a 50-foot waterfall, and then escape the crowds by hiking up to the Sifford Lakes, where tranquility and good swimming await. You can

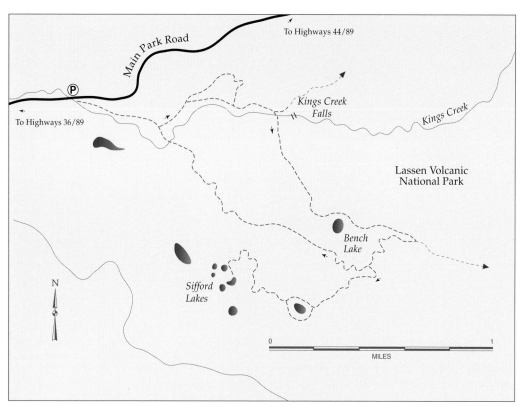

camp at the lakes. Overnight trips require a permit. Get one at the park or via email (530-595-4444; *www.nps.gov/lavo*). Drive to the Kings Creek Falls pullout on the main park road, which is 16.7 miles from the intersection of Highways 44 and 89 and 17.5 miles from the intersection of Highways 36 and 89. Park in the lot on the north side of the road.

The trail leaves from the road's south side and immediately parallels the meadow that borders the clear waters of Kings Creek. As you pass under the branches of mountain hemlock, red fir, western white pine, and lodgepole pine, look out into the meadow for grazing deer. Go left at a trail fork at 0.4 mile and right at another fork at 0.6 mile. The gentler left trail rejoins your trail before reaching the falls.

The path now descends a rocky stretch next to a series of small cascades; watch your step. The route levels after leaving the cascades behind and then meets the trail to Sifford Lakes at 1 mile. Go left for the last 100 yards to the top of Kings Creek Falls. Here you'll see the roaring water tumbling 50 feet from a lush meadow to the rocks below.

After steeping yourself in the beauty of this spot, retrace your steps and cross the creek on a wooden bridge at the trail fork for Sifford Lakes. After a stiff initial climb, the path passes under a talus cliff with two small caves near the top. At 0.6 mile from Kings Creek, it reaches shallow Bench Lake, which usually dries up by late summer. Ascend gently to a trail fork 0.4 mile past Bench Lake; go right and climb 0.3 mile to another trail fork. Go left for the final 0.4 mile to the first of the Sifford Lakes, a lake deep enough for swimming. A faint trail continues along the lake's edge and heads 0.4 mile northwest to the other Sifford Lakes. The next lake encountered offers excellent swimming and two campsites. You can easily visit the other small, shallow lakes in the flat basin by walking cross-country.

> **Kings Creek Falls plunges 50 feet from flowery meadow to hard rock.**

Once you've finished exploring the Sifford Lakes, head back down the main trail 0.4 mile below the first Sifford Lake to the trail fork. Go left and hike downhill 0.9 mile to Kings Creek. Cross the creek and rejoin the previously traveled path for the last 0.4 mile to the trailhead.

Kings Creek Falls

35 TWIN LAKES, HORSESHOE LAKE, AND GRASSY SWALE

Length: 15.2 miles round-trip
Hiking time: 2 days
High point: 7,150 feet
Total elevation gain: 1,800 feet
Difficulty: easy to moderate
Season: early July through early October
Water: available from lakes (purify first)
Maps: USGS 7.5' Reading Peak, USGS 7.5' Mount Harkness, USGS 7.5'
Prospect Peak, USGS 7.5' West Prospect Peak, park brochure
Information: Lassen Volcanic National Park

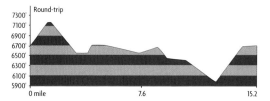

A long stroll through meadows, opportunities to explore six lakes, and a visit to a waterfall highlight this long day hike or easy backpack trip.

From the intersection of Highways 44 and 89, drive 13.5 miles on the main park road and turn east (at marker 36) into Summit Lake North Campground. From the intersection of Highways 36 and 89, drive 20.5 miles on the main park road. Park near Summit Lake's north shore at the day-use parking area if you're doing a day hike. If you plan on backpacking, park at the ranger station 0.3 mile north of the campground and take the path to the beginning of the hike. Overnight

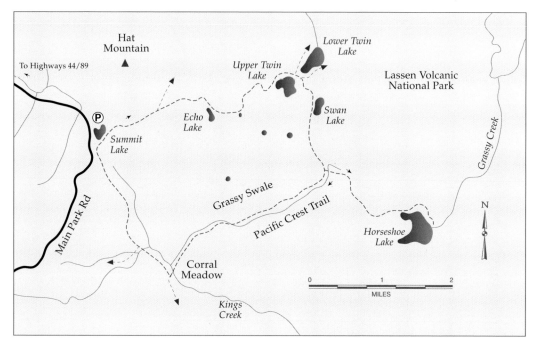

trips require a permit. Get one at the park or via email (530-595-4444; *www.nps.gov/lavo*).

Cross the wooden footbridge that leads to a trail sign, and then turn left and climb. Look left to inspect Hat Mountain, and gaze behind to observe the east faces of Lassen Peak, Crescent Crater, and Chaos Crags. Typical Lassen Volcanic National Park conifers abound here, including mountain hemlock, red and white fir, and lodgepole and western white pine.

Secluded Swan Lake is an excellent spot to spend the night.

At 1 mile you reach a broad plateau and bear right at the signed junction. The trail begins a moderate descent at 1.3 miles and reaches driftwood-lined Echo Lake at 1.8 miles (no camping allowed). The path climbs away from the lake at 2 miles, leads gently down to a pea-green, algae-laced pond on the right at 2.4 miles, and, after another 0.3 mile, borders the right side of a long, skinny pond lined with grass.

Reach the shore of Upper Twin Lake at 3.2 miles, and enjoy a scenic stroll past several campsites. The trail departs this forest-surrounded lake after 0.4 mile and leads to Lower Twin Lake a mere 100 yards farther. Bear right and pass by a number of flat spots suitable for camping.

Go right at the signed trail intersection at 4 miles, where the route promptly steepens. The dry, open hillside trail flattens 0.2 mile farther, staying mostly level to the attractive, secluded Swan Lake off the trail to the left at 4.5 miles. You can camp on all sides of this shallow lake as long as you are at least 100 feet from the high-water mark.

Turn left at the signed trail intersection 0.3 mile beyond Swan Lake. Reach a signed trail junction at 5.6 miles and bear left 1.4 miles to Horseshoe Lake. Horseshoe Lake is the biggest

The beginning of the journey

lake on this trip and has ample camping. To complete your trip, retrace your steps 1.4 miles and go left at the trail marker at 8.4 miles.

Slender stretches of Grassy Swale's meadow appear intermittently over the next 3.5 miles. Numerous flowers persist here into early October, and camping is permitted in the neighboring lodgepole pine forest.

The path crosses the meadow at 9.1 miles, where you bear left at a signed trail junction. Descend to a crossing of Grassy Swale Creek at 10.5 miles. The trail eventually topples into Kings Creek at 12.4 miles. Cross carefully and bear right at the signed trail junction near a cluster of campsites at Corral Meadow.

A steep climb ensues, rewarding you after 0.2 mile with an excellent view of a waterfall plunging 50 feet into Kings Creek. The trail then negotiates two consecutive stream crossings, followed by a signed trail junction at 13.1 miles, where you bear right.

A steady climb through forest takes you into a corn-lily-covered mini-meadow at 14.8 miles. The trail becomes the Summit Lake South Campground road 0.2 mile farther. Head north to the lake and choose either of two paths around Summit Lake's east and west shores to return to the north shore parking area at 15.2 miles.

36 TERRACE, SHADOW, AND CLIFF LAKES

Length: 8.4 miles round-trip
Hiking time: 5 hours
High point: 7,900 feet
Total elevation gain: 1,900 feet
Difficulty: moderate
Season: early July to mid-October
Water: available from lakes and streams (purify first)
Maps: USGS 7.5′ West Prospect Peak, USGS 7.5′ Reading Peak, park brochure
Information: Lassen Volcanic National Park

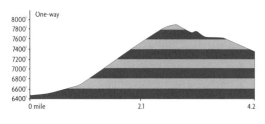

Hike through a dense forest by a rushing stream to a large, lush meadow, and then continue to three of Lassen Volcanic National Park's most beautiful lakes. Along the way you'll be treated to impressive views of Lassen Peak and numerous other high peaks and ridges.

From the junction of Highways 44 and 89, drive 10.2 miles on the main park road. Turn left into the parking lot across the road from the Hat Lake sign. Alternatively, reach the trailhead by driving 24 miles on the main park road from the junction of Highways 36 and 89.

The signed trail begins just east of what is left of Hat Lake. A large mudflow swept down from Lassen Peak in 1915 and dammed the West Fork of Hat Creek, creating Hat Lake; however, the lake quickly filled with stream sediments, and now only a small pond remains, which will eventually turn to meadow. Such a fate befalls most lakes but usually takes much longer.

After allowing a brief glimpse of Lassen Peak, the trail begins its climb to Paradise Meadows through a mixed forest of western white pine, red fir, and mountain hemlock. At 1.3 miles a 20-foot multistep waterfall awaits on the right.

Opposite: Cliff Lake and Lassen Peak

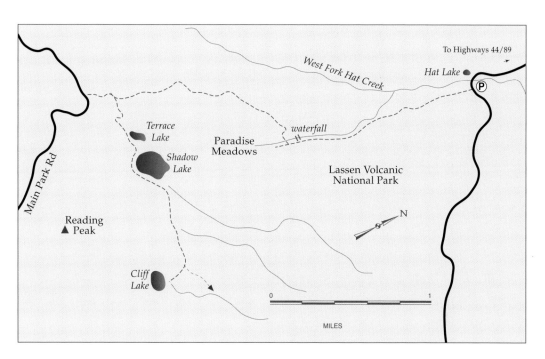

Continue to a trail fork just past the waterfall and bear left for the level 100-yard stroll to expansive Paradise Meadows. Here the swift waters of a tributary of the West Fork of Hat Creek slow to a lazy meander through grasses and a variety of wildflowers. The talus-sloped heights that house Terrace and Cliff Lakes stretch upward to the south, with Reading Peak rising even higher in the distance.

After absorbing the pleasant ambience of Paradise Meadows, go back to the trail fork, cross the creek, and head uphill. The trail eventually offers

excellent views of Lassen Peak looming to the west from gaps in the mountain hemlock forest. At 2.7 miles you'll reach a trail fork. (The right fork heads 0.3 mile uphill to the main park road, a good place to park if you want to do a much shorter hike to the three lakes. It's 20 miles southeast of the junctions of Highways 44 and 89 and 14 miles northeast of the junction of Highways 36 and 89.) Head downhill to the left

Shallow Hat Lake, a relic of Lassen Peak's 1915 mudflow, will eventually become a meadow.

for 0.3 mile to Terrace Lake, where a grassy beach area offers easy swimming access for those willing to brave the chilly waters. The much larger and deeper Shadow Lake lies 0.1 mile east. From the lake's east shore, you'll see the aquamarine waters reflecting a shimmering visage of Lassen Peak.

About 0.6 mile after leaving Shadow Lake, an unsigned path heads south on the right. Follow it 0.15 mile to the aptly named Cliff Lake. The namesake talus shoulders keep watch over the shallow corn lily- and red mountain heather-ringed waters. Note the red fir and mountain hemlock growing on the lake's island. This lake makes an excellent spot for a quiet picnic.

37 CHAOS CRAGS AND MANZANITA CREEK

Length: 4 miles round-trip for Crags Lake, 6.6 miles round-trip for Manzanita Creek
Hiking time: 6 hours or 2 days
High point: 6,800 feet for Crags Lake, 7,000 feet for Manzanita Creek
Total elevation gain: 1,000 feet for Crags Lake, 1,050 feet for Manzanita Creek
Difficulty: moderate
Season: mid-June through late October
Water: available from Manzanita Creek (purify first); best to bring your own
Maps: USGS 7.5' Manzanita Lake, USGS 7.5' Lassen Peak, park brochure
Information: Lassen Volcanic National Park

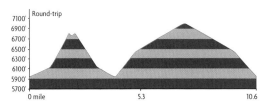

This easily accessible pair of trails in the northwest corner of Lassen Volcanic National Park offers vivid contrasts: You'll walk through serene forests and lush meadows that exist just 2 miles from stark and barren Chaos Crags and Lassen Peak, massive volcanoes that have been active within the last millennium. Manzanita Creek's clear and cold waters and numerous wildflowers also highlight the trip. For those who want to backpack, look for occasional level areas. You must camp at least a half mile from the campground. Overnight trips require a permit. Get one at the park or via email (530-595-4444; *www.nps.gov/lavo*).

Travel the main park road for 32.8 miles north of the junction of Highways 36 and 89 or 1.2 miles southeast of the junctions of Highways 44 and 89. Turn south onto the road to Manzanita Lake Campground and park 150 feet from the highway.

Stark and barren Chaos Crags formed a thousand years ago from a 1,500-foot-high lava surge.

Chaos Crags (Photo by John R. Soares)

The first trail takes you to Crags Lake. Climb past white fir and Jeffrey pine, with the occasional sugar pine thrown in. Leap across a shaded stream at 0.6 mile and climb steeply through chaparral thickets.

Your efforts are rewarded at 1.9 miles with a view of Crags Lake and Chaos Crags. The latter formed around a thousand years ago when thick, pasty lava surged 1,500 feet up from a vent.

Look north to Chaos Jumbles, an avalanche from Chaos Crags that occurred 300 years ago. You'll also see the Hat Creek Valley and the peaks of Thousand Lakes Wilderness, with more Cascade volcanoes leading westward to the Klamath Mountains.

It's easy enough to scramble down to the shore of Crags Lake. In years of heavy precipitation the waters are clear and invite you for a

refreshing, if chilly, dip. However, the lake can also dry up by early summer.

To reach the Manzanita Creek Trail, follow the campground road for 0.8 mile. Then take Loop F another 0.2 mile to the small parking area near site 31.

As you begin, you'll gain glimpses of Lassen Peak and Chaos Crags through Jeffrey pines. Climb to an open area at 1.1 miles, and then ascend through a fir and pine forest.

Cross Manzanita Creek on a wooden bridge at 2 miles and continue level. The jagged crest and colorful cliffs of Loomis Peak burst into view at 2.4 miles. This impressive volcano, just on the other side of the stream, will be with you for the remainder of the hike.

Farther on, small meadows nuzzle the creek. Saunter through a red fir forest before

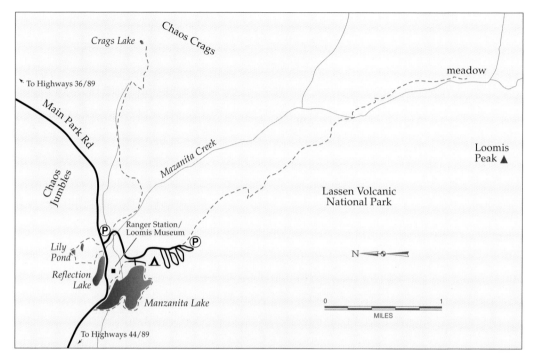

entering the first large meadow at 2.8 miles. Cross a brooklet and then gaze northward at the peaks of Thousand Lakes Wilderness. Another 0.5 mile brings you to the largest meadow—wet, lush, and ablaze with wild-flowers in summer.

38 CINDER CONE, SNAG LAKE, AND BUTTE LAKE

Length: 14-mile loop
Hiking time: 2 days
High point: 6,900 feet
Total elevation gain: 1,400 feet
Difficulty: moderate to strenuous
Season: late June through October
Water: available only from Snag Lake, Grassy Creek, and Butte Lake (purify first)
Maps: USGS 7.5′ Prospect Peak, USGS 7.5′ Mount Harkness, park brochure
Information: Lassen Volcanic National Park

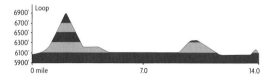

Cinder Cone's volcanic wonderland combines with a gently undulating trail around two of Lassen Volcanic National Park's largest lakes to make a good overnight backpacking trip. The journey offers open views of Lassen Peak and other prominent mountains from Cinder Cone's summit and the shores of both Butte and Snag Lakes. Overnight trips require a permit. Get one at the park or via email (530-595-4444; *www.nps .gov/lavo*).

To reach the trailhead, drive Highway 44 for 11 miles east of its junction with Highway 89. Turn right at the sign for Butte Lake, go 6 miles to the Butte Lake Campground, and park in the lot by the lake's north shore.

The trail begins by the boat launch. Grab the nature trail brochure from the trailhead box; it explains in detail the natural history of the route to Cinder Cone.

At the trip's beginning, you'll join the Nobles Emigrant Trail, a route used by thousands of California-bound pioneers in the 1850s and 1860s. Follow this historic path as it parallels the edge of the brooding black basalt hillocks of the Fantastic Lava Beds.

> West-bound pioneers traveled part of this trail in the mid-1800s.

The trail forks 0.4 mile from the trailhead. Bear left and gently ascend 1 mile to another fork. (Some backpackers may want to leave their packs at this trail fork before exploring the top of Cinder Cone. After returning, they can go right and then left to continue the hike.) Bear left again and gain 750 feet of elevation during the steep climb to Cinder Cone's sparsely vegetated 6,900-foot summit.

Formed over the last five hundred years, Cinder Cone last erupted in the 1600s. Massive basalt flows from the cone's base spread for several square miles to the south and east, creating the Fantastic Lava Beds. Oxidized cinders and ash account for the gray and orange Painted Dunes on the cone's south edges.

When you're done exploring, head down the trail on the south side. Once you leave the cone's flank, turn left at two successive trail junctures within 50 yards, and then head south 0.4 mile to another trail fork. Go left along the Fantastic Lava Beds 1.5 miles through a mixed forest of lodgepole pine, Jeffrey pine, and white fir to Snag Lake, which formed when lava flows from Cinder Cone dammed Grassy Creek. You can camp at any of the numerous sites near the lake's west and east shores, as long as they are at least 100 feet from the high-water mark.

After reaching Snag Lake, the trail travels 1.6 miles to a trail junction. Turn left here and again 0.3 mile farther. The way now heads east along the lake's south shore, crossing Grassy Creek and passing through a lush area to yet another trail fork after 0.5 mile. Turn left and walk 1.8 miles along

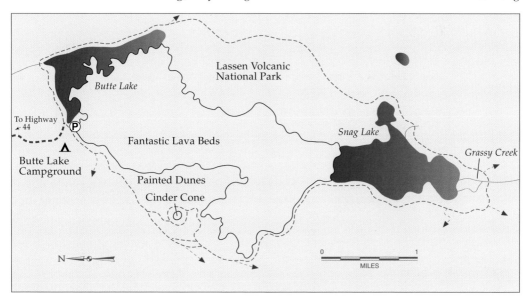

Painted Dunes viewed from the top of Cinder Cone

the lake's east shore, where you'll have good views of the Fantastic Lava Beds and Cinder Cone.

From Snag Lake's northeast shore, you'll initially travel by hundreds of aspen as the trail gently rises, levels, and then descends through 3 miles of forest. You'll encounter a trail fork (go left) just before reaching Butte Lake.

The trail then goes 1.8 miles along Butte Lake's shore, where you'll find aspen, black cottonwood, and willow that frame views of the Fantastic Lava Beds, Cinder Cone, Lassen Peak, and Prospect Peak. From the lake's outlet, climb steeply 150 feet and gently descend the last 0.3 mile to the parking lot.

39 MAGEE PEAK AND THOUSAND LAKES WILDERNESS

Length: 12.6 miles round-trip
Hiking time: 2 days
High point: 8,549 feet
Total elevation gain: 3,200 feet
Difficulty: moderate to strenuous
Season: mid-June through October; zillions of mosquitoes in June and July
Water: available only from Everett and Magee Lakes (purify first); bring your own
Map: USGS 7.5' Thousand Lakes Valley
Information: Hat Creek Ranger District, Lassen National Forest

This hike first takes you to two beautiful, cirque-surrounded, subalpine glacial lakes much less visited than lakes in nearby Lassen Volcanic National Park. It continues to the summit of Magee Peak, where you'll have a panoramic view that encompasses most of Northern California.

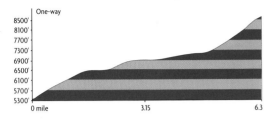

To reach the trailhead, turn west off Highway 89 onto Road 26, which begins 0.4 mile north of the Hat Creek Work Center and 10 miles south of Highway 299. Follow this road 7.5 miles through several junctions with lesser roads, as indicated by signs for Road 26, Thousand Lakes Wilderness, and Cypress Camp. At 7.5 miles turn left onto Road 34N60 for the last 2.6 miles to the parking area, marked by a "Thousand Lakes Wilderness–Cypress Camp" sign.

Walk up the rough road, bearing right and then left at two intersections within the first 200 yards, and then cross seasonal Eiler Gulch Creek. From here, the trail climbs southeast at a moderate grade under the partial shade of white fir, Jeffrey pine, and the occasional western juniper and levels at 1.7 miles upon reaching the Thousand Lakes Wilderness boundary.

You'll reach a trail fork 0.25 mile farther. Bear right at three trail forks within the next 0.7 mile. The path then climbs gently through a forest of red and white fir and lodgepole and western white pine. Pinemat manzanita covers the ground, but you'll also see greenleaf manzanita, bush chinquapin, tobacco brush, and numerous wildflowers.

> **Mountains and valleys ripple in all directions from the summit of Magee Peak.**

Forest-encircled Everett and Magee Lakes lie 1.8 miles past the last trail junction at an elevation of 7,200 feet. Both boast good views of the misnamed but magnificent Red Cliff to the south and the rest of the glacial cirque to the west. Both also offer excellent swimming opportunities in late summer. You can camp at either lake, although Magee has more sites.

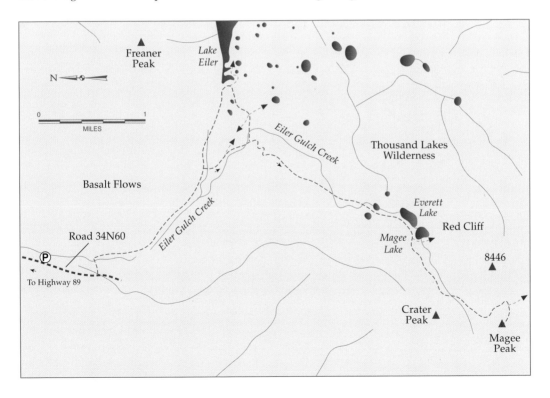

For the final 1.8-mile push to Magee Peak, bear right at the trail fork by Magee Lake. As you climb steadily and enjoy increasingly open views of the surrounding mountains, the red fir disappear as mountain hemlock and whitebark pine, which can better handle winter's fierce winds and heavy snow loads, take over. Note the various basaltic and other types of multicolored volcanic rocks.

You'll crest the ridge 1.5 miles from the lake. From here, take the faint path on your right 0.3 mile to the Magee Peak summit, elevation 8,549 feet. You're standing on the rim of an ancient volcano that encompassed 8,683-foot Crater Peak (0.5 mile north) and Peak 8446 (0.3 mile southeast), among others. Glaciers sculpted most of Thousand Lakes Wilderness, which stretches east to the Hat Creek Valley.

The 360-degree, long-range view will demand most of your attention. Lassen Peak (Hike 32) dominates the skyline to the southeast. Swinging northward, you'll see Lassen Volcanic National Park, the Fall River Valley, and Mount Shasta. West of Mount Shasta lie the Klamath Mountains, which stretch south to the Coast Range.

If you want to extend your trip on the way back, turn right at the first trail fork 1.8 miles below Everett Lake. Follow this path 0.7 mile through a trail junction and past a lily pond and other lush scenery to the shores of Lake Eiler, located at Freaner Peak's base. The lake, often visited by both hikers and mosquitoes, offers numerous campsites. From the water's west edge, follow the trail signed for Cypress Camp for 1 mile past the massive black basalt flows and turn right for the downhill roll to the trailhead.

Rain shower at Lake Eiler (Photo by John R. Soares)

40 | SUBWAY CAVE AND HAT CREEK

Length: 9.1 miles round-trip
Hiking time: 5 hours
High point: 4,350 feet
Total elevation gain: 500 feet
Difficulty: moderate
Season: early April through late November
Water: none; bring plenty
Map: USGS 7.5' Old Station
Information: Hat Creek Ranger District, Lassen National Forest

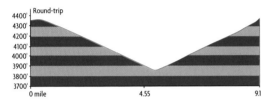

This hike offers two different natural experiences: First you'll travel underground through the dark and quiet of Subway Cave, and then you'll walk in the open air along Hat Creek with its open sky and rushing waters. It's always cool in Subway Cave, so bring a sweater and two flashlights per person.

To start your spelunking explorations, take the Subway Cave access road on the east side of Highway 89, across the road from Cave Campground and 0.3 mile north of the junctions of Highways 89 and 44 East.

Subway Cave, a 1,300-foot-long lava tube, formed around 30,000 years ago. Vast eruptions

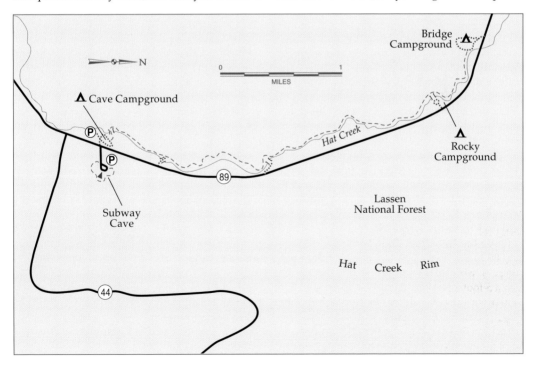

Hat Creek (Photo by John R. Soares)

of fluid basalt flowed northward through the Hat Creek Valley. Lava closest to the surface cooled more rapidly than the lava below, allowing the hotter lava to move farther before solidifying, leaving the cave as an empty space behind it.

Lighted information signs discuss the cave's natural history and explain the formation of such colorfully named features as Stubtoe Hall and Lucifers Cul-de-Sac. Several parts of the tunnel are completely dark though, so you'll be glad you brought the flashlights. When you emerge into daylight on the far side you have two options: Return through the cave or take the path back to the parking area.

To do the Hat Creek Trail, head across Highway 89 to the north side of Cave Campground, where a wooden footbridge spans the stream near a 5-foot waterfall. Cross over, turn right, and soon reach a massive sugar pine and its foot-long cones. Continue the mostly level stroll through vegetation that varies from open chaparral dominated by greenleaf manzanita to an open forest of incense cedar, ponderosa and Jeffrey pines, and white firs. Alders and willows flourish in the wet environs near the creek's banks.

Look for a small waterfall just beyond a bridge at 0.6 mile, and occasionally look behind you for tree-framed views of Lassen Peak. You'll also enjoy views of many other Cascade notables, including Mount Shasta, Burney Mountain, Crater Peak, Magee Peak, and Freaner Peak. The mountain to your immediate left is Sugarloaf Peak; its basalt talus often borders the trail.

Find two more small waterfalls at 2.2 and 2.4 miles as you and Hat Creek drop gently into a canyon. Reach another bridge at 3.7 miles, and finally reach the end of the path at 4.3 miles at Bridge Campground (3.6 miles north of Cave Campground if you're arranging a car shuttle).

> Cooling lava flowing through Hat Creek Valley created Subway Cave.

41 | BURNEY FALLS

Length: 4.9 miles round-trip
Hiking time: 3 hours
High point: 2,970 feet
Total elevation gain: 300 feet
Difficulty: easy
Season: year-round; occasional winter snow
Water: available near the visitor information center, in campgrounds, and
      from Burney Creek (purify first)
Map: USGS 7.5′ Burney Falls
Information: McArthur–Burney Falls Memorial State Park

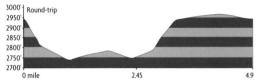

This state park offers an easy family hike year-round. Burney Falls is breathtaking, and everyone enjoys Burney Creek's lush coolness and the soothing sound of wind through the pine and fir.

From the junction of Highways 299 and 89, take Highway 89 north for 6 miles. Turn left and follow signs for McArthur–Burney Falls Memorial State Park. Park in the lot just beyond the check-in station.

First, buy a brochure that explains what you'll see at the twenty-four numbered posts along the Falls Loop Trail. Then follow your ears in the direction of roaring water, which brings you to the falls overlook. Springs from a vast

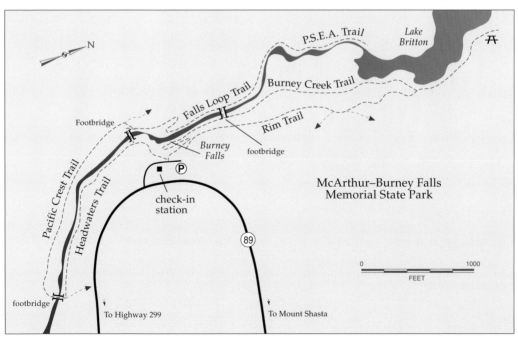

underground reservoir feed Burney Creek a daily supply of 200 million gallons of clear, cold water, which then crashes 129 feet over Burney Falls into a deep aqua-blue pool.

From the falls overlook, head downhill on the paved trail. After 300 feet it bends left, taking you to the edge of the huge pool at the base of the falls, where cool mists from the pounding water caress your face.

Follow the path downstream. Just before the Falls Loop Trail turns left and crosses a footbridge, stay straight and begin the Burney Creek Trail, which follows Burney Creek downstream 0.8 mile to Lake Britton. After passing through a forest of ponderosa pine, Douglas fir, and incense cedar, the trail skirts the edge of Lake Britton and then reaches a trail fork 0.5 mile from the bridge. Stay left and walk 0.3 mile down to the lake's shore, where you'll find a picnic area and swimming beach. (If you desire, take the right-hand Rim Trail, which climbs up to the canyon rim and back to the falls overlook.)

> Hot day? Spend a few minutes immersed in the chill mist created by the thunder of Burney Falls pounding an ice-blue pool.

Burney Falls (Photo by John R. Soares)

Return to the footbridge just below Burney Falls and cross it, pausing at the center to admire the cold water rushing below your feet. Turn right on the other side of the bridge onto the P.S.E.A. Trail. This path, well shaded by Douglas fir, white alder, and dogwood, stretches a level and peaceful 0.5 mile along Burney Creek. The trail ends at the P.S.E.A. camp and near some tranquil spots where you can picnic and watch the water flow.

When you're ready to continue, go back to the Falls Loop Trail and follow it uphill. A trail fork awaits at the top. A left would quickly bring you to the bridge across Burney Creek just above the falls and a quick route back to the parking area.

However, go right and immediately left onto the Pacific Crest Trail (PCT). Travel the famous PCT for 0.7 mile through the forest to a bridge across Burney Creek. (Burney Creek has very little water in summer; most of the springs that feed Burney Falls enter downstream.) Turn left just past the bridge onto the Headwaters Trail, which travels near the creek and reaches a trail fork after 0.5 mile. Turn left to a bridge, where you'll see the now-rushing waters of Burney Creek just before the big plunge. When you're finished, go back to the Headwaters Trail, turn left, and walk 0.1 mile back to the falls overlook and the parking lot.

42 McCLOUD RIVER'S THREE WATERFALLS

Length: 3.8 miles round-trip
Hiking time: 3 hours
High point: 3,500 feet
Total elevation gain: 400 feet
Difficulty: easy
Season: all; some winter snow; roads not plowed in winter
Water: available from Fowlers Camp Campground faucets or McCloud River
  (purify first)
Map: USGS 7.5′ Lake McCloud
Information: McCloud Ranger Station, Shasta–Trinity National Forest

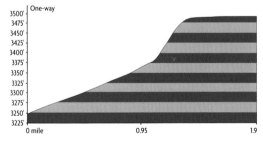

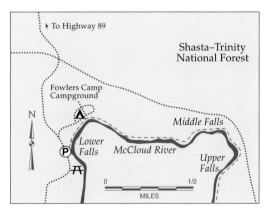

Get in tune with a wild river that sports back-to-back-to-back fantastic waterfalls. You'll also enjoy the scenic stroll's secluded forests.

From Interstate 5 south of Mount Shasta, take Highway 89 east 10 miles to McCloud and continue 5 more miles. Turn right onto the paved road signed for river access and Fowlers Camp Campground. Go 0.6 mile, stay straight at a road

fork, bear right 50 yards farther, and continue 0.6 mile to the trailhead at the Lower Falls of the McCloud River picnic area.

Taking the plunge at Lower McCloud Falls (Photo by John R. Soares)

Up to 40 feet wide in late spring, Lower Falls of the McCloud River (the hike's starting point) spill 15 feet into a foamy avalanche of white froth and then into a 25-yard-long pool. Picnickers and fishers relax along the rock slab overlooking the scene. Daredevilish youngsters sometimes leap 15 feet from the rocky edge into the swirl.

A wide asphalt path follows the river upstream past serviceberry, snowberry, thimbleberry, and ferns roofed mainly by Douglas fir and the occasional incense cedar, white fir, and ponderosa pine. Manzanita and ceanothus shrubs highlight the sunnier sections.

Fowlers Camp Campground borders the river's clear and cold water starting at 0.2 mile. Long ago, the Wintu Indians camped here seasonally to fish and hunt. Black oak, hazelnut, and dogwood join the forest as the trail converts to a wide dirt path at 0.4 mile. After you note an eroded and steep cliff face on the other shore at 0.8 mile, look for a 20-foot tall, rare Pacific yew conifer (redwoodlike needles) at trailside.

> Top off your internal batteries with McCloud River water power.

Reach the intermediate destination at 1 mile. Set in a steep and rocky canyon dotted with majestic Douglas firs, rectangular Middle Falls of the McCloud River are some 30 yards wide, with a spectacular drop-off. This is the favorite destination for most hikers: swimmers brave the chilly waters for a dip; fishers cast a line for trout; others just sit and admire the mighty roar and the cool swirling mists.

The trail then snakes up and away, reaches a prime vista down to the falls, and ascends to reach the Middle Falls overlook. Continue upstream along the path. (Watch children closely because of the steep cliffs.)

Look back for pleasing vistas of Mount Shasta and the Trinity Divide Mountains along this stretch. Inspirational views down into the river canyon continue for another 0.25 mile or so. At 1.5 miles you reach a shady section featuring a steep wall of lichen-covered rock on the left side

Fishing the pool at the base of the Middle Falls (Photo by John R. Soares)

of the trail. The first sighting of Upper Falls of the McCloud River ensues just past this 20-foot-high corridor.

Upper Falls aren't as photogenic as Middle Falls but are perhaps the most unique looking, and they certainly carry the most water force. Hemmed in on both sides by steep cliffs, these falls constitute an extremely powerful chute of pure white water. By looking down on them, it's easy to imagine a bursting dam. Make your way down the spur trail to the edge of a large, round, swirling pool. Retrace your steps and wander over to the falls' lip, where a 100-yard-long, all-white cascade plunges over the edge. The trail continues for several more miles. If you're interested in backpacking this stretch, contact the McCloud Ranger Station (530-964-2184; *www.r5.fs.fed.us/shastatrinity*).

43 MOUNT SHASTA SUMMIT

Length: 12 miles round-trip
Hiking time: 12 hours plus or 2 days
High point: 14,162 feet
Total elevation gain: 7,300 feet
Difficulty: very strenuous
Season: early May to late September
Water: none reliably available beyond Horse Camp except for snow
Maps: USGS 7.5' McCloud, USGS 7.5' Mt. Shasta, USFS Mt. Shasta Wilderness
Information: Mount Shasta Ranger Station, Shasta–Trinity National Forest

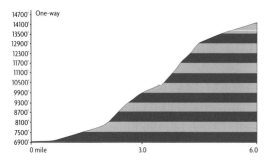

Looming 10,000 feet above its surroundings, Mount Shasta reigns as the dominant peak in Northern California. This Cascade volcano draws high-summit aspirants from around the country who attempt to reach its summit.

Although Avalanche Gulch provides the easiest route, do not take a casual approach to this climb. For starters, you need to be in good physical shape. You also must have the proper equipment and supplies: some form of shelter, such as a tent; boots; crampons; ice ax (make sure you know how to use it); warm clothes; food; water; a stove for melting snow; a climbing helmet; a wide-brimmed hat; good sunglasses; sunblock; compass; and a topographic map. Two businesses in the town of Mount Shasta rent and sell quality climbing equipment: the Fifth Season (530-926-3606; *www.thefifthseason.com*) and Shasta Base Camp (530-926-2359; *www.shastabasecamp.com*). Check the weather forecast before your ascent (530-926-9613; *www.shastaavalanche.org*) and quickly head back to the trailhead if the weather changes for the worse. You'll also want to get a predawn start so your crampons will have frozen snow to grip; as the snow warms you'll sink into the slush—which is definitely not good for climbing. Regulations require that you pack your feces out; special bags are available for free at the trailhead and at the Mount Shasta Ranger Station office in Mount Shasta. Many people choose to have a professional guide lead them on this dangerous climb. If this appeals to you, contact Shasta Mountain Guides (530-926-3117;

Mount Shasta from Gray Butte

www.shastaguides.com) or Sierra Wilderness Seminars (888-797-6867; *www.swsmtns.com*).

You'll also need a wilderness permit and a summit pass for climbing above 10,000 feet. They're available at the trailhead or from the Mount Shasta Ranger Station or McCloud Ranger Station. Dogs are prohibited.

Take the Central Mount Shasta exit off Interstate 5 and stop at the Mount Shasta Ranger Station office for your permit, climbing pass, pack-out bag, and advice regarding the route and climbing conditions. Then head east on Lake Street and curve onto Everitt Memorial Highway for the final 11 miles to the trailhead at Bunny Flat.

> At 14,162 feet, Mount Shasta is the undisputed mountain king of Northern California.

The first 1.8 miles travel through open area and some red fir forest to reach the historic stone cabin at Horse Camp. Here you'll find spring water, an outhouse, a Sierra Club caretaker, and a place to camp (fee charged, payable on site to the Sierra Club).

Resume the journey on a series of flat stones known as Olbermans Causeway. After that ends near the tree line, follow faint trails northwest. Put on your crampons once you reach snow. You'll soon be climbing along the west side of Avalanche Gulch, and then reach Helen Lake at 3.5 miles. This flat snow field, elevation 10,443 feet, is a common overnight site for those doing the two-day climb.

The tough part lies above Helen Lake as you labor up Avalanche Gulch, which increases in steepness as you gain elevation. The area is true to its name, so wear your helmet and keep an eye open for falling rocks. Near 12,000 feet you'll reach a bare area called The Heart. Skirt to its right and climb through the gap between the Red Banks and Thumb Rock. Konwakiton Glacier lies to the right and the Red Banks to the left as you continue. Late in the year, this part of the route becomes unsafe and better variations through the Red Banks are recommended. Call and/or visit the Mount Shasta Ranger Station (530-926-4511; *www.r5.fs.fed.us/shastatrinity*) for alternatives.

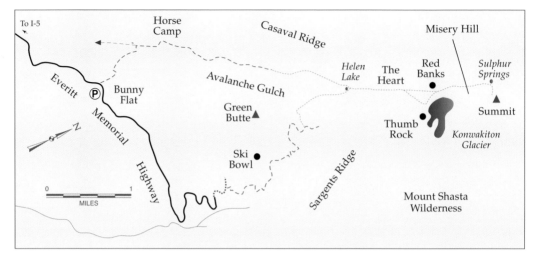

Misery Hill, just above the Red Banks, takes you from 13,000 to about 13,800 feet. If you've survived this long, you've nearly reached the goal. Continue northward, passing east of Sulphur Springs. A short scramble east brings you to the long-awaited summit.

A top-of-the-world panorama is now yours, limited only by atmospheric conditions and the curve of Earth. Cascade volcanoes march north to Mount McLaughlin, Crater Lake, and beyond, and also south to Lassen Peak, after which the northern Sierra begins. Range upon range of forested mountains lead south to the Sacramento Valley. The Klamath Mountains hold the west, with Castle Crags, the Eddy Range, and the Trinity Alps most prominent. To the east, volcanic mountains and plains give way to the desert peaks of northwest Nevada.

44 PANTHER MEADOWS, SOUTH GATE MEADOWS, AND GRAY BUTTE

Length: 8.6 miles round-trip
Hiking time: 5 hours
High point: 8,119 feet
Total elevation gain: 1,850 feet
Difficulty: moderate
Season: early July through mid-October
Water: bring your own
Maps: USGS 7.5' McCloud, USFS Mt. Shasta Wilderness
Information: Mount Shasta Ranger Station, Shasta–Trinity National Forest

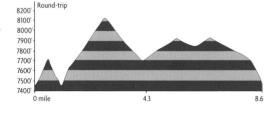

These three trails on the middle slopes of Mount Shasta take you through the beauty of delicate meadows, through the quiet of a red fir forest, and to the top of Gray Butte for excellent views of the behemoth volcano and the myriad peaks and valleys of far Northern California.

From the Interstate 5 Central Mount Shasta exit, go east 0.7 mile on Lake Street, and then curve left onto Everitt Memorial Highway. Travel 13.5 miles and park at Panther Meadows Campground. Dogs are allowed only on the trail to Gray Butte.

Before starting your explorations, read the flyers located at the trailhead. Panther Meadows and South Gate Meadows host numerous sensitive plants. Walk only on designated paths and protect the delicate meadows by stepping only on bare soil, rocks, and snow.

Upon reaching the west edge of Lower Panther Meadows, go left at a trail fork and climb gently past pink meadow heather, yellow monkey-flower, and red paintbrush, and then ascend steeply into forest at 0.2 mile. Enjoy a tree-framed view of Mount Shasta's south visage, go right at 0.5 mile into Upper Panther Meadows, and go right again just before a creek crossing. Head up to Panther Spring, a sacred Native American site; leave no trace of your visit. Retrace your steps back to the beginning of the hike.

> Walk softly here: Panther and South Gate Meadows shelter many delicate plants.

Now you cross Lower Panther Meadows and issue yourself a free wilderness permit on its far side. (You can also obtain a permit at the Mount Shasta Ranger Station or the McCloud Ranger

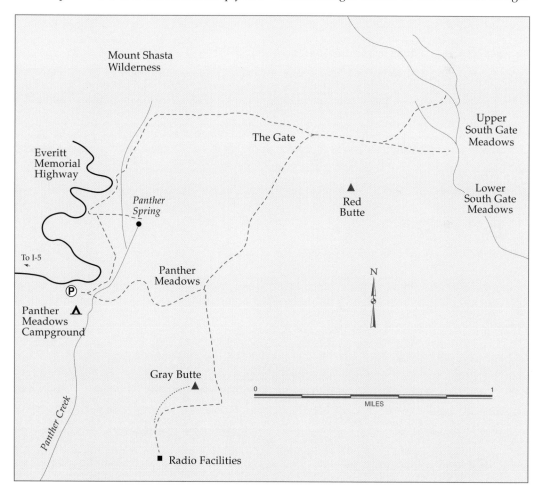

Station.) Leave the verdant expanse behind and climb 0.4 mile past red firs and mountain hemlocks with the mint scent of pennyroyal in your nostrils until you reach a trail fork.

Go right at the fork and travel Gray Butte's north ridge. Make a steep ascent through an area littered with talus boulders and then reach a saddle 1 mile from the trail fork. Turn right and take the faint path 0.2 mile to the summit of Gray Butte, where you'll find a weather-whipped, prostrate whitebark pine and a world-class view. Mount Shasta looms due north, and a line of volcanoes stretches southeast to Lassen Peak, with the Sierra Nevada stretching into the haze beyond. To the east lie the volcanic basalts of the Modoc Plateau. To the south, forested slopes lead to the Sacramento Valley. To the west rise the Klamath Mountains, spiked by

Castle Crags and Mount Eddy, with the Trinity Alps in the distance.

Retrace your steps to the trail fork above Lower Panther Meadows and take the other fork (now on your right) bound for South Gate Meadows. The trail disappears near the wilderness boundary at the base of a rocky cliff. Follow rock ducks (cairns) up the cliff and regain the obvious trail. After a short distance through the forest, the path drops into a valley along the west base of Red Butte.

The trail disappears in an open area of wildflowers and sand; stay near the boulders by the base of Red Butte for 0.2 mile. Reach the obvious trail and go right at a trail fork, reaching a saddle 0.1 mile farther.

Descend 0.3 mile to a trail fork. Both 0.4-mile paths lead to South Gate Meadows, where you'll find lush greenery and views of Mount Shasta.

Panther Meadows (Photo by John R. Soares)

45 BLACK BUTTE

Length: 5.2 miles round-trip
Hiking time: 4 hours
High point: 6,325 feet
Total elevation gain: 1,850 feet
Difficulty: moderate
Season: mid-May through mid-November
Water: none; bring plenty
Map: USGS 7.5′ City of Mount Shasta
Information: Mount Shasta Ranger Station, Shasta–Trinity National Forest

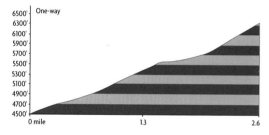

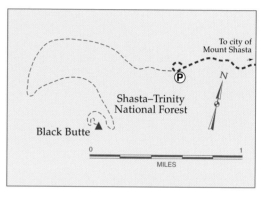

To those traveling Interstate 5 in far Northern California, Black Butte looms as a dark, impossibly steep visage rising 2,400 feet right beside the freeway. Surprisingly, a moderately graded trail can take you to the summit of this young volcano, where spectacular views await.

Take the Central Mount Shasta exit off I-5, head east through town for 0.7 mile on Lake Street, and curve left onto Everitt Memorial Highway. Drive 2.2 miles and turn left opposite the sign for Spring Hill Plantation onto Forest Road 41N18, an improved road surfaced with recycled asphalt grindings. Turn right after 0.1 mile, drive 1 mile, and swing 90 degrees to head straight for Black Butte. Go right (north) at a road fork 0.3 mile farther. After another 1.2 miles, turn left at a powerline undercrossing and continue the final 0.7 mile on a

> Black Butte, a relatively young volcano at a mere ten thousand years old, formed from four successive eruptions.

gravel and dirt road (41N18A) to the trailhead, which is a small turnaround in the road.

The path initially travels through a forest of Douglas fir, white fir, incense cedar, and ponderosa pine. Common trailside shrubs include bush chinquapin, huckleberry oak, and tobacco brush. As you continue the steady climb across talus slopes, the first of several sweeping vistas opens up to the north, where you'll see Shasta Valley and the town of Weed directly below and southern Oregon's Mount McLoughlin, a Cascade sibling of Mount Shasta. At 1.1 miles the path swings southwest, allowing views of Mount Eddy (Hike 52: Mount Eddy and the Deadfall Lakes) and the Klamath Mountains to the west and Castle Dome (Hike 49) and the rest of Castle Crags to the south.

At 1.6 miles the trail heads east, offering you the entrancing image of Mount Shasta, and eventually swings southeast past western white pine, mountain hemlock, and red fir. This is a good spot to search the far southeast horizon for

Black Butte (Photo by John R. Soares)

Magee Peak and Lassen Peak, which lie near the Cascades' southern boundary.

Climb northwest and then southeast again before switchbacking up the last stretch to Black Butte's summit at 2.6 miles, where all the previously encountered views come together in a 360-degree panorama. Mount Shasta will certainly demand most of your attention. This majestic peak, elevation 14,162 feet, is a stratovolcano formed by massive eruptions that began about one million years ago. Black Butte, a plug dome, formed from thick pasty lava extruded in four different eruptions about ten thousand years ago, making it quite young by geological standards.

46 PATTERSON LAKE AND SQUAW PEAK

Length: 18 miles round-trip
Hiking time: 3 to 4 days
High point: 9,350 feet
Total elevation gain: 3,350 feet
Difficulty: moderate
Season: mid-June through late October
Water: generally available from lakes and streams (purify first) but none for
the last 2.6 miles
Maps: USGS 7.5' Soup Creek, USGS 7.5' Eagle Peak, USGS 7.5' Warren
Peak, USFS South Warner Wilderness
Information: Warner Mountain Ranger District, Modoc National Forest

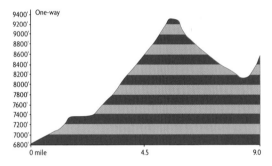

This hike takes you through dense fir forest to lush meadows and eventually to high sagebrush desert country. Along the way you'll visit beautiful Patterson Lake and enjoy expansive views of the mountainous landscape of northeastern California, southern Oregon, and northwestern Nevada.

From the junction of Highways 395 and 299 in Alturas, head south on Highway 395 for 1.1 miles, and then turn left onto County Road 56. Drive another 13.8 miles. Bear right at a major junction 0.3 mile past the point where the paved road changes to dirt. Follow this main dirt road another 10.4 miles and turn left where a sign directs you the final 1.5 miles to the Pine Creek Trail, your trailhead. Avoid other signed roads taking off from the main dirt road that have destinations with the word "pine" in them.

The trail begins its steady uphill climb, usually within earshot of tributaries of the South Fork of Pine Creek, under the shade of white fir, Jeffrey pine, and quaking aspen. However, by the time you pass a small, shallow pond on the left side of the trail at 0.6 mile, the latter two trees have been replaced by whitebark pine, a hardy species you'll encounter frequently from here on.

Reach a trail fork at 1.3 miles. The left-hand trail leads 50 yards downhill to a small but deep lake with campsites at the west and east ends. At 2.3 miles you'll pass another trailside pond on the right, also with campsites at the east and west ends. If other hikers have already claimed these, continue 100 yards due north of the pond to a lake with two sites on the east side.

Just past these two bodies of water, the trail leaves the white fir and whitebark pine forest. You now have the first open view of the Pine Creek Basin: a huge glacial bowl with 1,800-foot rock walls overlooking sagebrush-covered slopes and lush, verdant meadows.

About a hundred feet from the forest, the trail makes a 90-degree turn to cross the creek and then a 50-foot stretch of meadow. Look carefully for two rock cairns on the other side of the meadow, just in case the trail is obscured.

> A 360-degree view of northeastern California, southern Oregon, and northwestern Nevada stretches out from Squaw Peak's summit.

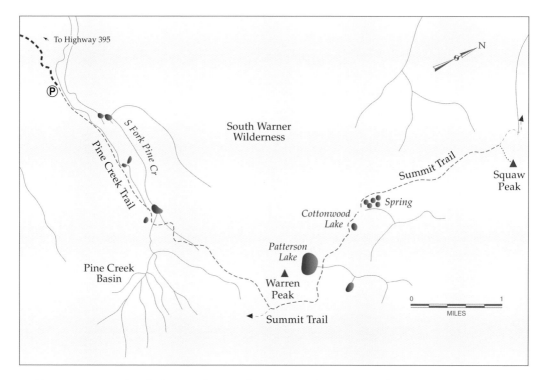

Your way immediately leaves the meadow behind and starts a steady ascent of 1,600 feet over the next 2.4 miles. Initially you travel through a white fir forest and then pass through an aspen grove. At 0.5 mile from the creek crossing, leave most of the trees behind and walk along the sagebrush-dotted open slope with mule ear, lupine, Indian paintbrush, and other flowers keeping you company. Be sure to look for the numerous antelope and deer that call this paradise home. You'll also encounter several small creeks along the way, but these can dry up by late summer.

After enjoying the spectacular view of the Pine Creek Basin as you climb, you'll be rewarded with even more stupendous views at 4.7 miles when you reach the ridge crest junction with the Summit Trail, which runs north-south along the crest of the South Warner Mountains. Look south to the commanding summit of 9,892-foot Eagle Peak, the highest mountain in the Warners. To the east lie the irrigated green fields of Surprise Valley, along with three large, dry alkaline lakes. The desolate stretches of

Nevada's Basin and Range dominate the landscape farther east. To the immediate north rise the steep sides of Warren Peak, and to the west and southwest Mount Shasta and Lassen Peak punctuate the skyline.

Once you've recovered from the climb and the awe-inspiring view, head left up to a saddle frequented by Clark's nutcrackers. Look northward for views of Squaw Peak, the North Warner Mountains, part of Goose Lake, and tall mountains stretching into southern Oregon. Also note the sedimentary rock layers here, which are overlain by volcanic basalts. The Warner Mountains were formed largely by volcanic eruptions over sediments that were then pushed up along faults as adjacent valleys, such as Surprise Valley, dropped down.

From the saddle the trail descends to the deep, cold, and clear waters of Patterson Lake at 5.5 miles. This beautiful body of water sits in a glacial cirque surrounded by 600-foot-high walls of basalt, crowned by 9,710-foot Warren Peak. You'll find several good campsites near the lake's west side.

The trail continues downhill 0.7 mile to the shallow waters of Cottonwood Lake. This small lake offers two campsites and good views of cliffs to the west.

Consider doing the last 2.8 miles to the summit of Squaw Peak as a day hike, using one of the two lakes as a base camp. The path enters a meadow filled with corn lilies and then passes a spring 0.2 mile past Cottonwood Lake, your last source of water for the remainder of the hike. Ascend briefly from here, and then walk along the crest of the South Warner Range past mountain mahogany, sagebrush, and numerous wildflowers as you enjoy the wide, open views to the west and east.

Once beside Squaw Peak, located 9 miles from the trailhead, you can easily pick a cross-country route to the top. From here, you'll have a breathtaking 360-degree view over all of northeastern California and large sections of southern Oregon and northwestern Nevada.

Quaking aspens

47 WHITNEY BUTTE

Length: 7 miles round-trip
Hiking time: 4 hours
High point: 5,010 feet
Total elevation gain: 500 feet
Difficulty: easy
Season: mid-April through mid-November
Water: none; bring your own and plenty of it
Map: USGS 7.5' Lava Beds National Monument
Information: Lava Beds National Monument

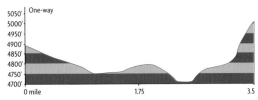

Hike through an open landscape past chunks of recently extruded dark lava to the top of a small volcano, where you'll have sweeping views of Mount Shasta, Lava Beds National Monument, and other volcanic landforms of far northeastern California.

Coming from the north on Highway 139, turn right 5 miles south of the town of Tulelake. Follow Lava Beds National Monument signs for 24 miles, turn right (west) at the sign for Merrill

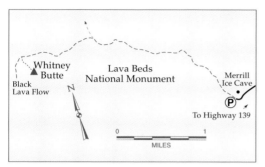

any access restrictions. If you do explore the cave, follow these rules: don't go alone; carry at least three sources of light; wear sturdy shoes, a hard hat, jacket, pants, and gloves; be careful not to harm rock formations; stay on existing paths; and leave quietly if you encounter bats.

> **Start the adventure by exploring the dark and frigid recesses of Merrill Ice Cave.**

Cave, and continue 0.6 mile to the trailhead. Coming from the south on Highway 139, turn left 26 miles northwest of Canby and follow Lava Beds National Monument signs 16 miles to the visitor center. From the visitor center, go north 1.2 miles, turn left (west) at the sign for Merrill Ice Cave, and drive the final 0.6 mile to the trailhead.

At the trailhead you'll see a short, paved trail to Merrill Ice Cave. Check with the visitor center for

Volcanic vista in Lava Beds National Monument (Photo by John R. Soares)

Various bunchgrasses and wildflowers line the path to Whitney Butte, as do sagebrush, bitterbrush, mountain mahogany, and western juniper. These plants can tolerate the dry, desert-like conditions of northeastern California, a region that sees little rainfall.

Along the trail's first mile lies black basaltic rock, which once oozed as a hot liquid from nearby fissures to eventually cool into the twisted shapes you see around you. You'll also be treated to views of Tule Lake and the irrigated fields to the lake's north, as well as 6,618-foot Mount Dome looming to the northwest and 9,495-foot Mount McLoughlin, a cousin of Mount Shasta, far off in southern Oregon.

The first sight of the steep, snow-clad slopes of 14,162-foot Mount Shasta awaits at 1.8 miles. Bear left at a trail fork at 2.2 miles and skirt the north flank of Whitney Butte. At 3.3 miles you'll see the Medicine Lake highlands just to the south, as well as the massive Black Lava Flow, a sheet of basalt covering several square miles. Your trail ends at the base of the Black Lava Flow, where you'll see lichens, sagebrush, and a few other plants gaining a tenuous foothold on the 20-foot-high sheet of inhospitable rock.

Be sure to climb to the top of Whitney Butte, a cinder cone. Begin by a trailside ponderosa pine about 3.3 miles from the trailhead, where you get the first good views of the edge of the Black Lava Flow. From the top you can view the cinder cone's collapsed center and also enjoy a 360-degree view of the entire volcanic landscape.

Consider exploring some of the Lava Beds National Monument's lava caves before leaving. Inquire at the visitor center about the best caves and proper safety procedures.

KLAMATH MOUNTAINS

A view east to Mount Shasta from the Pacific Crest Trail

Inspirational mountain remoteness not found anywhere else in California is all yours here. The jumbled clusters of jagged minarets and spires of the Klamaths are among the oldest and most rugged in the state. A long-lost geologic cousin of the Sierra Nevada, this mountain province includes the Trinity Alps, the Marble Mountains, the Siskiyou Mountains, the Eddy Range, and a vast assortment of metamorphic and granitic rocks. Explore this region and reap rich rewards: raging creeks plummeting over boulders and waterfalls in spring; profuse wildflowers at your feet and vast vistas on the horizon in summer; rich hues of dogwood, maple, and black oak leaves in autumn.

48 SULPHUR CREEK AND BURSTARSE FALLS

Length: 6.8 miles round-trip
Hiking time: 4 hours
High point: 3,350 feet
Total elevation gain: 950 feet
Difficulty: moderate
Season: year-round; occasional winter snow
Water: available from creeks (purify first)
Map: USGS 7.5' Dunsmuir, USFS Castle Crags Wilderness
Information: Mount Shasta Ranger Station, Shasta–Trinity National Forest

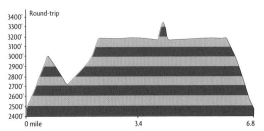

This hike offers solitude as you enjoy clear streams, a 40-foot waterfall, and extensive views of the steep granite spires of Castle Crags.

Drive Interstate 5 north of Redding 48 miles or south of Dunsmuir 6 miles to the Castle Crags/Castella exit. Head west on Castle Creek Road for 3.2 miles and turn into the large parking area on the right.

The trail begins on the northwest side of the parking area, quickly passes a grove of knobcone pine, and starts a steady climb through chaparral. Look south for views of Gray Rocks and Flume Creek Ridge on the other side of Castle Creek.

> Granite domes and spires loom high above.

You reach the Pacific Crest Trail at 0.6 mile. Turn right and climb gently to gain an exquisite northeasterly view of the massive granite bulk of Castle Crags. Continue downhill to the serene, shaded waters of Sulphur Creek at 1.2 miles, which originate in the high peaks above.

Retrace your steps and pass the previously encountered trail junction at 1.8 miles. The path now undulates gently under the shade of ponderosa pine, Douglas fir, incense cedar, and black oak and allows good views to the south and west. At 2.8 miles you reach Popcorn Spring, where bigleaf maple and black oak shade the small creek as it slides over smooth slabs of granite. The first meeting with Burstarse Creek occurs at 3.6 miles, but the waterfall awaits farther up the trail. Cross

Burstarse Falls

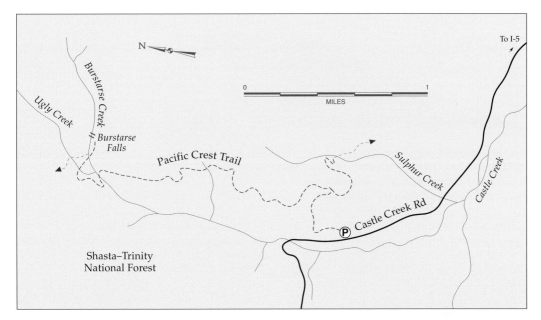

the misnamed Ugly Creek at 3.9 miles and continue another 0.1 mile to where the trail makes a 180-degree turn just above Burstarse Creek.

Leave the path here and carefully make your way down to the creek (watch for poison oak), taking note of a small wading pool as you cross to the creek's far side. Continue below the canyon wall 100 yards to Burstarse Falls. The greatest amount of water makes the 40-foot plunge in spring and early summer when snow melts, but the area at the falls remains lush, shaded, and cool even in late summer.

49 CASTLE DOME

Length: 5.8 miles round-trip
Hiking time: 3 hours
High point: 4,750 feet
Total elevation gain: 2,000 feet
Difficulty: strenuous
Season: early April through mid-November
Water: bring your own
Maps: USGS 7.5' Dunsmuir, USFS Castle Crags Wilderness
Information: Castle Crags State Park

The steep granite spires of Castle Crags entice many an Interstate 5 traveler into the wilderness for a trek. On this hike you'll climb through the forest to Castle Dome, a massive stone bulwark that anchors the crags and allows impressive views, including the brilliant white visage of Mount Shasta.

Leave Interstate 5 at the Castle Crags State Park/Castella exit, 48 miles north of Redding and 6 miles south of Dunsmuir, and follow signs

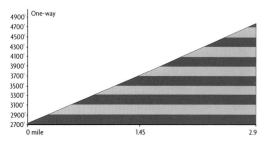

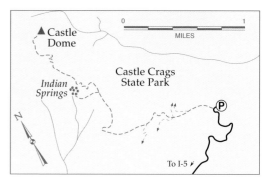

west to the state park's headquarters. Turn right and take the paved main road through the campground for 0.3 mile, following signs for photography and a vista point. It's another twisty mile from the campground to the trailhead.

The trail begins on the right, about 150 feet down the road from the parking area. A trail junction awaits after a flat 0.25 mile. Go left and begin a climb under a pine/fir canopy that doesn't end until you reach Castle Dome.

At 0.5 mile you briefly join the Pacific Crest Trail and then take a signed trail to the right. Go right again at another trail fork at 1 mile. Tantalizing glimpses of vertical granite slabs lure you upward and help you forget the vigorous climb. At 2 miles a path heads left 0.2 mile to lush and shady Indian Springs, the hike's only sure source of water. (If you visit the springs, be very careful not to pollute or disturb its fragile environment.) Stay right for the final 0.9 mile. Over the last 0.5 mile, you'll enter the crags proper, an area that's becoming increasingly popular with rock climbers.

> Castle Crags is a popular place to test rock-climbing skills.

At 2.9 miles, you reach the base of Castle Dome. Head to a chain-link fence at a small saddle on the dome's west side, where you'll have the best view of the broad shoulders and summit of 14,162-foot Mount Shasta, the undisputed mountain king of Northern California. Girard Ridge and other forested mountains stretch eastward; Grey Ridge, Shasta Bally, and Bully Choop lie southward; and the crags dominate the west.

You'll undoubtedly be tempted to climb to the top of Castle Dome. Do so only if you have rock-climbing experience, shoes with good tread, and dry rock. The least dangerous route begins on the dome's south side and then follows a crack around to the east. Be sure of your footing and the route, and remember that it's usually easier to climb up than down.

Granite spires near Castle Dome
(Photo by John R. Soares)

50 CASTLE LAKE TO HEART LAKE AND MOUNT BRADLEY RIDGE

Length: 5 miles round-trip
Hiking time: 5 hours or 2 days
High point: 6,050 feet
Total elevation gain: 1,300 feet
Difficulty: moderate
Season: mid-May through late October
Water: available from lakes (purify first)
Maps: USGS 7.5′ Seven Lakes Basin, USGS 7.5′ Dunsmuir, USFS Castle Crags Wilderness
Information: Mount Shasta Ranger Station, Shasta–Trinity National Forest

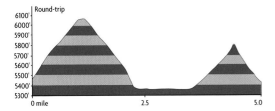

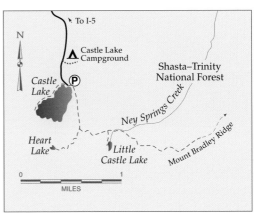

This hike gives you summer swimming in alpine lakes, opportunities to wander through lush meadows, and spectacular views of major California mountains, including Mount Shasta. Most hikers do the trek in one day, but you can certainly camp near Heart Lake or in the forest past Little Castle Lake.

Leave Interstate 5 at the Central Mount Shasta exit and head west and south on South Old Stage Road and W. A. Barr Road. Cross the dam at Lake Siskiyou and turn left 0.2 mile farther. Drive the paved road 7.1 miles to Castle Lake.

> Glaciers sculpted the Castle Lake landscape.

First examine the signboards that discuss the natural and human history of Castle Lake. Consider a swim if it's warm, and then take the trail across the lake's outlet.

The steep and rocky trail affords excellent views of Castle Lake and its glacially carved surroundings as you ascend. You'll pass numerous red and white firs before reaching a saddle at 0.6 mile. Keep your eyes peeled for an unmarked trail on the right

(about 100 feet before reaching a seasonal pond).

Follow the path with its accompanying meadows, flowers, and views for 0.5 mile to reach Heart Lake at 1.1 miles. Here you can swim in the warm, shallow waters and immerse yourself in the glorious view of Mount Shasta to the north and Castle Lake just below. Explore the lake's environs and find a small pond and a couple of level areas for camping.

Retrace your steps and rejoin the main trail at 1.6 miles. Drop through a rocky gully and enter a meadow at 2 miles. An unmarked trail on the right quickly brings you to the shallow waters of Little Castle Lake, encircled by dense vegetation. Make your way to the south shore for an impressive reflection of Mount Shasta on the surface.

Hop across the outlet stream, drop down, and then walk through a red fir forest. The way runs

Castle Lake and Mount Shasta from near Heart Lake (Photo by John R. Soares)

mostly level as you continue, bringing you to the spine of Mount Bradley Ridge at 3 miles. A 0.2-mile scamper northeast (left) brings you to a knob with the best views.

Look south at the immediate prospect of serrated granite crests of Castle Crags. Eastward Lassen Peak, Magee Peak, and numerous other Cascade volcanoes lead to Mount Shasta, with Mount Eddy to the west of the largest California volcano.

If you want more hiking, continue farther toward Mount Bradley or hike the 0.5 mile path that skirts the east side of Castle Lake.

51 SEVEN LAKES BASIN

Length: 6 miles round-trip
Hiking time: 5 hours or 2 days
High point: 6,825 feet
Total elevation gain: 1,200 feet
Difficulty: moderate
Season: early June through late October
Water: available only at Seven Lakes Basin (purify first); bring your own
Maps: USGS 7.5' Mumbo Basin, USGS 7.5' Seven Lakes Basin
Information: Mount Shasta Ranger Station, Shasta–Trinity National Forest

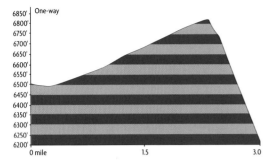

This hike gives you the best of the Klamath Mountains with little effort. You'll have 360-degree panoramas of far Northern California mountains, cool and clear mountain lakes to dip into, a varied palette of wildflowers, and several excellent campsites if you decide to do an overnighter.

To reach the trailhead, take the Central Mount Shasta exit from Interstate 5. Cross the freeway and go west and south on South Old Stage Road and W. A. Barr Road. Arc around Lake Siskiyou as the way becomes Forest Road 26. Follow this paved road to Gumboot Saddle, 18.3 miles from the freeway and 2.5 miles beyond Gumboot Lake and its campground.

Begin on the saddle's south side and head south on the Pacific Crest Trail (hikers and equestrians only). You quickly reach an open area with an unimpeded vista of the jagged

spires of the Trinity Alps to the west, with forested mountains filling in the northerly and southerly views.

Travel south, undulating gently along the spine of the ridge, occasionally shaded by a Jeffrey pine, western white pine, red fir, or white fir. Note the various flowers, including blue lupines and yellow sulfur flowers.

The first decent campsite appears on the left at 0.3 mile, followed by the inaugural view of Mount Shasta, with Mount Eddy and Gumboot Lake coming shortly thereafter. A westward glance shows Mumbo Lake and Mumbo Basin just below.

> Mount Shasta to the left, the Trinity Alps to the right —it doesn't get any better than this.

A trail fork on a saddle awaits at 2.4 miles and adds new peaks to your day's checklist. To the near east the granite spires of Castle Crags dominate, with Seven Lakes Basin just below and Boulder Mountain rising above Echo Lake. Far to the southeast are Lassen Peak, Magee Peak, and Burney Mountain.

To quickly reach the Seven Lakes Basin, ignore signs and go 30 feet farther on the Pacific Crest Trail. A faint and unmarked path drops down on the right, soon intersecting a four-wheel-drive road that you follow down to Upper Seven Lake,

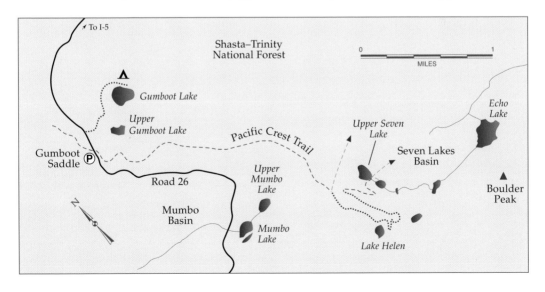

a total 0.5 mile distance. The lake's waters invite you to swim, but two campsites by the water are too close, so explore farther from shore for a level spot. Lower Seven Lake lies 100 yards to the south but has no campsites.

You can hike cross-country to explore the basin. The actual trail fades as it runs east toward Echo Lake. Do not attempt to visit this lake: It's privately owned, and the owner is notoriously cranky and very hostile to visitors.

Mount Shasta vista on the way to Seven Lakes Basin (Photo by John R. Soares)

52 MOUNT EDDY AND THE DEADFALL LAKES

Length: 10 miles round-trip
Hiking time: 6 hours or overnight
High point: 9,025 feet
Total elevation gain: 2,500 feet
Difficulty: moderate to strenuous
Season: early July through mid-October
Water: available from lakes and streams (purify first); none above Upper
    Deadfall Lake
Maps: USGS 7.5' Mt. Eddy, USGS 7.5' South China.
Information: Mount Shasta Ranger Station, Shasta–Trinity National Forest

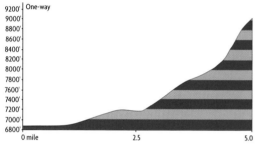

This hike features amazing wildflower displays and stupendous views from Mount Eddy's summit. You'll also visit the Deadfall Lakes, each surrounded by colorful metamorphic rocks.

On Interstate 5 drive north 3.4 miles beyond the Weed turnoff and take the Edgewood/Gazelle exit. Go under the freeway, turn right at the stop sign, and after 0.3 mile turn left onto Stewart Springs Road. At 4.7 miles turn right onto Forest Road 17, also known as Parks Creek Road. Park at the large trailhead clearing at Parks Creek Pass, 13.7 miles from the freeway exit.

Initially take the road that parallels the main road; it quickly turns to single track tread. The

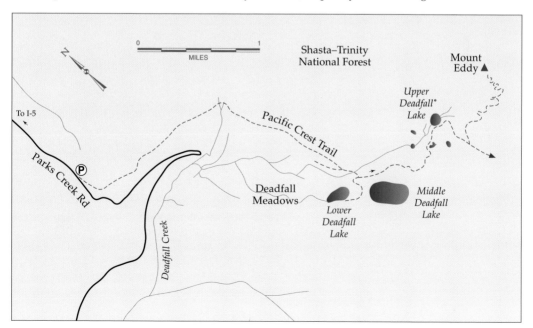

Middle Deadfall Lake (Photo by John R. Soares)

Pacific Crest Trail (hikers and equestrians only) stays mostly level at the onset and soon provides views of the Trinity Alps from a northeast vantage point. Red fir and white fir mix with Jeffrey pine and ponderosa pine to shade patches of dwarf larkspur and yarrow as you travel to a seasonal creek at 1.1 miles. Another stream gurgles down

> Yellow lupine, white angelica, red columbine: this hike is famous for its effusive floral display.

to scenic Deadfall Meadows at 1.8 miles, where yellow lupine and white-flowered angelica combine with sage for showy trailside color.

The wildflower displays keep coming, with corn lily and red columbine surrounding another brook at 2.1 miles. Western white pine dominates at 2.2 miles as you first sight Mount Eddy's southwest shoulder, along with the upper meadows where Deadfall Creek meanders. Reach a trail sign mounted on a huge western white pine at 2.6 miles. A right here would quickly lead you to Lower Deadfall Lake, which has a few campsites but loses a lot of water by late summer. Focus your attention on the prettier lakes farther on by going left and continuing uphill on the Sisson-Callahan Trail. You soon spot Middle Deadfall Lake on the right. Big rocks on the shoreline make great sunbathing and dipping spots, and you'll also find several campsites.

A marsh covered with marigolds empties into Middle Deadfall Lake's north side. Rejoin the Sisson-Callahan Trail near this colorful marsh, and then wander past a pure stand of western white pine on your way to Mount Eddy. At 3.1 miles, just before the first of three alpine ponds, foxtail pine appear. Three superb campsites exist at the first pond, which reflects the orange metamorphosed rock of the west flank of Mount Eddy.

Reach the meadow above Upper Deadfall Lake at 3.6 miles. A sand-bottomed brook wanders through the meadow, where wild onion, buttercup, and bird's-foot grow next to a spring. The path ascends to the southwest, allowing numerous views of the Deadfall Lakes and the Trinity Alps in the distance. At 4.2 miles you reach Deadfall Summit. Go left at a trail fork and climb relentlessly for the next 0.8 mile, gazing at displays of the upper Sacramento River drainage to the east and Castle Crags to the southeast, as well as a mix of shiny metamorphic stones and alpine wildflowers at your feet.

An excellent vista of Mount Shasta awaits at Mount Eddy's summit. In addition to all previously encountered views, you'll also see Black Butte (Hike 45).

53 BEAR LAKE

Length: 6 miles round-trip
Hiking time: 4 hours or overnight
High point: 5,550 feet
Total elevation gain: 1,750 feet
Difficulty: moderate
Season: mid-June through mid-October
Water: available at Bear Lake (purify first); bring your own
Map: USGS 7.5' Bear Peak
Information: Happy Camp Ranger District, Klamath National Forest

Hike into the heart of far Northern California's wild and remote Siskiyou Mountains; you'll visit the deep waters of Bear Lake and be treated to a panorama of high ridges and peaks.

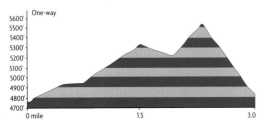

Take paved Road 15N19, which is on Highway 96's west side 72 miles north of Willow Creek, 10 miles south of Happy Camp, and 0.4 mile south of the Highway 96 bridge over Clear Creek. Always stay on the best road at intersections, and follow signs for the Bear Lake/Kelsey Trail. The pavement ends 6.5 miles from Highway 96. Drive 5 miles farther and turn right at the sign for Bear Lake. Continue the last 0.1 mile to the trailhead.

The path, a part of the nineteenth-century South Kelsey Trail that linked Fort Jones with the Pacific Coast, begins in a forest of Douglas fir, white fir, and incense cedar. It reaches the lush greenery of Elbow Spring at 0.2 mile and then climbs moderately past an understory of Sadler oak, huckleberry oak, manzanita, and tobacco brush. At 1.5 miles the trail nears a ridge and offers open views of the forested Siskiyou Mountains to the west and south.

As you continue northwest along the ridge, red fir, a few western white pine, and the rare Brewer spruce line the path, which is occasionally punctuated by granite outcroppings. Look for a lone red fir on the right 2.1 miles from the trailhead and just east of Bear Peak. From here, you have spectacular vistas of the Siskiyou Mountains stretching north into Oregon and east toward Mount Shasta, the Marble Mountains rising skyward to the southeast, and farther southeast the rocky spires of the Trinity Alps climbing up to 9,000 feet. Note the Brewer spruce to the north just below.

> This trek takes you deep into the Siskiyou Mountains and provides glimpses into Oregon.

Follow the trail another 0.2 mile to a Siskiyou Wilderness sign, where, in addition to the mountains seen from below the red fir tree, you can see Red Hill to the west, Twin Peaks and Rocky Knob to the northwest, and 7,309-foot Preston Peak (the tallest mountain in the region) to the north, with massive Cedar Crest guarding its south flanks. Just below you'll spy the glacial cirque enclosing Bear Lake along with an upstream pond.

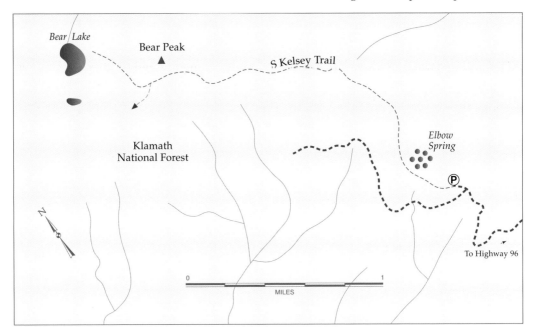

Go 10 feet past the Siskiyou Wilderness sign, take the unsigned trail on the right. Make note of the Alaska yellow cedar growing around the walls of the glacial cirque. This is the southernmost range of this tree species. Descend 750 feet over the next 0.7 mile to the shores of Bear Lake. Talus slopes border the deep lake's west side, and you'll find several campsites nestled in the forest that surrounds the other sides. If you want to hike more, take the South Kelsey Trail west along the ridge toward Red Hill.

Butterflies brighten a meadow.

54 PARADISE LAKE

Length: 15.2 miles round-trip from Kelsey Camp, or 2.1 miles one-way on Rye Patch Trail
Hiking time: 2 days
High point: 6,100 feet
Total elevation gain: 3,700 feet from Kelsey Camp, 1,400 feet from Rye Patch Trail
Difficulty: moderate to strenuous
Season: late June to mid-October
Water: plenty along Kelsey Creek Trail (purify first); none on Rye Patch Trail
Maps: USGS 7.5′ Grider Valley, USGS 7.5′ Marble Mountain, USFS Marble Mountain Wilderness
Information: Salmon/Scott River Ranger District, Klamath National Forest

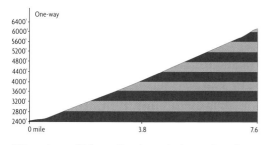

Hike along Kelsey Creek and through a long wildflower meadow to colorful Paradise Lake, where you'll have views of uniquely shaped Kings Castle, Cayenne Ridge, and other peaks in the Marble Mountains.

From Fort Jones on Highway 3, take Scott River Road and drive 16 miles. Turn left at Kelsey Camp immediately after a bridge. Bear right at 0.2 mile and park near the signed trailhead 0.2 mile farther.

Start your hike on the Kelsey Trail, a major supply route constructed in the 1850s that stretched between nearby Fort Jones to the east and Crescent City on the coast. The path initially climbs past sections of madly rushing water interspersed with serene pools and then reaches a sandy campsite with a makeshift table near a charred tree trunk at 2 miles.

The trail departs Kelsey Creek, only to return at 3 miles. Over the next 0.7 mile, it gently climbs past a seasonal streambed and two of Kelsey Creek's numerous tributaries. The next 2 miles travel near the creek most of the time, steadily climbing through a Douglas fir forest that includes a few sugar pine and incense cedar. Canyon live oak dominate the middle stretch, with an occasional black oak mixed in.

Packers Valley Creek tumbles into Kelsey Creek at 5.8 miles, promptly followed by a campsite next to a rustic wooden fence. From 6.1 to 6.8 miles, two unsigned scant trails lead westward up the hillside. Bear left at these cross trails, keeping close to Kelsey Creek.

> Kings Castle looks like a rook in a chess game.

A small grove of black cottonwood trees sways in the breeze 0.2 mile into a gently sloping meadow at 7 miles. From a small stream at 7.1 miles, the climb gets noticeably tougher as you pass a wildflower patch of blue lupine, white yarrow, orange Indian paintbrush, white angelica, western blue flax, and yellow meadow goldenrod. The slope eases along the meadowy mountainside when you make the final crossing of Kelsey Creek at 7.5 miles. The trail finally crests

California pitcher plant

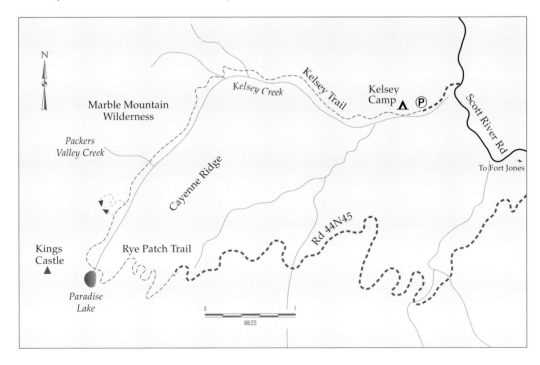

at 7.6 miles at Paradise Lake's scenic meadow, decorated by stonecrop and lupine.

A splendid campsite beneath a white fir community lies 120 feet from the east shoreline of the lake, from which you have fantastic views of numerous ridges and peaks, including Kings Castle, which resembles a rook in a chess game. A lone, grassy island invites you to wade out and sunbathe.

There's a backdoor shortcut to Paradise Lake via the strenuous Rye Patch Trail. It offers an excellent day hike option to the Cayenne Ridge and Paradise Lake area, or it can serve as a 9.7-mile, one-way route to Kelsey Camp.

To reach this trailhead, travel 13.5 miles on Scott River Road from Fort Jones. Turn left onto Road 44N45. Go right at a road intersection 6.4 miles farther, and continue on Road 44N45 another 5.6 miles.

The Rye Patch Trail climbs continuously and sometimes steeply in a well-shaded Douglas fir forest. The ascent finally eases when you reach a fern-covered hillside at 1.4 miles. At 1.9 miles you'll reach the colorful, open slope near the southeast section of Paradise Lake.

55 SKY HIGH LAKES AND SUMMIT LAKE

Length: 18 miles round-trip
Hiking time: 2 to 3 days
High point: 6,700 feet
Total elevation gain: 3,200 feet
Difficulty: moderate to strenuous
Season: mid-June to early October
Water: available only from lakes (purify first); have plenty on hand
Maps: USGS 7.5′ Marble Mountain, USFS Marble Mountain Wilderness
Information: Salmon/Scott River Ranger District, Klamath National Forest

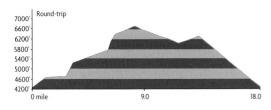

This hike boasts a lot of variety: Admire a white marble mountain, explore a big wildflower garden, swim in the attractive Sky High Lakes, and walk 5 miles along a high ridge with far-reaching views.

From Fort Jones on Highway 3, turn right on Scott River Road, and then drive 13.5 miles to Indian Scotty Campground, where you turn left. For the next 5.4 miles, stay on Forest Road 44N45, and then turn left onto Forest Road 43N45. Drive 1.7 miles farther to Lovers Camp, where you bear right and go 0.1 mile.

Climb gently for 0.2 mile to a dirt road and pick up the trail proper at an information kiosk 100 yards farther. The route weaves gently near Canyon Creek past dogwood, Douglas fir, sugar pine, and white alder. Go right on the Canyon Creek Trail next to a large dogwood at 0.8 mile. The next 3 miles climb gently under shade above the creek. Cross a terraced tributary stream featuring a slender cascade and two tiny soaking pools at 4.2 miles. Bear left 0.1 mile farther at a trail intersection. Climb another 0.3 mile and go left at another trail junction.

> Peak 6817 towers above Lower Sky High Lake's lime-green waters.

The countryside opens into a green sloping meadow with a striking view of Marble Mountain's escarpment, which sports a vertical band of shiny white marble. The black schist protrusion on the northernmost marble rim is Black Marble Mountain.

At 5.1 miles look down on tiny, inaccessible Gate Lake, and then reach Lower Sky High

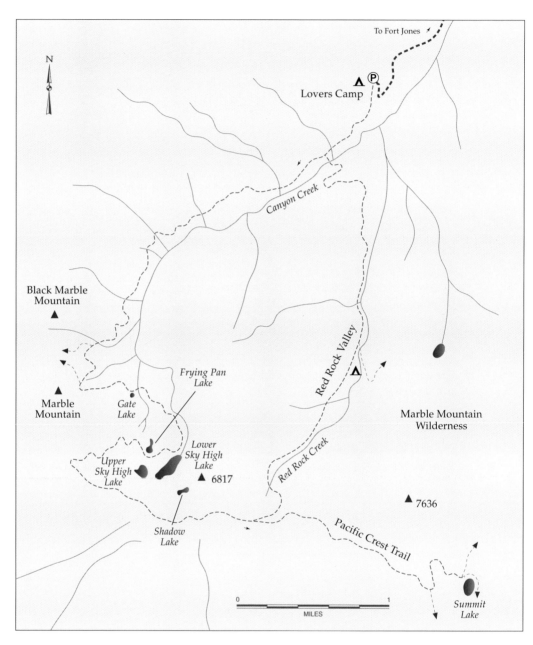

N

To Fort Jones

Lovers Camp

Canyon Creek

Black Marble Mountain

Red Rock Valley

Frying Pan Lake

Marble Mountain

Gate Lake

Marble Mountain Wilderness

Lower Sky High Lake

Upper Sky High Lake

6817

Red Rock Creek

Shadow Lake

7636

Pacific Crest Trail

0   1
MILES

Summit Lake

Lake at 6 miles, where ominous Peak 6817 towers above the lime-green waters. You'll find two campsites 200 feet from the northeast shore. Nearby Upper Sky High Lake, just to the west, is a nice side trip but has no campsites.

The trail then leads to a handful of white fir and hemlock that dot the exposed, meadowy shoreline of shallow, swimmable Frying Pan Lake. From here it climbs to the lowest saddle on the west ridge at 7.1 miles, where you bear left

Views of Mount Shasta are common from the Klamath Mountains.

twice onto the Pacific Crest Trail. Over a level, 1-mile ridge walk, enjoy open views of the surrounding Marble Mountains. Reach a signed trail fork at 8.2 miles, where you head left 0.4 mile to Shadow Lake. Obtain a view of Marble Mountain just a few footsteps from the lone campsite near the east shore and consider swimming near the boulder-strewn north shore.

To continue the journey, double back and go left onto the Pacific Crest Trail. Make note of the left turn down Red Rock Valley at a four-way intersection at 8.8 miles (your return route) and then go straight. The views instantly switch northward as you walk along the ridge, with occasional glimpses of massive, orange-rocked Peak 7636.

Turn left at the double-signed junction at the gap at 10 miles. Your new trail descends toward Peak 7636 and then abruptly swings toward the Shackleford Creek basin at 10.3 miles.

Look carefully for the signed trail junction 0.3 mile farther and head right to Summit Lake, where you'll find two campsites near the willow- and white-fir-lined shore.

Retrace your steps for 2.2 miles, and then turn right onto the signed Red Rock Valley Trail at 13.2 miles. The path plunges into a forest to pass below a tiny lake at 13.6 miles and then crosses a tributary of Red Rock Creek.

The path stays above and west of the creek for a while and then crosses it at 15 miles. Go left at a trail fork near a campsite, and then recross the creek at 15.1 miles. Depart the creek for good 0.7 mile farther, eventually crossing Canyon Creek at 17.2 miles. Bear right 100 yards farther onto the Canyon Creek Trail for the last 0.8 mile to the trailhead.

56 BIG BEAR LAKE

Length: 10 miles round-trip
Hiking time: 8 hours or overnight
High point: 5,850 feet
Total elevation gain: 2,800 feet
Difficulty: moderate
Season: mid-June through mid-October
Water: plentiful along most of the route (purify first)
Maps: USGS 7.5' Tangle Blue Lake, USFS Trinity Alps Wilderness
Information: Weaverville Ranger District, Shasta–Trinity National Forest

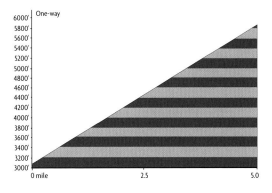

line the trail on the way up, you'll love the lake's clear waters and steep glacial cirque, and it's easily accessible from Highway 3.

From the west side of Highway 3 about 16 miles north of Trinity Center, take the north end of Bear Creek Loop Road. Follow this dirt road to the signed trailhead, which is near the road's crossing of Bear Creek.

> Mountain alder, ferns, and western azalea thrive in moist areas below the lake.

Granite-ringed Big Bear Lake makes a good overnight backpacking trip: A variety of plants

The trail begins the long climb to Big Bear Lake in a forest of incense cedar, Douglas fir,

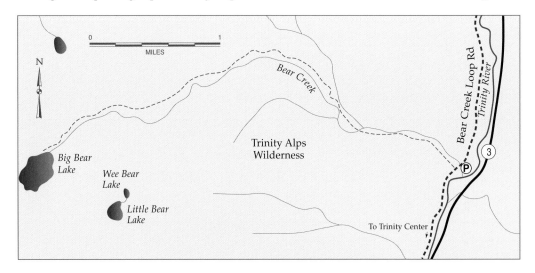

Bigleaf and vine maples

on the south, west, and north sides. You'll find good deep spots for swimming by walking to the steep granite on the east shore. Several adequate campsites, most shaded by mountain hemlock, western white pine, and red fir, sit above the lake on both sides of the outlet creek.

and ponderosa pine and travels close to Bear Creek for the first mile. At 0.9 mile you'll see a stock trail heading to the right. Continue straight another 200 yards and take a footbridge across the creek. The trail then switchbacks steeply up a ridge between Bear Creek and the smaller stream you just crossed. Manzanita and huckleberry oak, two common chaparral shrubs, line and occasionally intrude onto the path, while numerous black oak and an occasional stand of knobcone pine provide some shade.

Approach the creek again at 2.1 miles and begin alternating between a mixed white fir and western white pine forest and lush open patches with numerous ferns. The first open views of the glacial granite cirques harboring Big Bear Lake, your destination, and cousins Little Bear Lake and Wee Bear Lake, appear at 3.1 miles.

From here, the occasionally steep route passes through numerous moist areas inhabited by mountain alder, fern, and some western azalea. At 4.6 miles the trail crosses granite outcrops, where rock ducks (cairns) guide you. Be sure to look back for an exquisite eastward view of Mount Shasta.

At 5 miles you finally reach Big Bear Lake, where steep granite walls tower over 1,000 feet

Mount Eddy from Big Bear Lake

57 CARIBOU, EMERALD, AND SAPPHIRE LAKES

Length: 30.6 miles round-trip
Hiking time: 5 to 7 days
High point: 7,500 feet
Total elevation gain: 6,800 feet
Difficulty: strenuous
Season: early July through mid-October
Water: sporadically available (purify first); have at least a quart on hand at
all times
Maps: USGS 7.5' Caribou Lake, USGS 7.5' Thompson Peak, USFS Trinity Alps
Wilderness
Information: Salmon/Scott River Ranger District, Klamath National Forest

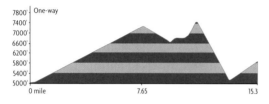

Take a long backpacking trip deep into the heart of the Trinity Alps, where you'll find expansive views, vertical granite mountain faces, deep glacial lakes, and numerous clear streams.

Drive west on Coffee Creek Road, which leaves Highway 3 about 8 miles north of the town of Trinity Center. Bear left at a road fork 19 miles from Highway 3, where a sign directs you to Big Flat Campground. Turn right 0.6 mile farther and park near the outhouses.

Follow the Caribou Lake signs as you head downhill to a log crossing of the South Fork of the Salmon River, and take the left trail that heads up the bank. After a brief climb, hike 200 yards through a meadow and bear right at a trail junction. From here, you begin a series of long switchbacks under the shade of white and Douglas fir, with a few open areas dominated by huckleberry oak, manzanita, and some tobacco brush. As you climb the gentle grade, occasional views of Preachers Peak and Red Rock Mountain open up to the east, and you'll also see the long granite ridge of Caribou Mountain to the south.

The saddle containing Caribou Meadows and a waterless campsite awaits 3.4 miles from the

trailhead. Just past the campsite, the trail crosses the old Caribou Lake Trail, which travels over a 7,400-foot ridge on its way to Caribou Lake. This trail, about 2 miles shorter than the new trail, may be difficult to follow because of lack of use and maintenance. From Caribou Meadows the new trail passes some small seasonal creeks and then gives a good view up a polished, glacial granite slope to the cirque that houses Little Caribou Lake. As you contour around a mountainside, the northern ranges of the Klamath Mountains appear on the right.

A small campsite sits just below the trail by a stream at 4.6 miles. From here, you travel past patches of red and white fir forest broken up by manzanita chaparral. At 5.4 miles you enter Browns Meadow, guarded by a steep wall of granite. These grass fields stretch up the mountainside and offer two campsites and a year-round stream.

As the trail climbs steeply, be sure to look behind you for a good view of Browns Meadow and snowy Mount Shasta. The trail levels at 6.6 miles, where gaps between red fir trees allow expansive westward views of Caesars and Thompson Peaks rearing their heads skyward. The long, granite spires of 8,575-foot Caribou Mountain appear as the trail undulates southward, and eventually you'll see rock-ringed Caribou and Lower Caribou Lakes. At 8.2 miles the old trail merges from the left just before your trail switchbacks down to Snowslide Lake.

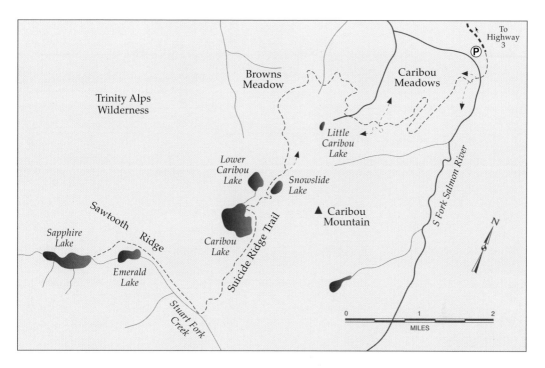

The deep, cold waters of Snowslide Lake nestle under the steep slopes of Caribou Mountain, whose highest pinnacles reach more than 1,900 feet above the lake's surface. You'll find at least five good campsites by the trail on the lake's west side, most partially shaded by red fir,

> Caribou Lake is the largest lake in the Trinity Alps and a strong contender for the most beautiful in the Klamaths.

lodgepole pine, and mountain hemlock. As you continue south across sheets of granite toward Caribou Lake, several faint paths head down to Lower Caribou Lake, which offers good swimming but only one campsite.

Continue up to Caribou Lake, which, at 72 acres, is the largest body of water in the Trinity Alps. Nestled in a glacial cirque 10 miles from the trailhead, it also makes a strong claim as the prettiest. Its deep blue waters reflect the metamorphic ridge crest to the south and west as well as the steep granite ridge to the east. To the north the Klamath Mountains stretch clear to Oregon.

If you're brave, take a chilly swim out to the two rock islands off the north shore. Several campsites lie near the north and east edges.

The trail, usually marked with rock ducks (cairns), continues along Caribou Lake's east shore and then climbs south up to jagged Sawtooth Ridge at 11.2 miles. From this aptly named point, you have a bird's-eye view of the territory hiked earlier; however, steep-sided Sawtooth Mountain towering over the Stuart Fork valley probably will capture your attention. The green of Morris Meadows glows downstream, and upstream you'll spy the crown jewels of the Trinity Alps: Emerald and Sapphire Lakes. Thompson Peak and Caesars Peak dominate the skyline to the west.

The next portion of your hike involves a 2-mile trek through chaparral and down the ninety or so switchbacks of the Suicide Ridge Trail, which loses 2,100 feet of elevation. Be sure you have plenty of water for this dry section, both going down and especially coming back up, and make sure you don't lose the sometimes faint trail.

At the bottom you'll reach the cool shade of Portuguese Camp and also have easy access to Stuart Fork Creek. Head upstream under

Caribou Lake

fir shade past a few small streams and several campsites. At 14.7 miles you'll see the sparkling surface of Emerald Lake, where you'll find a few campsites in the trees just below the dam.

The last stretch of trail borders Emerald Lake's north shore and then heads through chaparral to reach Sapphire Lake, a hefty 15.3 miles from the trailhead and this trip's final destination. Sapphire Lake receives far fewer visitors than its sister, and it has only one good campsite, located near the outlet. However, the lake and its surroundings will transfix you. The lake's depth is over 200 feet (the exact figure isn't known), and its waters gleam deep blue. A glacier carved the valley holding Emerald and Sapphire Lakes, leaving behind the steep sides of granitic Sawtooth Ridge, which forms a beautiful reflection in the lakes' waters.

58 HORSESHOE AND WARD LAKES

Length: 21.4 miles round-trip
Hiking time: 3 to 4 days
High point: 7,120 feet
Total elevation gain: 3,600 feet
Difficulty: moderate to strenuous
Season: mid-June through late September
Water: available from lakes and streams (purify first)
Map: USGS 7.5′ Covington Mill, USGS 7.5′ Siligo Peak, USGS 7.5′
Ycatapom, USFS Trinity Alps Wilderness
Information: Weaverville Ranger District, Shasta–Trinity National Forest

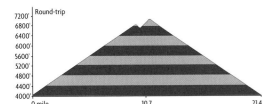

Powerful Swift Creek, miles of meadows, displays of Trinity Alps peaks, and two peaceful mountain lakes highlight this backpacking trip.

On Highway 3 by Trinity Center, turn west at the Swift Creek Trail sign. Drive 6.9 miles, following all signs indicating the Swift Creek trailhead along the mostly dirt road.

The Swift Creek Trail stays mostly level to the first visual attraction: granite slabs plunging into the cascades and clear pools of rushing Swift Creek at 0.7 mile. A sign on an incense cedar at 1.3 miles marks the trail fork to Granite Lake (Hike 59: Granite Lake and Seven Up Gap), but you bear right, staying on the Swift Creek Trail. From 1.3 to 3 miles, the route climbs gently past western azalea, Douglas fir, ponderosa pine, and incense cedar.

Hike across a wide basin, carefully negotiate the tricky crossing of Parker Creek at 4.2 miles, and note the debut of the towering Trinity Alps to the southwest. Bear right 0.1 mile farther at

Flowers, streams, lakes, forests, and peaks—it's all here.

the sign for "Fosters Cabin," go left at another trail fork just beyond, and reach Parker Meadow at 4.7 miles. You can choose from plenty of campsites along Swift Creek for the next 4 miles in Parker and Mumford Meadows. Fosters Cabin, hidden in the meadowy forest at 5.1 miles, contains several bunks and offers shelter during a thunderstorm.

Sawtooth Ridge from above Horseshoe Lake

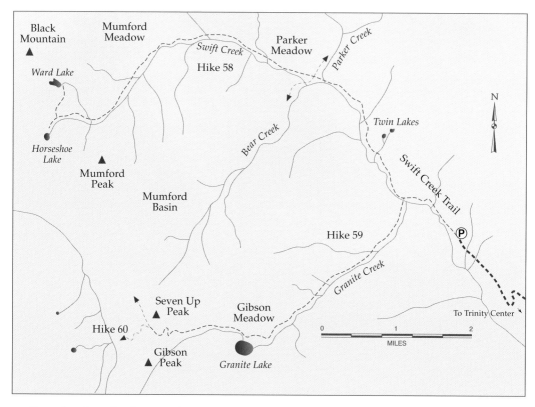

Cross Landers Creek at 6 miles and begin a 2-mile stroll through Mumford Meadow amid huge ponderosa pine and incense cedar. The path stays nearly level to 8.3 miles, traveling briefly into forests to return to the corn lily fields, marshes, and deer pastures of Mumford Meadow. Plan on frequent tributary crossings, and keep an eye on Mumford Peak as it looms on the left.

At 8.5 miles duck into a small forest, and then begin the steep part of the hike to Horseshoe Lake across loose talus. The narrow path borders dwindling Swift Creek at 9.3 miles, reaches a signed trail junction 0.1 mile farther (stay left), and leads you past three campsites to Horseshoe Lake, the creek's origin, at 9.7 miles.

Western white pine, mountain hemlock, and red fir grow between the lake's rock outcrops, and a couple of small ponds hide near the willow-choked outlet. Scamper up the rock outcrops for a picturesque view of Mumford and Parker Meadows and Mumford Peak to the southeast.

Buckwheat above Horseshoe Lake

To get to Ward Lake, retrace your steps 0.3 mile and bear left. You'll immediately traverse stepping stones next to marsh marigolds. At 10.8 miles, look down into the meadow below Ward Lake and look behind for a wide-open display of major Trinity Alps mountains, including Siligo, Gibson, and Seven Up Peaks.

Reach Ward Lake and its several campsites at 11 miles, where you'll enjoy small meadows and views of stark Black Mountain to the northwest.

If you want an extended trip, consider trekking to Granite Lake (Hike 59) and beyond to the Four Lakes Loop (Hike 60).

59 GRANITE LAKE AND SEVEN UP GAP

Length: 15.6 miles round-trip
Hiking time: 3 days
High point: 7,400 feet
Total elevation gain: 3,450 feet
Difficulty: moderate to strenuous
Season: late June through mid-October
Water: available from Swift and Granite Creeks (purify first)
Maps: USGS 7.5' Covington Mill, USGS 7.5' Siligo Peak, USFS Trinity Alps Wilderness
Information: Weaverville Ranger District, Shasta–Trinity National Forest

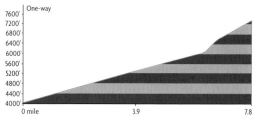

This trip takes you along the madly rushing waters of Swift and Granite Creeks, both blessed by the sweet fragrance of azalea blossoms in early summer. After visiting cool, clear Granite Lake, you'll climb to Seven Up Gap for a panoramic vista over the heart of the Trinity Alps. From here, you have the option of adding Hike 60 (Four Lakes Loop) and Hike 58 (Horseshoe and Ward Lakes) to your backpacking trip.

Turn left off Highway 3 at the Swift Creek sign, which is 0.2 mile north of the main turnoff for the town of Trinity Center. Bear left at two main road intersections. Park in the upper lot when you reach the Swift Creek trailhead, 6.9 miles from Highway 3.

The raucous roar of surging Swift Creek emanates from the left as you begin a steady climb under the shade of incense cedar, Douglas fir, sugar pine, and Jeffrey pine. A good campsite nestled above the creek awaits at 0.5 mile, and then you'll encounter three small, azalea-lined creeks. The trail then travels atop a steep canyon wall, from which you can see one of Swift Creek's cacophonous waterfalls crashing over a 40-foot drop into a deep pool. Go left at a trail junction at 1.3 miles (the right-hand trail is discussed in Hike 58: Horseshoe and Ward Lakes), pass by another large campsite, and cross Swift Creek on a large metal bridge at 1.5 miles.

You now trade Swift Creek for Granite Creek. After climbing a ridge, you'll encounter the first of numerous alder- and fern-bordered streams. At 2 miles the trail switchbacks away from the creek but rejoins it for a good view of a waterfall at 3 miles. As you continue up the trail, white fir replace Douglas fir, and yellow and blue lupine brighten the landscape, along with five-petaled white, pink, and red azalea flowers.

Seven Up Peak

A good campsite sits to the left just before the trail enters an area of downed trees at 3.3 miles, where the first good views of the granitic ridge to the south await. Over the next 1.5 miles you'll climb past another waterfall; enter a small, lush meadow; encounter yet another waterfall; then enter expansive Gibson Meadow.

After another 1 mile of climbing, reach Granite Lake, elevation 6,000 feet. Several campsites, shaded by incense cedar, western white pine, sugar pine, red fir, white fir, and mountain hemlock, lie near the trail on the lake's alder-enshrouded north side. You may prefer to cross the outlet creek on a log and head up to the campsites atop the granite hump on the lake's open east side. Besides easy swimming access, the best views of the clear, deep lake await you here. To the south and west you'll see the granite ridge that soars 2,400 feet from the lake's surface to the top of multispired, 8,400-foot Gibson Peak, and the reddish metamorphic mountains

that make up the north side of Granite Lake's glacial cirque.

If you aren't traveling over to the Four Lakes Loop (Hike 60), consider making the trip to Seven Up Gap a day hike, because climbing the steep trail takes a lot of energy. The path climbs above the north shore of Granite Lake and then crosses three small streams as it travels close to Granite Creek. At 6.4 miles enter a meadow, from which you have excellent views of the entire head of the Granite Creek drainage. Igneous granitic rocks rise skyward on the left, and jagged metamorphic rocks stretch upward on the right. Just a hundred yards into the meadow, you'll see one of the several small, shallow ponds across the creek. It's possible to camp on the flat granite slabs, a good option if the Granite Lake sites are crowded.

The trail eventually leaves the creek to rise steeply past numerous wildflowers to Seven Up Gap. Hardy foxtail pines join a few red firs and mountain hemlocks at the 7,600-foot saddle; however, it's the extensive views that will command your attention. To the east you'll see the north portion of Trinity Lake, and far beyond the forested Klamath Mountains rise the massive volcanic cones of the Cascades' Mount Burney, Magee Peak, and Lassen Peak. To the west you'll look far down to the Deer Creek Valley and then above it to Siligo Peak, which rises just south of the metamorphic ridge housing Luella Lake. Farther in

the distance, Sawtooth Mountain punctures the skyline, joined by its jagged siblings Mount Hilton, Wedding Cake, Thompson Peak, and Caesars Peak. Granitic Gibson Peak forms the south side of the Seven Up Gap saddle, and metamorphic Seven Up Peak shapes the north side.

To join the paths of Hike 60 (Four Lakes Loop), take the trail that switchbacks down the ridge for 1.1 miles to an intersection. You can then head left for Deer Lake or right for Luella Lake.

60 FOUR LAKES LOOP

Length: 23.9 miles round-trip
Hiking time: 3 to 4 days
High point: 7,500 feet
Total elevation gain: 5,700 feet
Difficulty: moderate to strenuous
Season: early July through September
Water: available from lakes and year-round streams (purify first)
Maps: USGS 7.5′ Siligo Peak, USGS 7.5′ Covington Mill, USFS Trinity Alps Wilderness
Information: Weaverville Ranger District, Shasta–Trinity National Forest

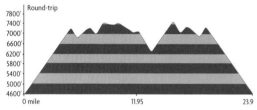

Glacial cirques, high mountain passes, and panoramas of the Trinity Alps and other mountain ranges await you on this hike, as do clear streams and flower-ringed, subalpine lakes.

From Weaverville drive northeast on Highway 3 for 14 miles, and then turn left 0.7 mile east of the bridge across Stuart Fork Creek onto a dirt road signed "Stoney Creek." Follow this dirt road 6.2 miles to the spacious trailhead.

The trail begins its steady climb up Stoney Ridge through a mixed forest of ponderosa pine, incense cedar, Douglas fir, white fir, and sugar pine. The trees part occasionally to allow views of Trinity Lake and the mountains to the south, as well as glimpses of Granite Peak and Red

Mountain just to the north. At 2.5 miles you'll pass through a chaparral thicket and then, at 3.7 miles, bear left at a trail fork. At 4 miles you'll reach the first decent campsite, located under a western white pine in Red Mountain Meadows. Nearby Stoney Creek has water year-round.

Stonewall Pass, 4.8 miles from the trailhead, features a magnificent vista: To the south lie Trinity Lake, Shasta Bally, and the Sacramento Valley; to the north, you're treated to views of granitic Sawtooth Mountain and Thompson Peak and nearer metamorphic summits such as Siligo Peak and Seven Up Peak.

The trail then descends for 1 mile as it skirts the upper edges of Van Matre Meadows and

> Take a break at Diamond Lake to admire the granite spires of Thompson Peak, Wedding Cake, Mount Hilton, and Sawtooth Mountain.

then climbs another 1 mile to Little Stonewall Pass. Just below the pass, a sign points the way to Echo Lake, only 250 yards to the right off the main trail. This flower-ringed lake, surrounded by metamorphic, red-tinged mountains, offers open vistas of the western Trinity Alps. You can camp by the lake's south side or on the ridge to the west.

From Little Stonewall Pass, the main path descends steadily past western white pine, fox-tail pine, and white fir for 0.7 mile to the edge of Lower Siligo Meadow. Cross the meadow and a year-round stream, and pick up the trail on the other side.

Bear left at a trail fork 0.3 mile from the meadow, and then climb through Upper Siligo

Diamond Lake

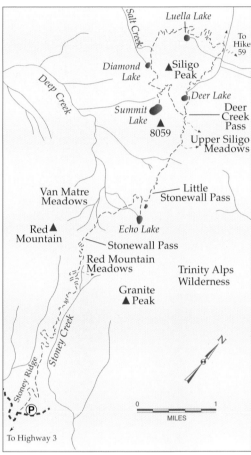

Meadow's multihued display of lupine, yarrow, and other wildflowers to another trail fork 0.5 mile farther. Bear left again and climb the last few yards to 7,500-foot Deer Creek Pass, from which you'll see Siligo Peak towering high above Deer Lake.

After you catch your breath, begin the clockwise loop of the four lakes by heading downhill for 0.2 mile and turning left at the trail fork. The way then gently switchbacks uphill to another trail fork 1 mile from Deer Creek Pass. Turn left here and follow the trail 0.5 mile to the deep blue waters of Summit Lake, snugly situated under the protective shoulder of Peak 8059. Several good campsites lie near the west shore, and near the south shore you'll have open views of the Stuart Fork valley, Monument Peak, and forested mountains marching westward to the coast.

Deer Lake

Back on the main trail, hike 0.2 mile to an impressive alpine view at a small saddle. If you wish, follow any of several faint trails along this 0.2-mile stretch up to the top of Siligo Peak, where you'll have a 360-degree view of far Northern California, including Mount Shasta and Lassen Peak.

From the saddle, walk 0.9 mile down a dozen switchbacks to the inviting waters of Diamond Lake, the crown jewel of the Four Lakes Loop. The lake rests on a shelf overlooking the Salt Creek and Stuart Fork valleys, but the most impressive sight is undoubtedly the jagged granite spires of Thompson Peak, Wedding Cake, Mount Hilton, and Sawtooth Mountain piercing the skyline to the west. A large western white pine near the lake's north edge guards the only decent campsite.

The trail then climbs 0.7 mile north to an open, grassy saddle with more stunning vistas and then drops via several switchbacks another 0.7 mile to Luella Lake. This lake offers views of Seven Up Peak, Deer Creek Canyon, and the mountains ranging east and north, but it has no good campsites.

The path continues its descent 0.8 mile to a trail fork near Deer Creek, where you turn right. After a 0.2-mile walk, you'll see a trail on the left climbing 1.1 miles up to Seven Up Gap and then on to Granite, Horseshoe, and Ward Lakes (see Hike 59: Granite Lake and Seven Up Gap and Hike 58: Horseshoe and Ward Lakes). The main trail ascends another 1.1 miles to Deer Lake. This deep, mountain-ringed lake lies at the base of Siligo Peak and offers meadow camping at its southeast edge. To get back to Deer Creek Pass, follow the trail 0.3 mile uphill and go left at the fork.

61 CANYON CREEK LAKES AND BOULDER CREEK LAKES

Length: 23.9 miles round-trip
Hiking time: 3 to 4 days
High point: 6,400 feet
Total elevation gain: 4,500 feet
Difficulty: strenuous
Season: mid-June to early October
Water: available from lakes and creeks (purify first)
Maps: USGS 7.5' Mount Hilton, USFS Trinity Alps Wilderness
Information: Weaverville Ranger District, Shasta–Trinity National Forest

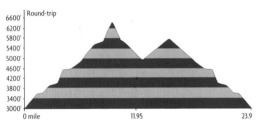

Surround yourself with steep, jagged granite peaks. Sunbathe on flat, house-size granite slabs. Wander through lush meadows. Swim in deep, cool lakes. This trip offers all this and more as it takes you deep into the Trinity Alps. It's also a very popular trek, so try to avoid weekends, especially the three- and four-day variety.

Take Highway 299 to Junction City, 8 miles northwest of Weaverville, and then turn east 75 yards southeast of the Junction City bridge onto Canyon Creek Road. Drive 13.2 miles on the paved road that follows Canyon Creek to the Canyon Creek trailhead.

The trail starts level amid ferns, dogwoods, bigleaf maples, madrones, Douglas firs, and canyon live oaks. It crosses Bear Creek at 0.3 mile

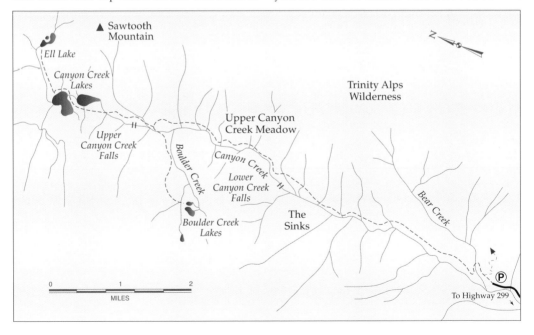

and then steepens. Pass a madrone tree at 0.8 mile and gently climb through a forest of ponderosa pine, black oak, incense cedar, and more madrone. Take the 10-yard spur trail to the left at 2.4 miles for a commanding vista of the sprawling basin, which contains a white-water stretch of Canyon Creek far below high granite peaks. At 2.8 miles, consider the 0.2 mile side-trail option to The Sinks, a series of swirling pools in Canyon Creek. Otherwise, bear right, climb past a lichen-carpeted gran-ite rock wall, and ascend a series of switch-backs that crosses the same tributary three times. Watch for a campsite on the left at 3.9 miles, where you can admire a small water-fall cascading into a round, clear pool. Look for Lower Canyon Creek Falls crashing into a deep pool a short distance downstream.

The trail climbs gently past a fern community for 0.8 mile and at 4.9 miles enters a small corn lily field in Canyon Creek Meadow. Cross sev-eral tributaries and climb through forest to a trail fork at 6.1 miles. The left trail goes 2.4 miles to Boulder Creek Lakes (description follows).

Go right to the more-visited Canyon Creek Lakes. Climb through a 0.6-mile stretch of open forest, followed by magnificent, misty Upper Canyon Creek Falls. The final leg to Lower Canyon Creek Lake gradually switch-backs between gran-ite boulders and across granite slopes and crosses Canyon Creek before reach-

> Find relief from the summer heat in the Boulder Creek Lakes.

ing the lake itself at 7.5 miles. Be very careful crossing Canyon Creek, especially during peri-ods of high water flow. Once on the west side of Lower Canyon Creek Lake, you'll find several campsites with good eastward views of Sawtooth

Upper Canyon Creek Lake

Mountain. On hot days, this clear, deep lake offers chilly refreshment to swimmers.

To get to less-visited Upper Canyon Creek Lake, follow the rock ducks (cairns) past the campsites on the west side, travel a faint path through forest, and then reach several campsites near Upper Canyon Creek Lake's south shore. The path continues, at 8.2 miles crossing the stream linking Upper Canyon Creek Lake with its lower sibling. From the lake's east shores, you'll have magnificent views of the meadow surrounding the higher reaches of Canyon Creek and the high granite peaks and ridges to the north, including Thompson Peak, the highest mountain in the Trinity Alps at 9,002 feet.

Continue northeast to Ell Lake from Upper Canyon Creek Lake's north side. The moderate 1-mile-long climb requires following rock ducks that lead directly to the lake, which is tucked into a narrow, glacier-carved slot bordered by steep granite. Seldom-visited Ell Lake offers a few campsites on the west side. Explore the meadows next to the north shore that encompass a circular pond.

For the 2.4-mile climb to Boulder Creek Lakes, retrace your steps to the trail junction you negotiated at 6.1 miles. Wade Canyon Creek very carefully, and only do this side trip if you are very confident in your stream crossing skills. Go left on the other side of Canyon Creek. (The spur trail on the right leads to a campsite.) The trail heads southwest past a marsh and then ascends moderately through ceanothus and manzanita chaparral and a few stands of sugar pine, western white pine, ponderosa pine, and incense cedar. It eventually carves steeply through a thicket on the south-facing mountainside, routing you to a sheer, black cliff. Follow the rock ducks here near the cliff for another 0.3 mile to the lakes.

Boulder Creek Lakes, nestled in a glacial bowl and surrounded by high granite peaks, feature moist meadows, red mountain heather, yarrow, dwarfed western white pines, red firs, mountain hemlocks, and the rare weeping spruce. Tiny pools and little brooks surround the small lower lake on the southeast section of the basin. Look for powerful waterfalls that pour from large Boulder Creek Lake's outlet and topple off a granite cliff.

You'll find a few campsites near the east shore of Boulder Creek Lake and a couple of makeshift spots near three ponds. The shallow lakes and ponds receive a lot of summer sun, making long swims in the warm water very pleasant.

62 MILL CREEK/TOWER HOUSE HISTORICAL DISTRICT

Length: 5.6 miles round-trip
Hiking time: 3 hours
High point: 2,050 feet
Total elevation gain: 800 feet
Difficulty: easy
Season: year-round
Water: available from Mill Creek (purify first)
Map: USGS 7.5' French Gulch
Information: Whiskeytown–Shasta–Trinity National Recreation Area

This hike initially takes you through an area rich in Northern California's pioneer history and then enters a nature lover's paradise as it travels through mixed pine/fir forest and riparian habitat along Mill Creek, a year-round stream that courses in cool shade over granite boulders.

The parking area is on the south side of Highway 299, just east of the highway's bridge across

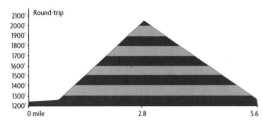

Clear Creek. The bridge is 0.1 mile east of Trinity Mountain Road (signed for French Gulch) and 1.3 miles west of the Carr Powerhouse turnoff.

Take the footbridge across Clear Creek, and then do the same for Willow Creek. The sandy path heads northwest along Willow Creek through the heart of the Tower House Historical District. Camden House and smaller outlying buildings to your right were built in the 1850s. The caretaker house and barn across the meadow to your left were built around 1913. The path reaches Levi Tower's shady gravesite after a level 0.25 mile. From here, turn left and follow the Camden Water Ditch, which brought water from nearby Crystal Creek to the meadow's former orchard and garden. After another 0.25 mile,

bear right and join a dirt road that leads you to the El Dorado Mine at 0.7 mile. This gold mine, in operation until 1967, still has much of the original machinery.

As you continue up the dirt road paralleling Mill Creek, all signs of civilization drop away. A small swimming hole on the left just beyond the mine allows you to cool off on hot days. At 1 mile take the path to the right and walk in the shade provided by ponderosa pine, incense cedar, and Douglas fir. The trail follows very near the creek and makes you rock hop on granite boulders at nineteen creek crossings. At 2 miles you'll reach the second and best

Explore an important area of California gold-mining history.

swimming hole: 15 feet in circumference, 5 feet deep, and fed by a 5-foot waterfall.

After you've absorbed the beauty of this spot, follow the trail as it bends 90 degrees to the left, passes through a dogwood grove, and then crosses Mill Creek at 2.2 miles. The path

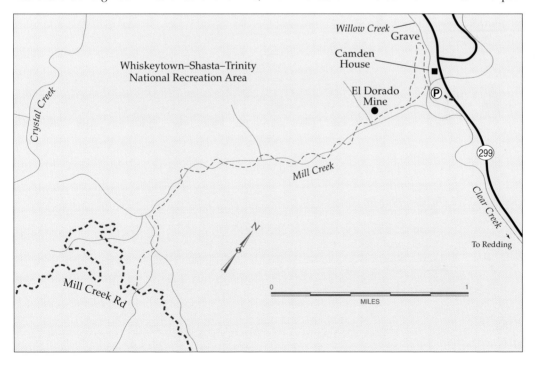

Tower House Historical District (Photo by John R. Soares)

now follows a seasonal tributary uphill until finally reaching Mill Creek Road at 2.8 miles. If you want to extend your hike, walk this seldom-traveled dirt road in either direction. When you return, follow the road past the El Dorado Mine all the way to the parking area.

63 NORTH YOLLA BOLLY TRAILS

Length: 16.1 miles round-trip
Hiking time: 9 hours or overnight
High point: 7,900 feet
Total elevation gain: 3,900 feet
Difficulty: moderate to strenuous
Season: mid-June through mid-October
Water: available from lakes and streams (purify first)
Maps: USGS 7.5' Black Rock Mtn, USGS 7.5' North Yolla Bolly Mtn, USFS
  Yolla Bolly Middle Eel Wilderness
Information: Yolla Bolly Ranger District, Shasta–Trinity National Forest

This hike's trail system takes you into the heart of the North Yolla Bolly Mountains, the southernmost section of the vast Klamath mountain range. You can choose from four different trails that leave the central trail—the lower two visit secluded lakes, the upper two climb high summits with extensive views.

From Redding drive 40 miles on Clear Creek Road (off Highway 273) to Platina. From Red Bluff drive 47 miles on Highway 36 (off Interstate 5) to

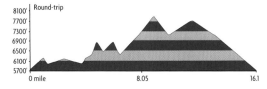

Platina. From Platina drive west 11 miles on Highway 36. About 0.25 mile west of the Hayfork Creek bridge and about 81 miles east of Highway 101, turn south onto Wildwood–Mad River Road (Road 30). Go 9 miles to Pine Root Saddle, and turn left onto Road 35. Drive 10 miles to the intersection of several roads. Take the one signed for Stuart Gap trailhead for the last 1.8 miles to the parking area. All roads are paved except for the last 1.8 miles.

From the parking area, take the Pettijohn Trail, the central path for this hike. It climbs gently for the first mile and then much more steeply for the final 1.5 miles to a broad ridge. Several small streams cross it and usually provide water until late summer.

Black Rock Lake Trail. The right-hand trail leaves the Pettijohn Trail 1 mile from the trailhead. It quickly descends to the Pettijohn Basin, an expansive meadow with a good view of North Yolla Bolly Mountain, one of this hike's destinations. The basin also holds several campsites and the fledgling South Fork of the Trinity River, a sure source of year-round water. Cross the river and continue on the gently rolling path through a forest of Jeffrey pine, incense cedar, and red fir. Shallow Black Rock Lake awaits 1.5 miles from the Pettijohn Trail. You'll find several campsites near the water that offer southward views of looming Black Rock Mountain, another hike destination.

North Yolla Bolly Lake Trail. This lake is both more attractive and more secluded than Black Rock Lake. It also requires a bit more effort

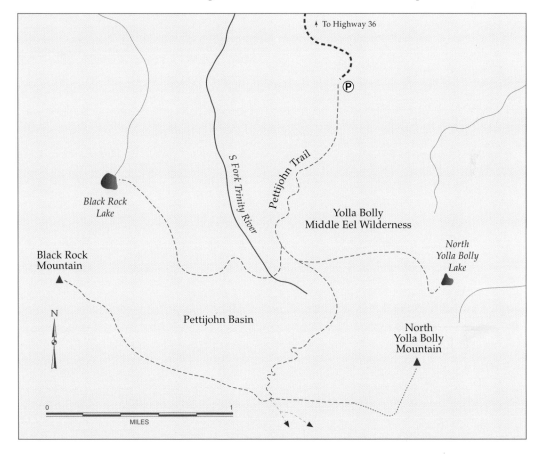

to reach. Take the trail on the left off the Petti-john Trail 1.2 miles from the trailhead. Climb 0.7 mile to the ridge and look for a rock outcrop with vistas to the east, north, and west. From here, descend 0.4 mile to the lake, which offers good swimming, good campsites, and a view of a 1,000-foot cliff stretching up to the south.

North Yolla Bolly Mountain Trail. The trail goes left from the Pettijohn Trail 2.5 miles from the trailhead; look for a sign directing you to North Yolla Bolly Station Spring. Head east 0.5 mile to the spring, where you'll find a lush meadow, a campsite, and ice-cold water flowing from a pipe, the ridge's only reliable source of water. Continue east 0.1 mile and head cross-country uphill (southeast) where the trail fades. Reach a ridge and turn left (northeast) for the final climb to the 7,900-foot summit, 1 mile from the Pettijohn Trail. Note that you began the climb in the company of red fir, but at the summit you'll find primarily foxtail pine, a hardy species that can withstand extreme conditions of wind and cold. Most people climb this mountain for the spectacular panoramic vistas: the Trinity Alps and the rest of the Klamath mountain range to the north; Mount Shasta, Lassen Peak, and the rest of the Cascades to the northeast; the Sacramento Valley and the Sierra Nevada to the east and southeast; and row upon row of Coast Range mountains stretching south and west.

Black Rock Mountain Trail. This 1.8-mile path on the right also leaves the Pettijohn Trail 2.5 miles from the trailhead. It initially travels west along

Pettijohn Basin (Photo by John R. Soares)

the open, lupine-covered ridge and allows good views to the north and south, including Mount Linn and the Ides Cove area. After 1.2 miles, it begins a gentle climb to the summit. Once at the top of the 7,755-foot peak, you'll have views similar to those from North Yolla Bolly Mountain.

COAST RANGE AND NORTH COAST

The Lost Coast

The world's tallest redwoods await here, towering over clear creeks that climax at the Pacific Ocean. Explore pristine beaches and walk atop remote bluffs where Roosevelt elk roam near wave-blasted rocks. You'll also find the rugged and isolated Lost Coast, one of the most coveted getaway paradises in the country. This region is a place of peculiar pygmy forests, profuse ferns, and rugged low-elevation mountains often shrouded in summer fog or dripping with winter rain. California gray whales surface in coastal waters in winter, while autumn offers the best far-reaching views of pounding ocean waves, flowing grasslands, and conifer-clad coastal mountains.

64 HIDDEN BEACH AND FALSE KLAMATH ROCK

Length: 8 miles round-trip
Hiking time: 4 hours
High point: 600 feet
Total elevation gain: 600 feet
Difficulty: easy to moderate
Season: year-round
Water: none; bring your own
Map: USGS 7.5′ Requa
Information: Redwood National and State Parks, Crescent City
    Information Center

This excursion features vistas of notable high-lights, including the mouth of the Klamath River, the Pacific Ocean, Hidden Beach, and False Klamath Rock.

Turn west on Requa Road 2 miles north of the town of Klamath on Highway 101. Go 2.3 miles on Requa Road to the trailhead next to a stop sign.

The Coastal Trail drops at the onset as you view the wide mouth of the Klamath River. Look

for California gray whales and barking sea lions. Commanding eagle's-eye views continue as the trail travels 0.7 mile past open grasslands, where bracken fern, horsetail, and lupine grow.

Take a break at 0.7 mile by a trailside bench to admire the Klamath River valley to the south, where the river, loaded with sediment washed down from the interior and coastal mountains, joins the Pacific Ocean. Proceed

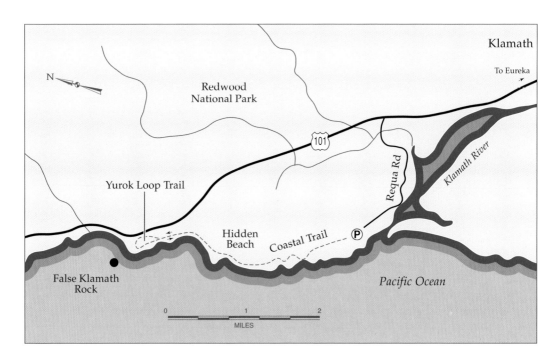

into a red alder forest highlighted by Sitka spruce.

The main attraction of the hike awaits at 2.7 miles, where a spur trail takes you to driftwood-covered Hidden Beach. Spend some time exploring this secluded area, featuring dark gray sand, wildflowers, and large waves exploding on jagged rocks.

Regain the Coastal Trail, which at 2.8 miles descends to near beachside and then enters grasslands as a steady surf chant accompanies continuous open views of the ocean. A spectacular view of Hidden Beach awaits at the end of a 50-yard loop spur trail to the left at 3.3 miles.

Go right onto the signed Yurok Loop Trail 0.1 mile farther, which takes you under a dense canopy of willow, oak, and

> Hidden Beach provides seclusion for seaside explorers.

Hidden Beach

alder. The freshwater pond on Lagoon Creek on the right provides a setting for yellow pond lilies and native and migrating birds. Spot massive False Klamath Rock offshore to the north at 3.8 miles. The trail winds westward at 4 miles to rejoin the main path back to the trailhead.

65 OSSAGON ROCKS AND GOLD BLUFFS BEACH

Length: 7 miles round-trip
Hiking time: 4 hours
High point: 50 feet
Total elevation gain: 100 feet
Difficulty: easy
Season: year-round
Water: none; bring your own
Map: USGS 7.5' Fern Canyon
Information: Prairie Creek Redwoods State Park

Admire massive Roosevelt elk as you stroll leisurely through spruce and alder forests. Then picnic amid Gold Bluffs Beach's rugged Ossagon Rocks and breathe the cool mist from the Pacific Ocean.

Turn west on Davison Road 2 miles north of Orick on Highway 101, and then drive 6.8 miles to the Fern Canyon trailhead parking lot.

The slender, level Coastal Trail (also called the Beach Trail here) starts by crossing Home Creek to travel through a red alder forest for 0.2 mile

and then hugs the bottom of cliffs with constant views of the grass-covered sandy plain on the left and numerous strips of Sitka spruce. The grassy areas provide perfect habitat for the small herds of Roosevelt elk, named for President Theodore Roosevelt. These grazers, native to the north coast, are California's largest land animals: A bull can weigh a half ton. All elk are potentially dangerous, so stay well away from them.

At 1.6 miles the trail skirts a marsh, and then 0.2 mile farther you pass near Ossagon Creek

Primitive Camp (for bicyclists). Native grasses reach 6 feet here, and Ossagon Creek swirls by, soon to reach the Pacific Ocean.

At 2.1 miles a 50-yard cobblestone section of the trail leads into a dark and moist jungle that hosts banana slugs, California salamanders, frogs, and pigeons. Reenter the sandy plain 0.2 mile farther.

When you reach a small brook at 3 miles, the Ossagon Trail heads inland and upward. However, stay left near Gold Bluffs Beach. Hike 0.5 mile along the open plain, staying near, but never in, the dense alder.

Sand verbena and fescue grasses flourish in the dunes along the short scamper to wild, wave-worn Ossagon Rocks, where the surf sprays white water onto the massive outcrops. You'll also find an ideal section of beach for watching California gray whales and sea-birds while collecting sand dollars and sea-shells—you can only collect empty shells; leave those with live creatures alone.

> **Look for Roosevelt elk, the state's largest land animals, grazing in grassy areas.**

To complete this varied journey, beachcomb your way back to the Fern Canyon parking area via secluded Gold Bluffs Beach.

Ossagon Rocks

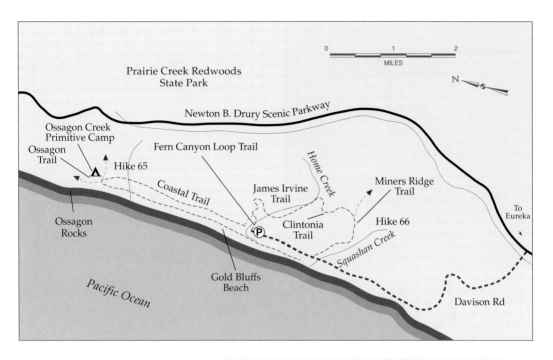

66 FERN CANYON AND GOLD BLUFFS BEACH

Length: 6.3 miles round-trip
Hiking time: 4 hours
High point: 500 feet
Total elevation gain: 500 feet
Difficulty: moderate
Season: year-round
Water: available from Home and Squashan Creeks (purify first)
Map: USGS 7.5' Fern Canyon
Information: Prairie Creek Redwoods State Park

Walk through an extensive redwood forest featuring a floor blanketed with sea-misted ferns. Finish the peaceful journey along scenic Gold Bluffs Beach.

Travel 2 miles north of Orick on Highway 101, turn left onto Davison Road, and drive 6.8 miles to the Fern Canyon trailhead parking lot.

The Fern Canyon Loop Trail continually crosses Home Creek as you walk through misty, dark Fern Canyon. (Planks are in place from around Memorial Day until about mid-October; otherwise you will need to cross on rocks and logs.) Note that storms knock down trees in Fern Canyon, occasionally requiring you to walk around or climb over them.

Five-finger and sword fern, with a small mix of lady and bracken fern, coat 60-foot walls that shade thimbleberry and salmonberry. Near the end of 30-foot-wide Fern Canyon, a large red alder fronts a spiral staircase that leads to a smaller side canyon flourishing with five-finger

Roosevelt bull elk

ferns and highlighted by a 12-foot trickling waterfall. At 0.4 mile a walkway departs the canyon and ascends past groves of redwood trees. Bear right at the ridge top onto the signed James Irvine Trail.

Five-foot-tall sword ferns lead you to a footbridge at 0.8 mile, where a waterfall tumbles 20 feet into Home Creek, viewable from two thronelike redwood chairs. The tallest redwood and Douglas fir on this hike await at 2.2 miles near the signed junction of the James Irvine and Clintonia Trails, where you head right on the latter. The 1-mile jaunt on this snaking trail turns narrow, dark, and quiet as it leaves Home Creek and links with the Miners Ridge Trail, where you bear right at 3.1 miles.

The next 2.2 miles feature whisper-still solitude and wooden walkways as the path crosses babbling brooks that merge with nearby Squashan Creek. Observe the ground here for long, yellow banana slugs and orange, lizardlike Pacific giant salamanders.

At 5.3 miles cross Davison Road, and bear right when you reach Gold Bluffs Beach, named long ago when prospectors found gold in the black sands. Gold Bluffs Beach offers opportunities to beachcomb, wave watch, and observe wildlife, including Roosevelt elk. When you spot the red alder forest that surrounds Home Creek at 6.3 miles, turn right and walk 150 feet to the trailhead.

67 REDWOOD CREEK TO TALL TREES GROVE

Length: 18 miles round-trip
Hiking time: 1 to 3 days
High point: 800 feet
Total elevation gain: 800 feet
Difficulty: easy to moderate
Season: late May through mid-October only; Redwood Creek impassable
    in winter
Water: available from Redwood Creek (purify first)
Maps: USGS 7.5' Orick, USGS 7.5' Rodgers Peak, USGS 7.5' Bald Hills
Information: Redwood National and State Parks, Thomas H. Kuchel
    Visitor Center

Take a pleasant, shaded day hike or backpack trip near the banks of Redwood Creek on your way to visit some of the world's tallest trees. Be aware that Redwood Creek often swells to uncrossable depths from November into May, so do not do this trip then. Movable bridges allow easy crossing in the busy warmer months. Call ahead to find out the status of the creek height and bridges. You can camp on the creek's numerous gravel bars. Wear long pants to avoid rubbing against trailside plants, which include stinging nettles. Consider a one-way hike by arranging for a car shuttle at the south end of Tall Trees Access Road (9 miles farther on Bald Hills Road, and then right). You must stop by the Thomas H. Kuchel Visitor Center 1 mile south of Orick on Highway 101, the Prairie Creek Redwoods State Park Visitor Center, or the Redwood National and State Parks office in Crescent City for a permit and the combination to the locked gate.

> S-t-r-e-t-c-h your neck looking up at the towering redwood trees.

Just north of Orick and 0.1 mile north of the Redwood Creek bridge, turn east off Highway 101 onto Bald Hills Road. Turn right after 0.25 mile and drive another 0.5 mile to the Redwood Creek Trail parking lot.

The flat trail takes you past red alder to cross a seasonal creek at 0.4 mile, where a towering big-leaf maple bears thick moss. In late spring and early summer, you can pick salmonberries here or blackberries a little farther on. Briefly depart the red alder forest at 1.6 miles to enter a gravel plain covered with wild mustard, and then cross Redwood Creek via the bridge.

Attractive views down on Redwood Creek greet you at 2 miles, where the few redwood trees outgrow huge bigleaf maple that shade sorrel and fern communities. At 2.7 miles, two huge, lightning-charred redwoods grow together. The trail is briefly overgrown at 3 miles; look for the moss-covered maple next to a prime picnic spot at a scenic gravel bar in this vicinity. From 4.2 miles on, a series of seasonal streams drains into Redwood Creek until you cross Bond Creek at 5.6 miles. A mile farther, admire lush, shaded canyon walls as you cross Forty-Four Creek.

At 8.2 miles you reach the alluvial flat where Redwood Creek bends and the soaring giants tower high above. Cross the creek and take the 0.7-mile Tall Trees Trail to spend some time underneath these natural wonders.

Climb out of the grove and follow the Tall Trees Trail up to the end of Tall Trees Access Road if you've arranged a car shuttle. Otherwise, retrace your steps to the trailhead.

If you wish to do a much shorter 3-mile hike to see the Tall Trees, stop by one of the visitor centers for the free permit and combination to the gate. Go just north of Orick and turn right on Bald Hills Road. Go 9 miles and turn right onto Tall Trees Road, using the combination for the locked gate. Drive 6 miles to the trailhead. The trail then descends 700 feet over 1 mile to reach the Tall Trees Trail, which is a 1-mile loop. It's another mile uphill back to the car.

Vine maples and Bond Creek

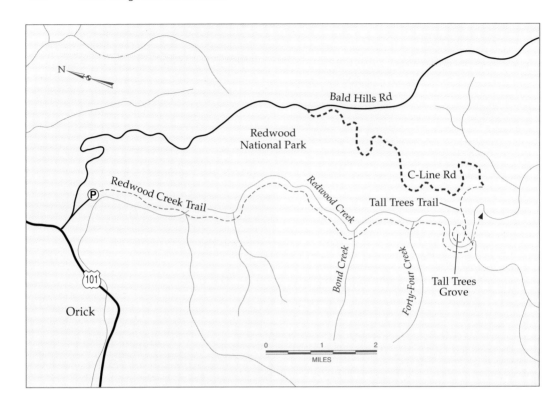

68 PUNTA GORDA LIGHTHOUSE

Length: 6 miles round-trip
Hiking time: 3 hours
High point: 25 feet
Total elevation gain: 100 feet
Difficulty: easy
Season: year-round
Water: bring your own
Map: USGS 7.5' Petrolia
Information: Bureau of Land Management, King Range National
   Conservation Area Project Office

Hike along one of California's wildest stretches of ocean shoreline, the Lost Coast, past the Punta Gorda promontory to an abandoned lighthouse. An abundance of wildflowers grows on the sea-hugging, steep hills, and numerous animals of the sea and coast inhabit the ocean waves, the rocky tide pools, and the beach.

To reach the trailhead, you must first get to Petrolia. Take the Honeydew exit off Highway 101 and drive 38 miles along Honeydew Road and Mattole Road to Petrolia, or drive 30 miles southwest from Ferndale on Mattole Road to Petrolia. Once in Petrolia, go 50 feet south of the bridge across the Mattole River, turn west on Lighthouse Road, and drive 4.9 miles to the parking area.

Before heading for the lighthouse, be sure to walk 0.25 mile north of the parking area to the Mattole River's mouth. Here you'll

Several ships crashed onto the rocks before the Punta Gorda lighthouse was built.

see a wide variety of waterbirds where the mountains' freshwater meets the ocean's saltwater.

To begin the main portion of the hike, let your ears lead you over low dunes to the ocean's roar. As you walk south along Mattole Beach's black sand, observe numerous pelicans, cormorants, seagulls, and other birds skimming between the ocean's tall waves or perching on the sea stacks that puncture the surf zone. Also watch for otters spying on you from just offshore during the entire journey.

After passing a sea lion rookery, at 2 miles you'll see a small cave in the cliff side near Punta

Shoreline near Punta Gorda

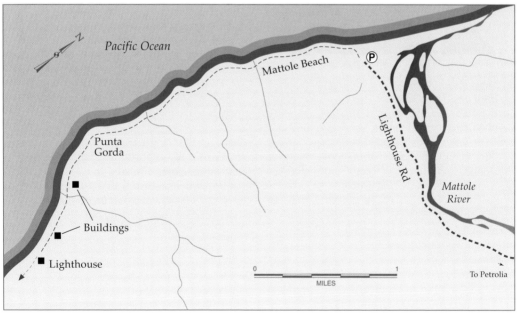

Gorda (Spanish for "Thick Point"). Walk a 0.5-mile stretch of actual trail from here if you want firmer tread.

Shortly after spotting the lighthouse in the distance at 2.5 miles, you'll reach two old ranch cabins on private property beside a year-round stream. Walk along a dirt road past another cabin and a barn to reach the lighthouse at 3 miles. The lighthouse, in operation from 1911 to 1951, was built after several ships wrecked on the rocks offshore. You can see a remnant of one unlucky vessel embedded in the beach below.

If you want to extend your hike, walk farther down the beach. The Lost Coast extends another 21 miles to Shelter Cove and makes an excellent backpacking trip, especially if you can arrange a car shuttle. Contact the Bureau of Land Management for a detailed map and more information.

69 LOST COAST: BEAR HARBOR TO USAL CAMP

Length: 33 miles round-trip
Hiking time: at least 3 days
High point: 1,150 feet
Total elevation gain: lots of up and down for a total of 10,600 feet round-trip
Difficulty: very strenuous
Season: year-round
Water: available from a variety of creeks (purify first)
Maps: USGS 7.5′ Bear Harbor, Sinkyone Wilderness State Park Map
Information: Sinkyone Wilderness State Park

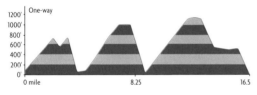

So many folks dream about finding themselves on the Lost Coast, but only lucky souls get the chance. This is the land with jaw-dropping perpendicular views, black sand beaches, and brilliant wildflower displays. On this journey, you'll encounter many fern-encased creeks, experience relaxing seclusion, and discover numerous stately redwood groves.

Get to Redway on Highway 101 (about 60 miles south of Eureka). From there, travel 12 miles on Briceland Road. Turn left at Whitethorn, after 4 miles go straight at the Four Corners junction, and then go 3.6 miles (this dirt road is now labeled County Road 435) to the visitor center. The next 2.4 miles to the Bear Harbor trailhead are very narrow, potholed, and winding.

Gain the trail and cross Orchard Creek beneath a cluster of tall red alders. Pass Railroad Camp (0.2 mile) and continue on the Lost Coast Trail along the creek and into a meadow decorated by horsetails. Bear Harbor features an excellent campsite and a knoll revealing breathtaking views up and down the Lost Coast.

The Lost Coast Trail wanders east next to a gulch laden with sword fern and cow parsnip beneath towering red alder. California bay laurel shows up near a stream crossing, shading redwood sorrel and profuse sword fern. Higher up, the clean evergreen foliage of California huckleberry shrubs appears. Cross shaded Duffys Gulch (2.2 miles), a peaceful brook babbling over mossy boulders beneath a massive bigleaf maple and some old-growth redwoods.

The trail then leads past grasslands awash in spring with lupines, blue-eyed grass, and poppies to steep bluffs overlooking the sea. Pass a garden of orange bush monkey-flower before alternating between grasslands and dark forests

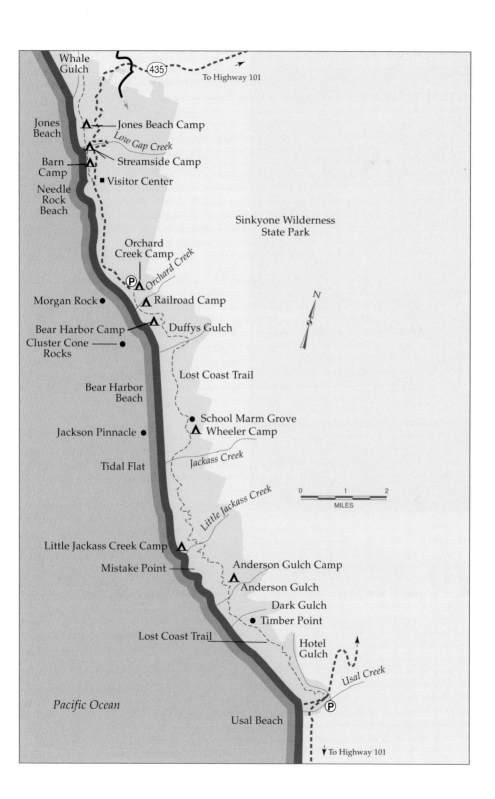

Whale
Gulch

(435)

To Highway 101

Jones
Beach

⛺ ——Jones Beach Camp

Low Gap Creek

⛺

Barn ——
Camp

⛺ ——Streamside Camp

■ Visitor Center

Needle
Rock
Beach

Sinkyone Wilderness
State Park

Orchard
Creek Camp

Orchard Creek

Ⓟ △

Morgan Rock ●

△ Railroad Camp

Bear Harbor Camp ——
Cluster Cone ——●
Rocks

△ Duffys Gulch

N

Lost Coast Trail

Bear Harbor
Beach

● School Marm Grove
△ Wheeler Camp

Jackson Pinnacle ●

Jackass Creek

Tidal Flat

0   1   2
◼◼◼◼◼◼◼◼◼◼◼
MILES

Little Jackass Creek

Little Jackass Creek Camp —— △

Mistake Point ——

Anderson Gulch Camp
△
Anderson Gulch

Dark Gulch

● Timber Point

Lost Coast Trail ——

Hotel
Gulch

Usal Creek

Pacific Ocean

Ⓟ

Usal Beach

To Highway 101

until reaching an almost pure redwood forest at 3.3 miles. More old-growth redwoods highlight cool and tranquil School Marm Grove, just before Wheeler Camp.

Strenuous up-and-down climbing over the next 8 miles leads to view-loaded Timber Point. Sally Bell Grove features campsites at Little Jackass Creek (9 miles), two shaded by majestic old-growth redwoods and another pair near a shiny black sand beach. Capture the photogenic views of Anderson Cliffs to the south from Mistake Point, where you can look down on barking sea lions swimming near a pretty pocket beach.

> The Lost Coast Trail explores a remote and wild section of California.

Reach Timber Point at 12.6 miles, and the rest of the journey is a cakewalk. The Lost Coast Trail stays mostly flat along the grassy ridges, with glimpses of beautiful bluffs and steep cliffs. The final 2 miles descend to Usal Camp, which features a big beach, a meadow, and Usal Creek.

If you wish to arrange a shuttle, you can reach Usal Camp by driving Highway 101 to mile marker 90.88, which is about 15 miles west of Leggett and about an hour north of Fort Bragg. From here drive 6 miles on the unpaved and steep road.

Bear Harbor

70 BULL CREEK FLATS

Length: 9.4 miles round-trip
Hiking time: 5 hours
High point: 300 feet
Total elevation loss: 100 feet
Difficulty: easy
Season: year-round
Water: available from Bull Creek (purify first)
Maps: USGS 7.5' Weott or park brochure
Information: Humboldt Redwoods State Park

Take a leisurely stroll through the heart of a virgin redwood forest, where the deep quiet complements the majesty of the massive trees soaring skyward.

Take the South Fork/Honeydew exit off Highway 101, about 23 miles north of Garberville and 15 miles south of Scotia. Following signs for Honeydew, travel west on Mattole Road. After 4.8 miles, turn left at the sign for the Giant Tree day-use area, and go 100 yards down to the parking area.

From the picnic site near the parking area, cross the clear waters of Bull Creek on a temporary bridge that's not in place during the winter season. Be sure to pause at the bridge's midpoint to admire the bigleaf maple and white alder that grow in the moist soil near the stream's banks.

Immediately on the other side, turn left onto the Bull Creek South Trail, which offers a nearly level downstream descent through a forest of redwood trees that measure over 10 feet in diameter and tower up to 300 feet. You'll soon reach the aptly named Giant Tree, cross Squaw Creek at 0.3 mile, and bear left at a trail fork at 0.5 mile.

The Bull Creek South Trail continues east under the shade of redwoods. You'll see a variety of plants that have adapted to the paucity of sunlight on the forest floor. Look for redwood sorrel and, in spring, trillium and calypso. As you cross Miller Creek at 1 mile, look for Douglas fir trees that have managed to make an inroad into the dense redwood forest.

> The shaded path wanders near Bull Creek and through a thick redwood forest.

The path eventually crosses Connick Creek at 1.6 miles and Tepee Creek at 2.9 miles. At 3.9

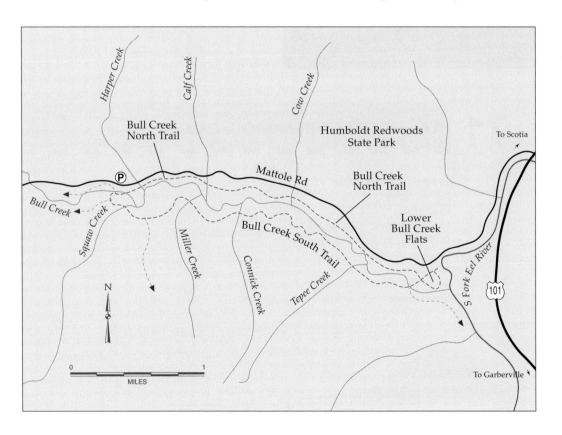

miles turn left onto a trail that leads down to a bridge across Bull Creek. (This bridge is only in place during summer. In winter you'll have to wade.)

On the creek's far side, head right at a trail fork up to Lower Bull Creek Flats and the Rockefeller Loop Trail. This 0.5-mile loop passes through a dense redwood grove, and on the far side a trail goes 150 yards to a bridge across the South Fork of the Eel River. If you want to arrange a car shuttle, the Lower Bull Creek Flats parking area (from which the Rockefeller Loop Trail begins) is 1.5 miles west of Highway 101 on Mattole Road.

If you are returning to the trailhead, consider taking the first left after crossing the bridge across Bull Creek onto the Bull Creek North Trail. This path travels between Bull Creek and Mattole Road and leads back to the trailhead. Although not as pretty and private as the Bull Creek South Trail, it does offer an alternative to retracing your footsteps.

Giant coast redwoods (Photo by Dionne Soares)

71 TAN OAK SPRINGS/DURPHY CREEK LOOP

Length: 4.4-mile loop
Hiking time: 3 hours
High point: 1,450 feet
Total elevation gain: 1,100 feet
Difficulty: easy to moderate
Season: year-round
Water: bring your own
Map: USGS 7.5' Garberville
Information: Richardson Grove State Park

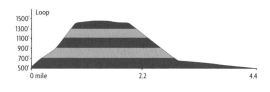

This hike takes you far away from the noise and traffic of Highway 101's heavily traveled Avenue of the Giants. You'll climb past redwoods to a ridge, visit a small spring, and then walk near the banks of a year-round stream.

Enter Richardson Grove State Park, which is on Highway 101's west side 8 miles south of

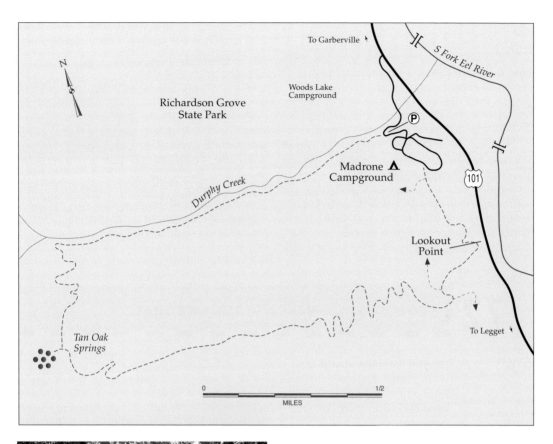

N

To Garberville

S Fork Eel River

Woods Lake
Campground

Richardson Grove
State Park

P

Madrone ▲
Campground

101

Durphy Creek

Lookout
Point

Tan Oak
Springs

To Legget

0   1/2
MILES

Garberville and 17 miles north of Leggett. Drive along the main road and find the designated parking area.

Walk through the campground to campsite 58, where you'll find the trail, signed for Lookout Point. Go 100 feet, turn left, and begin a gentle climb, initially skirting behind campsites. You'll enter a fire-scarred area in the vicinity of a seasonal creek shaded by tall redwoods and then reach Lookout Point at 0.3 mile. From the wooden railing, you can look west and south over the South Fork of the Eel River and part of its mountainous, heavily forested watershed.

You'll encounter two trail forks over the next 0.1 mile; go left at the first and right at the second. The trail now begins a steep climb over the next 0.5 mile and then undulates along a ridge

Madrone tree

shaded by Douglas fir, tan oak, and madrone. As you walk the leaf-littered path, you'll have occasional views of the forested slopes on the north side of Durphy Creek.

At 1.9 miles the trail begins a steep descent. Shortly thereafter, an unsigned trail heads left for 100 yards to Tan Oak Springs, a small, lush area of ferns, cattails, and other water-loving plants.

Back on the main trail, continue downhill 0.9 mile to where the trail approaches Durphy Creek just downstream of the confluence of its two forks. You now head east, following the white alder-lined creek downstream as bigleaf maple and California laurel join Douglas fir and tan oak as the primary tree species. The path passes ever-increasing numbers of massive red-

wood trees as it alternates between level creek-side stretches and steep but brief climbs along the mountainside.

Cross several small wooden bridges across seasonal streams as you continue. A redwood-ringed picnic spot lies just below the previous one, and you'll find a similar picnic site 0.1 mile farther, at 3.8 miles. These picnic sites, located at 0.4 and 0.5 mile from the trailhead, make good destinations if you only want a short, level hike into tall redwood groves.

> Enjoy a leisurely afternoon picnic among the redwood groves.

72 ECOLOGICAL STAIRCASE NATURE TRAIL

Length: 5.4 miles round-trip
Hiking time: 3 hours
High point: 450 feet
Total elevation gain: 500 feet
Difficulty: easy
Season: year-round
Water: bring your own
Maps: USGS 7.5' Fort Bragg, USGS 7.5' Mendocino
Information: Jug Handle State Reserve

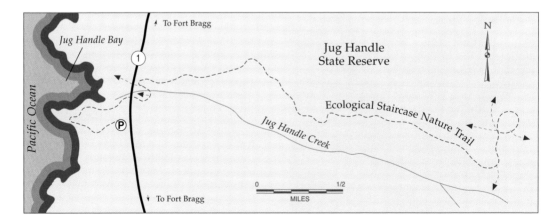

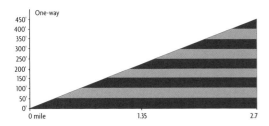

One-way

Enjoy spectacular views of sea stacks attacked by the pulsing waves of the Pacific Ocean, and then climb past a series of different ecological communities, each with a diverse array of plants. Be sure to invest in the immensely informative brochure for this self-guided nature trail. It explains the 500,000-year interaction of land, ocean, and biological processes that created the five different terraces and the plant communities that now grow upon them. It's available from a machine by the parking lot.

To reach the trailhead, turn into the signed Jug Handle State Reserve, which is 5 miles south of Fort Bragg on the west side of Highway 1.

The trail begins by an interpretive signboard near the parking lot. Follow it due west, where you'll find the first of thirty-two numbered posts corresponding to natural history descriptions in the nature trail brochure. Out near the cliff edge beyond post 2, you'll have an excellent view of beach, sea stacks, Jug Handle Bay, and the coastline stretching to the north and south.

The trail then heads toward Highway 1, eventually passing underneath it. In this section you'll see first a small path heading downhill to the beach at Jug Handle Bay and then, just after crossing Jug Handle Creek, another small path traveling along the creek to the same destination. Both paths make excellent side trips.

From here, the main trail begins a gentle northward climb, initially passing under the native two-needled Bishop pine and then the introduced three-needled Monterey pine, which is native to the central California coast. Grand fir and Sitka spruce eventually join the forest.

About 2.4 miles from the trailhead, the trail meets a dirt road just before encountering post 23. Turn left on the dirt road, follow it for 200 yards, and then look for the continuation of the

Beach along Jughandle Bay

trail on the right. You now enter the pygmy forest, which is an association of bolander pine, manzanita, and other plants that can tolerate the highly acidic hardpan soil, though just barely, as their small stature indicates.

From post 32, the nature trail's last post, go right and follow the ditch to a dirt road. Go west for about 200 feet on this road, and then turn left onto another dirt road. Follow this previously encountered road for 200 yards south, turn right onto the actual trail, and return to the trailhead.

> The nature trail describes the interaction of land, ocean, and biological processes that created the area's different terraces and plant communities

169

73 FERN CANYON TRAIL TO PYGMY FOREST

Length: 7.9 miles round-trip
Hiking time: 4 hours
High point: 600 feet
Total elevation gain: 500 feet
Difficulty: easy
Season: year-round
Water: available from Little River (purify first); best to bring your own
Map: USGS 7.5' Mendocino
Information: Van Damme State Park

This path travels through the lush environs of multiferned and redwood-shaded Little River canyon and then heads up to the ecologically intriguing Pygmy Forest.

Drive to Van Damme State Park, which is 3.5 miles south of Mendocino on the east side of Highway 1. Follow the paved main road past the campground for 0.8 mile to the trailhead. You can drive into the park and pay a fee, or you can park at the day-use lot for free and walk in.

As you begin the walk down the signed Fern Canyon Trail, you'll surely agree that it's aptly named: sword, bracken, five-finger, and several other species of fern flourish in the moist soil of the Little River canyon. Numerous berry-producing shrubs compose the understory, and redwood and Douglas fir tower high above.

The mostly level trail makes the first of several crossings of Little River at 0.8 mile. If you hike here during periods of high water flow (winter and spring), you might have to get your feet wet. At 1.7 miles you'll pass ten environmental campsites designed for hikers and bikers (inquire at park headquarters if you want to camp here), and then meet a trail fork at 2.3 miles. Go either way: The two halves rejoin 0.2 mile farther,

> The redwoods cluster in Little River's sheltered valley, while the Pygmy Forest inhabits the ridge.

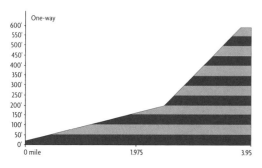

Redwoods and ferns

where you'll find another fork. Go right where a sign directs you the final 1.3 miles up an old dirt logging road to the Pygmy Forest.

Cross Little River and then climb moderately under redwood and Douglas fir. As you approach the Pygmy Forest, bishop pine becomes the dominant tree species.

The 0.3-mile-long Pygmy Forest Discovery Trail, this hike's destination, lies 3.8 miles from the trailhead. It begins from the paved parking lot just off Airport Road. (You can drive to this lot by going 3.5 miles down Airport Road, which leaves Highway 1 about 0.7 mile south of Van Damme State Park.) Grab the brochure available at the trail's beginning, which explains the interaction of geological and biological processes that led to the formation of pygmy forests and also identifies Mendocino cypress, rhododendron, and five other plant species.

You can extend your walk back to the trailhead by taking the trail that leaves the logging road about 0.1 mile below the Pygmy Forest. This trail heads northeast to Fern Canyon and eventually leads you back to the trail fork encountered at 2.5 miles. It adds another 1.1 miles to the round-trip hiking distance.

74 SNOW MOUNTAIN

Length: 8 miles round-trip
Hiking time: 6 hours or overnight
High point: 7,056 feet
Total elevation gain: 2,150 feet
Difficulty: moderate
Season: mid-June to early October
Water: none; bring your own
Maps: USGS 7.5' Potato Hill, USGS 7.5' Fouts Springs, USGS 7.5' St. John
Mountain, USGS 7.5' Crockett Peak, USFS Snow Mountain Wilderness
Information: Grindstone Ranger District, Mendocino National Forest

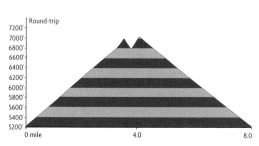

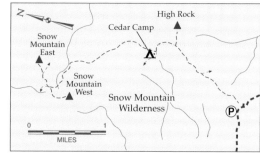

The trip to the twin summits of Snow Mountain offers scenery that includes serene forests of pine and fir, a psychedelic assortment of multihued rocks, and sweeping vistas of mountains and valleys stretching to the far horizons.

Reach the town of Stonyford by exiting Interstate 5 at either Maxwell or Willows. Take Road M-10 (18N01), which is initially called Fouts Springs Road, and follow signs for Snow Mountain and Summit Springs. After 24 miles turn right at a "Trailhead 1" sign for the final, steep 1.4 miles to the Summit Springs trailhead parking area.

The path begins in a small forest of Jeffrey pine and white fir and quickly enters open areas created by a huge 1987 fire. As you climb over the next mile, note the variety of shrubs and other plants that have begun a long process of succession, which should eventually restore much of this area to forest.

Go left at a trail fork at 0.7 mile, and then cross two small, seasonal creeks at 1 mile. Next, switchback uphill to a ridge at 1.5 miles. Look to the right for High Rock, about 300 yards east of the trail; it offers expansive westward, southward, and eastward views similar to those of the Snow Mountain summits, lacking only a northward vista.

East Snow Mountain from West Snow Mountain (Photo by John R. Soares)

The path now climbs along the ridge, passing through a forest of Jeffrey pine and red and white fir. Ignore the faint trails that disappear into the trees, and continue to Cedar Camp at 2 miles, which has an excellent campsite beside a small pond, a green meadow, and no cedars. Bear right here at a trail fork, taking the path signed for Snow Mountain.

After a steady ascent through the forest, enter the open, glaciated basin below Snow Mountain's summits. Climb steadily 0.7 mile to the saddle between the two summits, and then turn left at a three-way trail junction.

After a brief climb, reach the 7,038-foot summit of Snow Mountain West. From here, you have northward views of Mount Linn, Mount Shasta, and the Klamath Mountains; eastward views of Stony Creek Gorge, the Sacramento Valley, Sutter Buttes, the Cascades, and the Sierra Nevada; and southward and westward views of endless chains of Coast Range ridges and peaks. Be sure to look at the odd assortment of green, gray, and purple rocks at your feet.

After you've rested and enjoyed the view, go back to the saddle and take the right-hand trail up to the 7,056-foot summit of Snow Mountain East, which offers views similar to those of its sibling.

> Nature has strewn a psychedelic assortment of metamorphic rocks across the twin summits of Snow Mountain.

If you have the ambition, consider camping on one of the summits. You'll have far-reaching, earthly views during the day and an open universe above at night. Bring all the water you'll need, be prepared for possible high winds, and head downhill into the relative safety of the forest if a thunderstorm threatens.

Blue oak above Anderson Marsh

75 ANDERSON MARSH

Length: 5 to 6.5 miles round-trip
Hiking time: 3 hours
High point: 1,500 feet
Total elevation gain: 300 feet
Difficulty: easy
Season: year-round
Water: bring your own
Maps: USGS 7.5' Clear Lake, USGS 7.5' Lower Lake
Information: Anderson Marsh State Historical Park

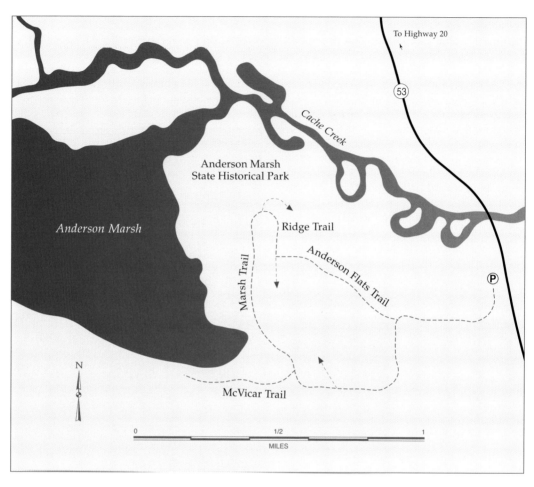

Visit oak woodlands before exploring a marsh shoreline that hosts a variety of birds. Wear long pants and a long-sleeved shirt, and be prepared for some mud along Anderson Marsh.

From the junction of Highways 20 and 53 on Clear Lake's east side, drive south 7 miles on Highway 53, turn right onto Anderson Ranch Parkway (0.7 mile north of Highway 29), and turn right again at the entrance to the park.

Pick up the trail by heading west across the field next to a chain-link fence. Go left at a trail junction at 0.4 mile and continue alongside another chain-link fence past the occasional valley oak.

The path gradually climbs a hill under the shade of blue oak and greenleaf manzanita to a signed trail junction at 0.9 mile, where you bear left. As you bisect the grassy meadow next to the marsh, watch for a herd of deer. Gray pines hug the foothill on the left, and cottonwood and willow surround the marsh on the right.

Without warning the trail becomes mucky and jungled, with 2-yard-high grasses, teasel, and sporadic patches of poison oak. Quite soon the marsh extends next to your feet near wood rose bushes. Pause quietly for a few moments and observe an impressive variety of waterbirds, including pelicans, green herons, and blue herons.

At 1.5 miles bear left onto the McVicar Trail. Although moist and clogged with weeds, it

The marsh area is a bird lover's paradise: look for pelicans, green herons, and blue herons.

goes for 0.6 mile alongside the marsh, offering ample opportunity for further bird-watching.

When you've had enough of this path, retrace your steps and bear left at a rattlesnake sign onto the Marsh Trail, which allows you to explore the east side of Anderson Marsh.

Depart the blue oak belt after 0.4 mile and move slightly closer to the marsh and a tall stand of valley oak on the right. After another 0.2 mile, the trail abruptly departs the marsh and climbs 20 yards to another unsigned trail junction, where you head straight on the Ridge Trail toward a huge valley oak.

The trail soon heads south to a picnic table under a massive valley oak. Pause here to admire the moist lowlands to the northeast that stretch to the riparian habitat bordering Cache Creek. Turn left and follow the unsigned Anderson Flats Trail east through the oak-studded meadow for another 1 mile to the trailhead.

76 MOUNT SAINT HELENA

Length: 10 miles round-trip
Hiking time: 6 hours
High point: 4,343 feet
Total elevation gain: 2,300 feet
Difficulty: moderate
Season: year-round
Water: bring plenty
Maps: USGS 7.5′ Detert Reservoir, USGS 7.5′ Mount St. Helena
Information: Bothe–Napa Valley State Park

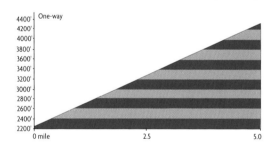

The journey to Mount Saint Helena's summit takes you high above the Napa Valley vineyards and through territory that inspired some of Robert Louis Stevenson's writing. Upon reaching your lofty goal, you'll see Northern California's hills, ridges, and mountains stretching in all directions. Bring binoculars.

To reach the trailhead, drive to Robert Louis Stevenson State Park, located on both sides of Highway 29 at a saddle 8 miles north of Calistoga and 31 miles south of Highway 20.

The trail begins on the west side of Highway 29 near some old building foundations. Initially, you gently switchback uphill under the shade of Douglas fir, madrone, black oak, and California laurel, accompanied by an understory of tan oak, interior live oak, and the sharp-needled California nutmeg.

At 0.7 mile the trail enters a small, level clear-

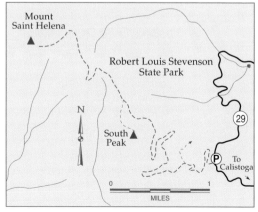

Chamise thickets on Mount Saint Helena

ing and then ascends steeply up a slippery slope 0.2 mile to meet the dirt road, which you follow uphill all the way to the summit. This is where you first encounter the large forests of knobcone pine stretching up the flank of Mount Saint Helena. Note the numerous cones tightly bound to the trunks and branches.

As you climb you'll see more and more of the surrounding country. Initially, the road travels past manzanita, chamise, and other chaparral plants, and then by abundant outcroppings of volcanic rock. Mount Saint Helena, though composed primarily of volcanic rock, has never been an active volcano.

At 3 miles you reach the 0.5-mile spur trail to the top of 4,003-foot South Peak. Continue up the main path another 2 miles to the summit of Mount Saint Helena, elevation 4,343 feet, which offers exquisite views in all directions. To the north lies Snow Mountain, and on an exceptionally clear day you can even see Northern California's two most famous volcanoes: Mount Shasta and Lassen Peak. To the east are the mountains leading to the Sacramento Valley and the Delta, with the Sierra Nevada in the far distance. The Napa Valley vineyards lie immediately south, with the Bay Area and Mount Diablo farther away. To the west, low mountain ranges stretch seaward.

> The vineyards of Napa Valley stretch out below Mount Saint Helena.

77 BALD MOUNTAIN

Length: 6.4-mile loop
Hiking time: 4 hours
High point: 2,729 feet
Total elevation gain: 1,700 feet
Difficulty: moderate
Season: year-round
Water: bring your own
Maps: USGS 7.5' Kenwood, USGS 7.5' Rutherford
Information: Sugarloaf Ridge State Park

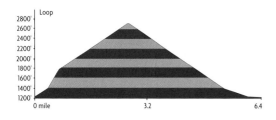

Before you tour Sonoma Valley's famous wineries, climb Bald Mountain for a panoramic view of the Sonoma Valley and many of Northern California's high mountains.

Reach Adobe Canyon Road, located on Highway 12 midway between Santa Rosa and Sonoma, and then go 3.6 miles to Sugarloaf Ridge State Park and park on the left just past the kiosk.

The Bald Mountain Trail begins by a large signboard containing a map of all the park's trails. As you begin the trek along the ever-climbing path, you'll pass briefly through an oak forest and then turn left at two trail forks to travel along an open hillside that hosts a multihued wildflower display in spring. At 0.6 mile the trail continues through a lush forest of coast live oak, madrone, and California laurel, which eventually gives way to drier chaparral. This pattern of alternating between oak woodland forest and brushy areas repeats throughout the hike.

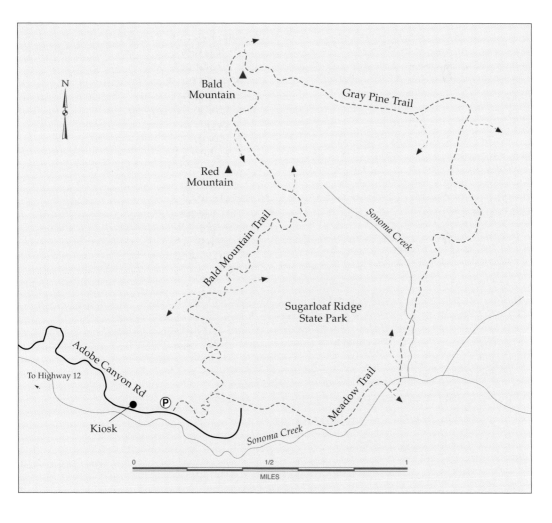

At 1 mile the dirt path meets a paved road. Turn right and head uphill. As you climb, note the blue-green serpentine rock exposed by the road cuts. Stay on the pavement past the Vista and Red Mountain Trails.

At 2.3 miles turn right at the signed junction for Bald Mountain onto a wide dirt path. Follow this steep trail up grassy slopes for another 0.4 mile to a three-way trail junction just below Bald Mountain's summit. Follow the Gray Pine Trail for 200 feet and turn right for the last 150 feet to the summit.

Bald Mountain, part of the Mayacamas Mountains, offers broad vistas in all directions. To the north rises Mount Saint Helena, and even farther beyond, to the northwest, is Snow Mountain. The Napa Valley lies to the northeast, and on exceptionally clear days you can even see high peaks rising over 10,000 feet in the Sierra Nevada 125 miles away. Beyond nearby Red Mountain's microwave station, Mount Diablo looms. The San Francisco Bay area, including Mount Tamalpais, anchors the southeast horizon. Mount Hood, 1 foot higher than Bald Mountain, rises 3 miles due west, and just beyond is the Sonoma Valley.

To complete the loop trip, take the Gray Pine Trail as it travels along the ridge past California laurel and large black oak. Follow this dirt road as it descends, staying on it at 0.7 mile from Bald Mountain's summit when the Red Mountain Trail comes in from the right.

You'll first encounter the crazily twisted trunks and branches of gray pine about 1 mile from the summit, just before the Brushy Peaks Trail. Head right at this junction and go downhill for another 1.4 miles, where you'll meet Sonoma Creek and the turnoff for the Vista Trail (stay left). After crossing the creek and walking another 0.1 mile, turn right onto the Meadow Trail (a gravel road) and follow it 0.8 mile through the broad, flower-filled Sonoma Creek valley to a parking lot by a campsite. Cross through the lot, bear left at two trail junctions within the next 0.1 mile, and then hike the last 0.3 mile back to the trailhead.

> Bald Mountain offers a panoramic view of Sonoma Valley, a famous wine region.

Bald Mountain vista

SAN FRANCISCO BAY AREA

East Bay foothills

Tucked away from the skyscrapers of the San Francisco skyline and the vast sprawl of the Bay Area are tens of thousands of acres of remote marshes, shorelines, foothills, and mountains. In the following pages, you'll discover routes to scenic and secluded bluffs, bays, and coves; through foothills dotted with mighty, crook-limbed oak trees; and into deep-shade redwood groves and clusters of Douglas fir and California laurel. You can hike this region year-round, reveling in foothill wildflowers in spring, strolling ocean beaches in summer, enjoying the spectrum of leaf color in autumn, and exploring forest and ridge in winter.

78 TOMALES POINT

Length: 9.4 miles round-trip
Hiking time: 5 hours
High point: 530 feet
Total elevation gain: 900 feet
Difficulty: easy
Season: year-round
Water: bring your own
Map: USGS 7.5' Tomales
Information: Point Reyes National Seashore

This excursion along gently rolling, slender Tomales Point offers premium views of the Pacific Ocean and Tomales and Bodega Bays and the chance to observe tule elk and various seabirds.

From Point Reyes on Highway 1, drive northwest on Sir Francis Drake Boulevard for 8.5 miles and then turn right on Pierce Point Road. Go 9.2 miles farther to the Tomales Point trailhead.

Tule elk herd

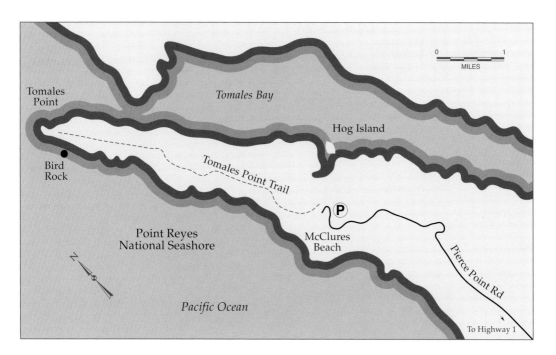

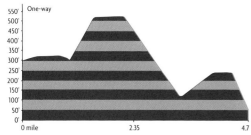

This herd was brought to this sanctuary after nearly a century-long absence from the area.

Views of the tiny town of Dillon Beach come from just above the pond. The worn ranch road trail transforms into a scant footpath 0.3 mile farther as you begin another gentle climb. At 3.3 miles the trail reaches open ocean vistas at a crest.

The tread becomes sand at 3.7 miles, where a sign indicates Tomales Point. Stay with the barely discernible path to the final crest at 4.2 miles. Wander west from here past bush lupine, and get out the binoculars for great views of birds perched atop aptly named Bird Rock, which rests just offshore.

> Tule elk and seabirds are some of the wildlife inhabiting Tomales Point.

At 0.2 mile you'll see striking scenes of Tomales Bay to the right and the Pacific Ocean to the left as you walk past yellow bush lupine and purple-flowered Canada thistle. Stroll gently upward to 0.3 mile for your first view of McClures Beach (a recommended destination, 0.6-mile from the trailhead).

The path gradually climbs, revealing White Gulch and Hog Island on Tomales Bay at 0.7 mile. Reach a crest at 1.5 miles, punctuated by a 7-foot-high boulder on the left. You'll see Bodega Bay at 2 miles where it joins Tomales Bay at Avalis Beach.

Study Bodega Bay through tall lupine from 2.6 miles and beyond. The trail snakes east at 2.8 miles near a small pond where tule elk come to drink.

The final 0.5 mile gradually descends to the Tomales Point bluffs, which slid nearly 20 feet north during the 1906 earthquake. Spend time in solitude with ocean and cliff before returning to the trailhead.

79 HOME BAY, DRAKES ESTERO, AND SUNSET BEACH

Length: 7.8 miles round-trip
Hiking time: 4 hours
High point: 220 feet
Total elevation gain: 800 feet
Difficulty: easy to moderate
Season: year-round
Water: bring your own
Map: USGS 7.5' Drakes Bay
Information: Point Reyes National Seashore

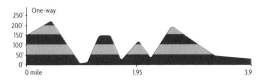

Bring your binoculars for close-ups of shorebirds and packs of basking harbor seals on this journey along mudflats and *estero* (Spanish for "estuary"). The spectacular views include Inverness Ridge and numerous overlooks of Home Bay and Drakes Estero.

From Highway 1 in Point Reyes (14 miles north of Stinson Beach), turn west on Sir Francis Drake Boulevard. Drive 9.9 miles to a sign marked "Estero," then turn left and drive 0.9 mile to the trailhead.

The obvious trail starts level near cattle ranchlands where clover grows among pasture grasses, native bunchgrasses, and rushes. It

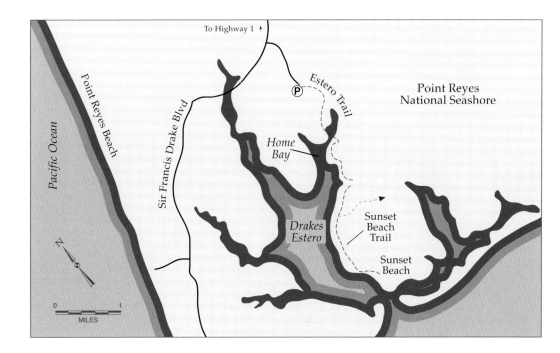

Home Bay (Photo by Dionne Soares)

twists sharply right at 0.5 mile near a small community of Scotch broom, offering good views of Inverness Ridge eastward beyond the fields.

Proceed past a thick forest of Monterey pines, all the same height because they were planted simultaneously as a Christmas tree farm. At 0.6 mile, stroll past a gateway and travel briefly alongside this small forest's outskirts.

Your first view of Home Bay arrives at 1 mile next to a boggy pond. At 1.1 miles cross the bridge dividing the pond and Home Bay. From here, the trail ascends past cow parsnip and bush lupine. As you continue climbing gradually to 1.9 miles, keep checking Home Bay's mudflats and water's edge for a variety of waterbirds, including widgeons, ducks, blue herons, godwits, and willets.

The trail levels to a pasture and then heads southeast to two ponds and your first sighting of Drakes Estero. At 2.2 miles go straight at a trail fork, pass several stands of rushes that front premium views of the estero below, and skirt two dinky ponds at 2.5 miles.

The trail stays flat the rest of the way as it overlooks the estero, where freshwater runoff meets the ocean's saltwater, creating rich habitat for numerous shorebirds. A pond at 3.9 miles marks your arrival at Sunset Beach, which offers seclusion, rocky bluffs, beachcombing opportunities, and possible harbor seal sightings.

> Harbor seals often frolic in the waters off Sunset Beach.

80 BEAR VALLEY AND ARCH ROCK

Length: 12 miles round-trip
Hiking time: 6 hours
High point: 370 feet
Total elevation gain: 850 feet
Difficulty: easy
Season: year-round
Water: seasonally available from creeks (purify first); best to bring your own
Maps: USGS 7.5′ Inverness, USGS 7.5′ Double Point
Information: Point Reyes National Seashore

This journey, suitable for the whole family, stays shaded along Bear Valley and Coast Creeks most of the way and then leads to Arch Rock on a coastal bluff, where you'll admire views of the Pacific Ocean before strolling on a gorgeous beach.

From Highway 1 near Point Reyes (14 miles north of Stinson Beach), turn west onto Bear Valley Road, drive 0.5 mile, and then turn into the Bear Valley Visitor Center parking lot.

Pick up the Bear Valley Trail, a dirt road, by walking south past the Morgan Horse Ranch. The climb to Divide Meadow travels under the

shade of Douglas fir and alder and follows Bear Valley Creek. Divide Meadow supports an assortment of tall annual grasses that dry up by early summer.

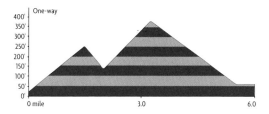

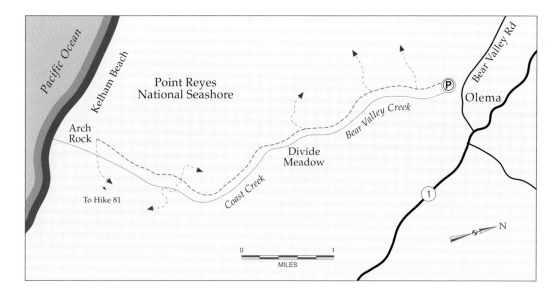

Once past the meadow, the native tree habitat expands. Look for alder, California laurel, buckeye, coast live oak, willow, and Douglas fir. Now follow Coast Creek on its gradual descent to the Pacific Ocean. Continue on the wide Bear Valley Trail past all signed trail junctions, watching for five-finger fern, chain fern, sword fern, thimbleberry, stinging nettle, poison hemlock, cow parsnip, and thistle.

At 5.6 miles you break out of the shaded, riparian habitat and into an open chaparral section where coyote brush dominates along with young Douglas fir. Gather the first view of the sea 0.1 mile farther, quickly followed by a signed trail junction, where you go right for 0.3 mile to prominent Arch Rock. There you'll enjoy splendid views of beach and ocean, enhanced by rock outcrops that host a variety of seabirds.

For an excellent backpacking trip, take the Coastal Trail (retrace your steps 200 yards from Arch Rock and bear right at the signed trail junction) 3.5 miles southeast to Wildcat Beach (see Hike 81: Pelican Lake and Wildcat Beach). This side trip allows continuous views of the ocean from high chaparral-clad bluffs.

> The Pacific Ocean and a sky full of seabirds make Arch Rock the highlight of this easy hike.

Kelham Beach

81 PELICAN LAKE AND WILDCAT BEACH

Length: 10.2 miles round-trip
Hiking time: 5 hours
High point: 670 feet
Total elevation gain: 1,100 feet
Difficulty: moderate
Season: year-round
Water: bring your own
Map: USGS 7.5' Double Point
Information: Point Reyes National Seashore

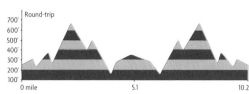

Stinson Beach and 8.6 miles south of Olema, turn west on an unsigned road (signed "Olema/Bolinas Road" farther on) that's just north of Bolinas Lagoon, where a Golden Gate National Recreation Area sign stands next to a big white house, both on the east side of the highway. After 1.8 miles on Olema/Bolinas Road, turn right on Mesa Road. Travel 3.5 miles, turn right where the pavement ends, and go 1.3 miles to the Palomarin trailhead.

The trail quickly reaches a tall eucalyptus forest and then stays mostly level for the first 1.1 miles as it offers views of the Pacific Ocean. Climb to a signed trail fork at 2.1 miles. Continue left on the Coastal Trail. Spur trails lead to three freshwater ponds on the left.

A quarter mile past the third small pond, you'll spot swimmable Bass Lake. At 3.2 miles, you arrive at a westward view down on Pelican Lake, enhanced by the Pacific Ocean appearing through a rock hillside archway just beyond. For the next 0.5 mile, you're treated to view after view of the lake's dark gray waters, inaccessible because of dense chaparral.

At 4 miles you'll reach a signed trail junction next to profuse coyote brush and orange sticky monkey-flower. Make a mental note of the left-hand trail (the return loop), and then continue straight on the Coastal Trail for the 1.3-mile stroll past Wildcat Lake to Wildcat Camp and Wildcat Beach.

Near Alamere Falls and Wildcat Beach

This varied journey leads past three ponds and four freshwater lakes to attractive, secluded Wildcat Beach. On the way you'll admire continuous vistas of the Pacific Ocean and its rugged shoreline. If you prefer a backpack trip, register for Wildcat Camp at the Bear Valley Visitor Center (for directions, see Hike 80: Bear Valley and Arch Rock).

From Highway 1 about 4.1 miles north of

Wildcat Camp, a huge field, is an excellent backpacking camp facility. You'll find several picnic tables and benches and a spring-fed water spigot, plus easy access to pristine Wildcat Beach. (To gather more views of the ocean and beaches, continue along the Coastal Trail past Wildcat Camp to Arch Rock [see Hike

> Situated near pristine Wildcat Beach, Wildcat Camp is an irresistible lure for backpackers.

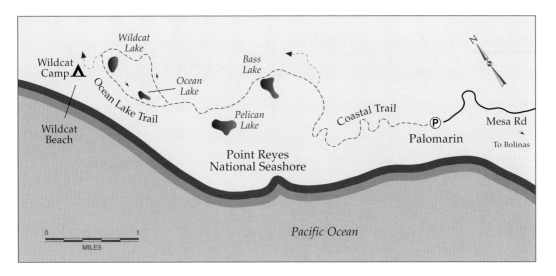

80: Bear Valley and Arch Rock] for 3.5 miles along chaparral-covered bluffs.)

To return, double back to the north side of Wildcat Lake and take the lower loop trail past Ocean Lake. This slender footpath (0.2 mile from Wildcat Beach) quickly climbs to a series of perches offering inspiring oceanic vistas. Poppy and yarrow decorate the area, but thistles and poison oak occasionally intrude on the trail, so proceed cautiously. Gain an eastward view of Wildcat Lake, followed by a brief drop that takes you next to rush-lined Ocean Lake, and then rejoin previously encountered trails for the final 4 miles to the trailhead.

82 BOLINAS RIDGE

Length: 10.2 miles round-trip
Hiking time: 5 hours
High point: 1,329 feet
Total elevation gain: 1,100 feet
Difficulty: easy to moderate
Season: year-round
Water: bring your own
Maps: USGS 7.5′ San Geronimo, USGS 7.5′ Inverness
Information: Golden Gate National Recreation Area

The Bolinas Ridge Trail provides commanding views of bald hills, wooded ridges, and expansive Tomales Bay as it escorts you past large coast live oak and eventually through Douglas fir.

From Olema on Highway 1, turn east on Sir Francis Drake Boulevard, go 1.1 mile, and then park off the road at the signed trailhead.

At the outset, pick up the dirt road, which promptly ascends to an old corral next to a patch of cypress trees at 0.1 mile. Then travel past tree-less rolling hills covered with pasture grasses, yellow-flowered mustard, plantain, and low-growing filaree.

Reach the first crest at 0.6 mile. A lone boulder

Coast live oak on Bolinas Ridge

outcrop and a single coast live oak impressively frame a northwesterly view of Tomales Bay and the Point Reyes Peninsula. Barnabe Peak stands guard to the east. Turn right and head up the

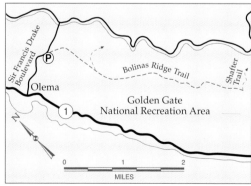

bare hillside at a signed trail junction at 1.3 miles.

A ridge-top field rewards you 0.2 mile farther with a splendid westward view of lush, dark-forested Inverness Ridge, which hides the Pacific Ocean. The dirt road now hugs a double-barbed wire fence, affording intermittent glimpses of the slender Olema Valley below Inverness Ridge. At 2.4 miles you walk past a long stretch of Douglas fir on the left, fronted by coyote brush. Pass a rush-lined pond on the right at 3.6 miles, and 0.2 mile far-

> Take in the great views of rolling hillsides and Tomales Bay.

ther climb gently past another pond. Reach the open ridge top at 4.1 miles, where you'll enjoy great northward views of rolling hillsides and Tomales Bay. The trail gains its highest point when you pass a row of five huge eucalyptus trees at 4.8 miles and capture another view of Tomales Bay.

An excellent vista point awaits at 5.1 miles. At the Shafter Trail junction, climb any knoll on the right for spectacular views of Inverness Ridge and the Pacific Ocean.

83 | MOUNT TAMALPAIS: PANTOLL RANGER STATION TO STINSON BEACH

Length: 7.5-mile loop
Hiking time: 4 hours
High point: 1,650 feet
Total elevation gain: 1,700 feet
Difficulty: moderate
Season: year-round
Water: bring your own
Maps: USGS 7.5′ San Rafael, USGS 7.5′ Bolinas
Information: Mount Tamalpais State Park

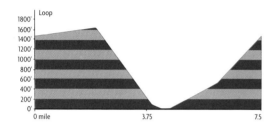

This hike takes you from open views on the slopes of Mount Tamalpais to Stinson Beach and the Pacific Ocean and, finally, under the shade of tall redwoods.

From Stinson Beach on Highway 1, turn east on the Panoramic Highway, drive 3.8 miles, and park at the Pantoll Ranger Station.

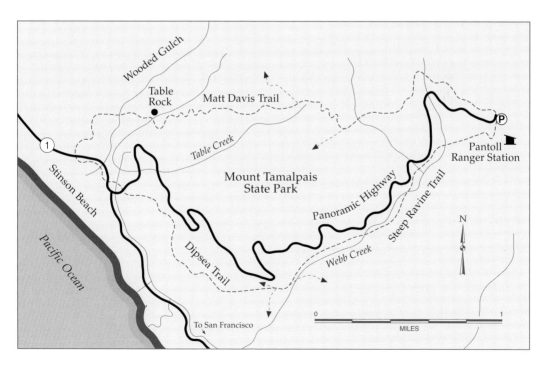

Looking north from the slopes of Mount Tamalpais

From the Golden Gate Bridge on Highway 101, drive 5 miles north and take the Muir Woods/Mount Tamalpais exit, go west for 3 miles on Highway 1, turn right onto the Panoramic Highway and go 5.5 miles to the Pantoll Ranger Station.

To begin the hike, cross the Panoramic Highway and turn left onto the signed Matt Davis Trail. After 0.1 mile stroll under the shade of Douglas fir, California laurel, and alder. After you cross a seasonal creek at 1.2 miles, look south for a view of San Francisco Bay joining the Pacific Ocean. Go straight at a signed trail intersection 0.1 mile farther.

At the far end of a California laurel grove at 1.6 miles, bear left at a signed trail junction. Reenter forest at 2.1 miles, and descend past sword ferns, coast live oak, Douglas fir, and California laurel. At 2.7 miles the continuous roar of the Pacific Ocean ahead accompanies the steady rumble of

Table Creek on the right. Depart Table Creek's riparian habitat at 3.4 miles, and continue downhill past chaparral to forested Wooded Gulch just before reaching a signed trail fork at 3.7 miles, where you go right.

The trail ends at a paved street at 4.1 miles. At all street junctions, take the road that heads downhill to popular Stinson Beach, which offers excellent swimming, beachcombing, and picnicking. After enjoying the beach, pick up the signed Dipsea Trail at the intersection of the Shoreline and Panoramic Highways just south of town (0.1 mile south of Arenal Avenue).

After a short climbing burst in shaded woods, enter open chaparral country, which allows continuous views of the sprawling sea behind you. Ignore the first unsigned dirt road 1.3 miles from Stinson Beach, and continue straight 0.1 mile farther at a trail junction. Follow the sign directing you to the Steep Ravine Trail.

You soon approach Webb Creek. The Dipsea Trail crosses the creek; you stay on the Steep Ravine Trail as it continues to follow Webb Creek upstream. The shaded footpath crosses the stream five times via wooden bridges as it travels past bouldery cascades that slide gracefully into small pools. You'll duck under toppled redwood archways several times, pass through profuse communities of thimbleberry and sword fern, and climb a fifteen-rung ladder during the 1.8-mile climb back to the Pantoll Ranger Station. If you want to hike more, see Hike 84 (Mount Tamalpais: The Summit to Pantoll Ranger Station).

> Climb to the top of the bar knoll and gaze out over the Pacific Ocean and San Francisco Bay.

84 MOUNT TAMALPAIS: THE SUMMIT TO PANTOLL RANGER STATION

Length: 9 miles round-trip
Hiking time: 5 hours
High point: 2,571 feet
Total elevation gain: 1,400 feet
Difficulty: moderate
Season: year-round
Water: bring your own
Map: USGS 7.5' San Rafael
Information: Mount Tamalpais State Park

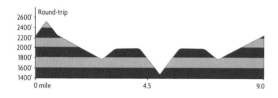

This hike features commanding vistas of the entire San Francisco Bay area from the summit of Mount Tamalpais and then alternates shaded forest with open views of city, hills, and ocean. Note that you can eliminate the climbing by arranging to be picked up at the Pantoll Ranger Station.

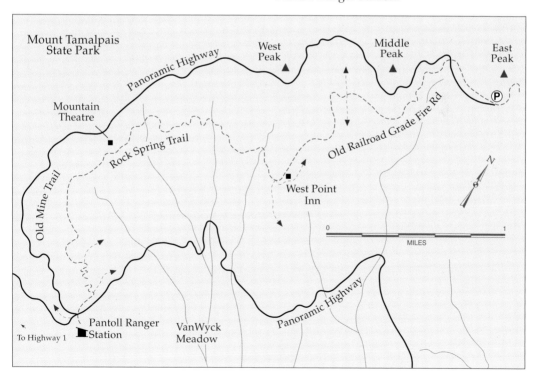

Bon Tempe Lake from Mount Tamalpais

Five miles north of the Golden Gate Bridge on Highway 101, take the Muir Woods/Mount Tamalpais exit. Continue west on Highway 1 for 3 miles and then turn right onto the Panoramic Highway. Follow all obvious signs labeled "Mount Tamalpais" for another 10.2 miles to the parking lot near East Peak.

From Highway 1 in Stinson Beach, turn east onto the Panoramic Highway and drive 3.8 miles to the Pantoll Ranger Station. Turn left onto Pantoll Road, go 1.3 miles, and then turn right on East Ridgecrest Boulevard for the final 3.3 miles to the parking lot near East Peak.

From the parking lot, first take the 0.4-mile Plank Walk Trail to Mount Tamalpais's East Peak. From this well-known landmark, you'll have far-reaching views of Marin County, San Francisco, Mount Diablo, and the entire Bay Area.

Return to the parking lot and take Old Railroad Grade Fire Road from the main road near the entrance sign for East Peak. Douglas firs, numerous oaks, and yerba santa combine with sweeping scenes of the Pacific Ocean at the onset. Then the path travels past chaparral, highlighted by orange sticky monkey-flower. At 0.5 mile, near where a graceful Douglas fir highlights a view of the Bay Bridge, San Francisco skyscrapers, and Alcatraz Island, you'll come to a sign for the West Point Inn. Next to a wooden water storage tank at 1.2 miles, you'll get views of San Pablo Bay and Mount Diablo.

At 1.8 miles turn right onto the signed Rock Spring Trail next to the West Point Inn. At 2 miles the path ascends gently, with views of the West Point Inn framed by the Golden Gate Bridge and Angel Island. Cross the first of three wooden bridges at 2.8 miles on the Rock Spring Trail, where you'll find fern and California laurel along a tiny brook. At 3.3 miles reach Mountain Theatre, featuring seat rows built from rocks.

The trail becomes a rocky theatre row. Follow this row and cross a paved maintenance row. Continue on the path, cross a paved road, and take the Mountain Theatre Fire Trail. Stay on the Mountain Theatre Fire Trail for 50 yards and go left at a Y intersection. You soon reach the Old Mine Trail. This path travels along a vast hillside of pure oat grass and coast live oak with sweeping views of the sea and bay for another 0.8 mile to the Pantoll Ranger Station.

Views and more views: the San Francisco skyline, the Golden Gate and Bay Bridges, Alcatraz and Angel Islands, and Mount Diablo

From here, you can continue all the way to Stinson Beach (see Hike 83, Mount Tamalpais: Pantoll Ranger Station to Stinson Beach) or return the way you came.

85 MUIR WOODS

Length: 6-mile loop
Hiking time: 3 hours
High point: 1,240 feet
Total elevation gain: 1,200 feet
Difficulty: easy to moderate
Season: year-round
Water: available from faucets at the visitor center and along trails
Maps: USGS 7.5′ San Rafael, park brochure (available at the visitor center)
Information: Muir Woods National Monument

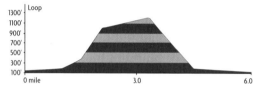

This hike in Muir Woods begins with an informative self-guided interpretive nature trail displaying spectacular redwood trees, followed by quiet creekside walking, climaxed by bird's-eye views of some of the tallest redwoods in California.

Five miles north of the Golden Gate Bridge on Highway 101, go west on Highway 1 at the Stinson Beach exit. After 3.3 miles turn right on Muir Woods Road and go 2.5 miles to the visitor center parking lot (follow signs).

The paved, populated path (starting as the self-guided interpretive nature trail) begins through a level old-growth redwood forest. In this high-usage first 0.5 mile, posted signs provide interesting information about redwoods. Cross any of the four wooden bridges over Red-

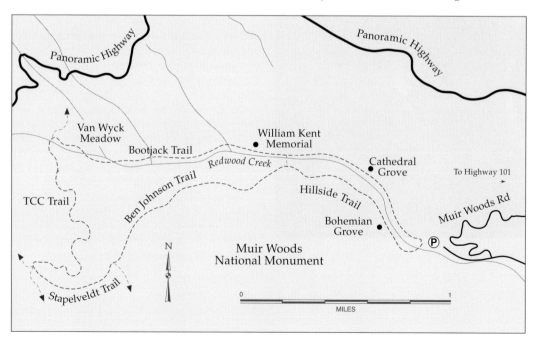

Stillness in the redwoods

wood Creek that lead to several redwood groves (all paths shortly rejoin the main trail). Wander into Cathedral Grove, highlighted by tall redwoods, and then make a side trip up Fern Creek to visit the William Kent Memorial beside a fallen Douglas fir.

> Leave the crowds behind as you journey down serene and shady Bootjack Trail.

Refreshing seclusion awaits at 0.9 mile as you take your first steps onto the Bootjack Trail and leave the crowds behind. The quiet solitude is comforting: The steady splash of tumbling Redwood Creek is virtually the only sound you hear.

The path climbs past bigleaf maple and bracken, sword, and lady ferns to reach a large wooden bridge across Redwood Creek, which originates near the top of Mount Tamalpais's west peak. The trail cuts a steep course up the hillside, reuniting with a bouldery section of Redwood Creek at 1.9 miles.

The climb persists 0.4 mile to small Van Wyck Meadow and its surrounding Douglas fir, coast live oak, and California laurel. From the meadow, bear left onto the TCC Trail. It provides a 1.4-mile level excursion across a series of canyon sides in tranquil, shady woods. Teasing glimpses of Mount Tamalpais appear intermittently beyond the low-hanging limbs of majestic Douglas fir.

At 3.6 miles, reach a wooden bridge and bench, where you make two successive left turns on the Stapelveldt Trail. This trail descends past two huge redwoods that form an archway at 4.1 miles. Reach a signed trail intersection 0.1 mile farther, and bear left onto the Ben Johnson Trail.

Depart this gradually descending trail at 5.2 miles with a right turn onto the signed Hillside Trail. This scenic, level trail offers several vistas of Redwood Creek and its surrounding massive redwoods before reaching the parking lot.

86 TENNESSEE VALLEY BEACH

Length: 4 miles round-trip
Hiking time: 3 hours
High point: 100 feet
Total elevation gain: 100 feet
Difficulty: easy
Season: year-round
Water: bring your own
Map: USGS 7.5' Point Bonita
Information: Golden Gate National Recreation Area

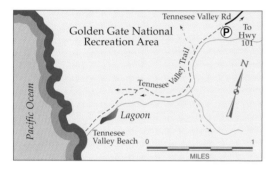

The Tennessee Valley gradually unfolds into the Pacific Ocean on this family journey as you trek past wildflowers and grasslands to a lagoon and scenic Tennessee Valley Beach.

On Highway 101 about 5 miles north of the Golden Gate Bridge, take the Highway 1 exit marked Muir Woods/ Mount Tamalpais. Follow the highway 0.5 mile, and then turn left onto Tennessee Valley Road, which takes you to the large parking lot 2.2 miles farther.

A freshwater lagoon, popular with birds, is encircled by bush lupine and cow parsnip.

The trail (an old road) begins paved and level as it travels past numerous flowers, including wild radish, mustard, fennel, dock, and California poppy. Wild oat grass mingles with cow parsnips at 0.3 mile, where you bear left at the

Tennessee Valley Beach

marker indicating Tennessee Valley Beach.

For the next 1.7 miles, head down and directly west in the bottom of the U-shaped canyon to the beach. Ignore the two trails on the right along the way, staying instead on the wide gravel path that hugs the creek.

At 1.8 miles you reach a waterbird-frequented freshwater lagoon surrounded by bush lupine and cow parsnip. Continue 0.1 mile farther to popular Tennessee Valley Beach for picnicking, wave watching, beachcombing, and castle building.

87 MOUNT DIABLO LOOP

Length: 7.1-mile loop
Hiking time: 4 hours
High point: 3,849 feet
Total elevation gain: 2,050 feet
Difficulty: moderate
Season: year-round
Water: bring your own
Maps: USGS 7.5' Clayton, park brochure
Information: Mount Diablo State Park

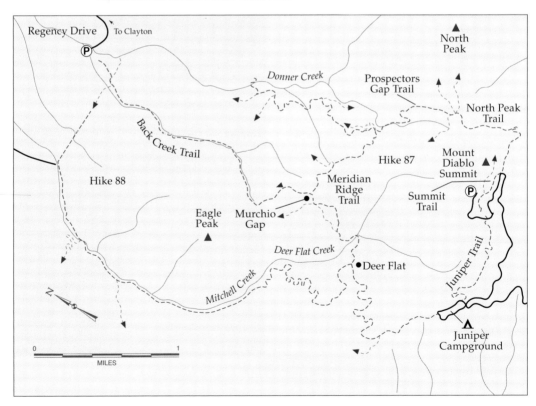

View from Deer Flat

This hike begins at Mount Diablo's summit, which offers a far-reaching panorama encompassing more square miles than any other view in the United States. You'll then take a loop trip along the flanks of this famous mountain, encountering a vast array of different plant species suited to different elevations along the way.

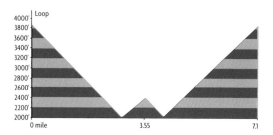

If driving south on Interstate 680 toward Walnut Creek, take the Treat Road exit and go east. In 1.2 miles turn right onto Bancroft Road, which crosses Ygnacio Valley Road after another 0.6 mile and then turns into Walnut Avenue.

If driving north on Interstate 680, drive north from the Highway 24 interchange, take the Ygnacio Valley Road exit, and drive 2.6 miles east on Ygnacio Valley Road to Walnut Avenue.

From either approach, drive Walnut Avenue for 1.6 miles, go right onto Oak Grove Road, and take an immediate left onto North Gate Road. From here, it's 12.4 curvy miles to the trailhead at the summit of Mount Diablo.

Alternatively, you can reach the summit by taking the Diablo Road exit off I-680 in Danville, traveling Diablo Road for 3.4 miles, and turning left onto South Gate Road. From here, it's 6.6 curvy miles to the junction with North Gate Road. Go right and proceed another 4.5 miles to the summit.

Before starting the hike, absorb the fantastic view from the 3,849-foot summit of Mount Diablo. On an exceptionally clear day, you can see the Delta, the Sacramento Valley, the Sutter Buttes, and Lassen Peak to the north; the San Joaquin Valley and the Sierra Nevada (including Half Dome in Yosemite) to the east; Mount

Hamilton and its surrounding hills and valleys to the south; and the East Bay hills, San Francisco Bay, the Santa Cruz Mountains, and Mount Tamalpais to the west.

Take the Summit Trail downhill from the southeast side of the lower parking area, and at 0.3 mile turn left at the unsigned North Peak Trail, which is also close by the main road and offers an alternative starting point. Descend past California laurel, interior live oak, scrub oak, orange California poppy, blue lupine, and purple brodiaea. At 1.4 miles you reach a four-way junction at Prospectors Gap, an excellent spot to picnic under the shade of blue oak and gray pine as you enjoy open views to the east and west.

> You won't want to miss the panorama from Mount Diablo: It encompasses more square miles than any other in the United States.

Head downhill on the dirt Prospectors Gap Trail toward Deer Flat, one of your intermediate destinations. You'll pass several side trails along the way; always stay on the main dirt road. At 2.2 miles you'll reach seasonal Donner Creek and then stroll past chaparral to Murchio Gap at 3.3 miles, where you can connect with the trails of Hike 88 (Mount Diablo's Back and Mitchell Canyons) trails. Near the road, look for a low knob, which offers good westward views.

Cross seasonal Deer Flat Creek, and then reach Deer Flat at 4.1 miles, where you can rest under the shade of large blue oak. Go left at a road fork and start the occasionally steep ascent. Stay left at a road fork at 4.9 miles, and continue to climb as you enjoy the open views and wildflowers.

Juniper Campground awaits at 5.9 miles. Head left on the paved road past the restrooms and drinking fountain, and then turn left on the signed Juniper Trail. This trail initially passes through a large grove of tall California laurel trees and then climbs to a ridge, which hosts chaparral shrubs, gray pine, and interior live oak. You'll pass a radio tower and then reach the main road to the summit at 6.9 miles. Go right for 100 feet, and then turn left and take the unsigned trail uphill 0.1 mile to the lower parking lot. From here, you can proceed across the parking lot to your car.

88 MOUNT DIABLO'S BACK AND MITCHELL CANYONS

Length: 8.6 miles round-trip
Hiking time: 4 to 6 hours
High point: 2,400 feet
Total elevation gain: 1,800 feet
Difficulty: moderate to strenuous
Season: year-round
Water: bring plenty of your own
Maps: USGS 7.5' Clayton, park brochure
Information: Mount Diablo State Park

This hike halfway to the top of the Bay Area's most-seen mountain hosts the largest variety of flora of all hikes in this book. Wander in two distinctly different canyons and explore chaparral hillsides, oak woodlands, meadows, and dense riparian habitats.

From Interstate 680 in Walnut Creek, take the Ygnacio Valley Road exit and drive east 7.8 miles. Bear right onto Clayton Road, travel 2.8 miles, and turn right onto Regency Drive, where you go 0.5 mile to its dead end.

Descend an embankment, cross the park gate, and take a right at the dirt road fork that leaves Donner Creek. Go past valley oaks, bear right at

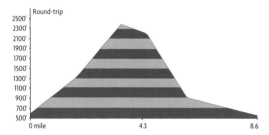

Wildflower meadow near Murchio Gap

an unsigned road fork, and then promptly turn left at another unsigned trail junction.

Back Creek flows below sensational eroded rock and is framed by buckeye, blue oak, interior live oak, and gray pine for the first 0.5 mile. Cross a gate and continue past orange bush monkey-flower, fragrant sage, toyon, and yarrow. A bit farther, several spur trails break to the left amid chamise, wild grape, poison oak, and yerba santa; always stay right and resume climbing Back Canyon, which steepens at 1.3 miles. From 2.1 to 3.2 miles, chamise dominates, interspersed with yerba santa and eventually thickets of whiteleaf manzanita recovering from a major fire that ravaged this area in 1977.

Upon reaching isolated Murchio Gap (3.5 miles), you can climb another 1,500 feet in elevation to Mount Diablo Summit (Hike 87: Mount Diablo Loop). To bypass the summit, head south from Murchio Gap 0.8 mile to Deer Flat, the most abundant wildlife and birding area in the park. Bear left here and descend 1 mile to gently swirling Mitchell Creek. Promptly reach a grassy flat where canyon and coast live oaks grow magnificently tall near creekside.

Follow alder- and bigleaf-maple-lined Mitchell Creek for 2.4 miles, taking a fire road on the right. This trail passes through grasslands featuring Coulter and gray pines to reunite with your trailhead.

89 BRIONES REGIONAL PARK TRAILS

Length: 8.4-mile loop
Hiking time: 5 hours
High point: 1,483 feet
Total elevation gain: 1,300 feet
Difficulty: easy to moderate
Season: year-round
Water: bring your own
Maps: USGS 7.5' Briones Valley, USGS 7.5' Walnut Creek
Information: East Bay Regional Park District

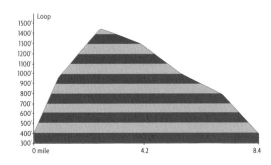

Explore a creek and a pond, and then climb Briones Peak for views of rolling hillsides, Mounts Diablo and Tamalpais, and San Pablo and Suisun Bays.

From Highway 24 in Lafayette, take the Pleasant Hill Boulevard exit, go north for 0.6 mile, and then turn left on Reliez Valley Road. Drive 4.8 miles, turn left onto the road signed for the Alhambra Creek Staging Area, and then go 0.8 mile to the parking lot.

From Highway 4, take the Alhambra Avenue exit south, and then go right onto Alhambra Valley Road. Drive 1.7 miles, turn left on Reliez Valley Road for 0.5 mile, and then go right for 0.8 mile.

Take the Alhambra Creek Trail past riparian habitat, buckeye, live oak, and blue oak to a signed trail junction at 0.9 mile, where you bear right onto the Spengler Trail. Climb away from the creek past coast live oak, poison oak, coyote brush, and California laurel to two ponds called Maricich Lagoons at 1.6 miles, where you turn left onto the Old Briones Road Trail. Climb gradually along gently rolling grassy hillsides that typify the Briones region to a signed trail junction at 1.9 miles, where you bear left on the Briones Crest Trail.

> **Smooth-sloped, grassy hillsides highlight the Briones region.**

Take the spur trail on the left at 2.5 miles to a bench marking the top of 1,483-foot Briones Peak, the highest spot in Briones Regional Park. To the north you can see the San Joaquin and Sacramento Rivers converge into Suisun Bay; San Pablo Bay sprawls northwesterly, Mount Tamalpais looms westward beyond the Berkeley hills, and Mount Diablo juts to the east.

Bear left at the next signed trail junction, and then climb briefly and go right onto the signed

View from Briones Peak

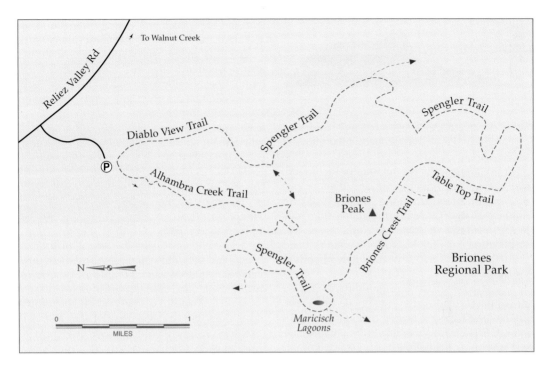

Table Top Trail. Walk past chaparral and scattered coast live oak to a signed trail junction at 3.3 miles, where you turn left back onto the Spengler Trail. This wide road plunges steeply at times through a canyon shaded by coast live oak, huge toyon, buckeye, California laurel, and the occasional bigleaf maple.

Ignore an unsigned trail junction near a water tank and continue left to a signed trail junction at 5.7 miles, where you turn right. Bear right at an unsigned trail junction and then left at a signed trail junction at 6.3 miles. Continue left on the Spengler Trail at a three-way, unsigned trail junction 25 yards farther. The trail stays shaded while dropping 0.4 mile to an unsigned fork, where you bear left for a brief climb. Go right onto the Diablo View Trail at 7.3 miles. Turn left at a signed trail junction 0.5 mile farther. After 100 yards the trail drops to the Alhambra Creek canyon and to the trailhead at 8.4 miles.

90 WILDCAT CANYON REGIONAL PARK TRAILS

Length: 11.5 miles round-trip
Hiking time: 6 hours
High point: 1,250 feet
Total elevation gain: 1,400 feet
Difficulty: moderate
Season: year-round
Water: bring your own
Map: USGS 7.5' Richmond
Information: East Bay Regional Park District

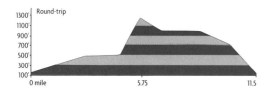

Stroll alongside scenic Wildcat Creek, and then climb Wildcat Peak to enjoy spectacular views of the Bay Area.

From Interstate 80 northbound in Richmond, take the Amador/Solano exit, and then go east on Amador Street. Drive three blocks and turn right on McBryde Avenue. Go another 0.5 mile to the trailhead at Alvarado Park. From I-80 southbound, take the McBryde Avenue exit and go east on McBryde Avenue until it dead-ends at the trailhead.

The Wildcat Creek Trail promptly climbs on an old paved road that eventually becomes dirt. Continue straight at a signed trail junction at 0.5 mile. At 0.9 mile the sprawling Wildcat Creek canyon appears on the right. Large coast live oak and

mature California laurel coat the canyon sides, and alder and willow cover Wildcat Creek.

The first union with Wildcat Creek occurs near a wooden bridge at 2.1 miles amid eucalyptus trees. Continue straight, and then begin a brief climb at a signed three-way intersection a few yards farther. Note that you can substantially shorten your trip here by going left onto the Havey Canyon Trail for 1.2 miles to the Nimitz Way Trail.

Admire Bay Area natural landmarks from the peace grove platform atop Wildcat Peak.

The main path remains mostly flat over the next 2 miles past a sequence of gullies choked with willow and blackberry bushes; all empty into Wildcat Creek during winter and spring's wet months.

At 4.1 miles, and a few yards before reaching a duck pond called Jewel Lake, bear left onto the unsigned Wildcat Peak Trail next to two signposts (one is labeled "9"). Your climb

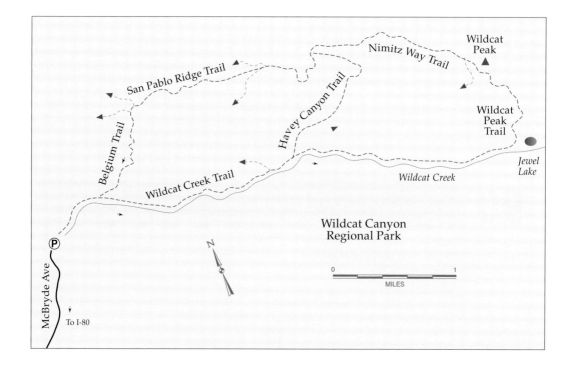

San Pablo Reservoir from Wildcat Peak

commences through a eucalyptus forest and then open chaparral. Be sure to follow sign arrows with drawn pictures of the peak at the numerous intersections.

Reach the peace grove platform atop 1,250-foot Wildcat Peak at 5.6 miles, and admire extensive views: Mount Diablo towers to the east beyond San Pablo Reservoir, and to the west you'll see Mount Tamalpais, Angel Island, the Golden Gate, the San Francisco skyline, and San Francisco Bay. Choose one of the numerous footpaths and head north down to the obvious asphalt intersection of the Conlon and Nimitz Way Trails, where you go north on the Nimitz Way Trail.

Scattered Monterey pine and coyote brush adorn the open grasslands along this ridge-top path. At 8.2 miles, stay on the Nimitz Way Trail as it goes left and becomes a dirt road. When you pass a corral at 8.5 miles, bear left, and then right 100 yards farther onto the signed San Pablo Ridge Trail. This secluded dirt road climbs a few knolls, which provide pleasing panoramas of rolling hills and the Bay Area.

Bear left onto the Belgum Trail at 10 miles. The path gives great vistas of San Pablo Ridge behind you and San Francisco Bay ahead. Cactus, eucalyptus, and palm trees precede a right turn onto the signed Wildcat Creek Trail at 10.9 miles, which returns you to the trailhead.

91 LAS TRAMPAS REGIONAL WILDERNESS

Length: 15.5 miles round-trip (Rocky Ridge, 6.3 miles; Las Trampas Ridge, 9.2 miles)
Hiking time: 4 hours for Rocky Ridge, 6 hours for Las Trampas Ridge
High point: 2,000 feet
Total elevation gain: 1,150 feet for Rocky Ridge, 2,100 feet for Las Trampas Ridge
Difficulty: moderate
Season: year-round
Water: bring your own
Maps: USGS 7.5' Las Trampas Ridge, park brochure
Information: East Bay Regional Park District

Las Trampas Ridge and foothills

The steep hills of Las Trampas Regional Wilderness host a variety of plant communities—flower-dotted meadows, vast thickets of multiscented chaparral, lush streamside habitat, oak-studded hillsides—and they allow extensive vistas of the Bay Area.

To reach the trailhead, first get to the intersection of Crow Canyon Road and Bollinger Canyon Road by traveling east 7.3 miles on Crow Canyon Road from Interstate 580 in Castro Valley or by traveling west 1.6 miles on Crow Canyon Road from I-680 in San Ramon. Then take Bollinger Canyon Road 4.4 miles northwest to its end. Be sure to grab the park brochure; it'll help you navigate the trails.

The 6.3-mile loop on and around Rocky Ridge begins with a long climb on the paved Rocky Ridge Trail. Groves of live oak and California laurel dot the open hillside, interrupting extensive meadows. At 0.4 mile the Cuesta Trail comes in on the left. You'll use this path to complete the loop journey, but for now continue up to a road gate at 0.7 mile and turn left onto the Upper Trail.

You now travel just below Rocky Ridge. A look eastward shows Bollinger Canyon below, with chaparral-cloaked Las Trampas Ridge just above and Mount Diablo looming in the distance beyond. As you continue, look for fossil clam shells embedded in the sandstone rock.

Turn right onto the Sycamore Trail at 1.5 miles and enjoy views of the East Bay hills, San Francisco Bay, the entire peninsula, including San Francisco, and the Santa Cruz Mountains and Coast Range stretching to the south.

Reach a shoulder at 1.7 miles and drop past chaparral, grassy hillsides, and coast live oak groves to a seasonal creek at 2.7 miles, which is amply shaded by California laurel, canyon live oak, and a few California sycamores. Stay on the main trail at a fork just beyond the creek, and then turn left onto the Devils Hole Trail at 2.8 miles.

Climb steeply, regain the spine of Rocky Ridge, and turn left onto the Upper Trail at 4.1 miles. Take a right onto the Cuesta Trail at 4.5 miles, cross a trail, and hike downhill to connect

> The sandstone contains numerous fossilized clam shells.

with the paved Rocky Ridge Trail at 5.9 miles. Go right for 0.4 mile back to the trailhead.

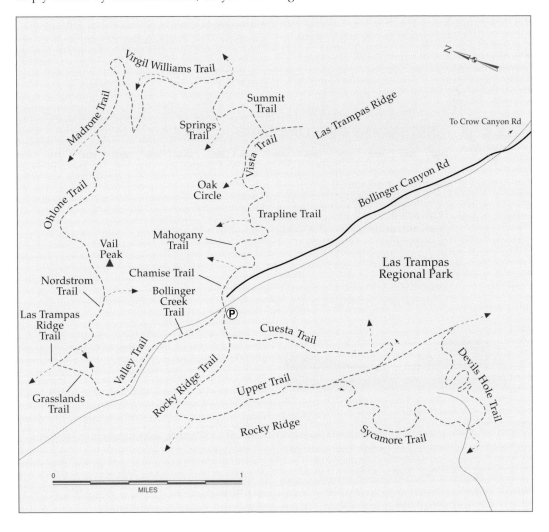

The 9.2-mile hike on and around Las Trampas Ridge begins with the Bollinger Creek Trail on the west side of Bollinger Creek next to a huge coast live oak. Cross the creek at 0.6 mile underneath some California laurel trees, and then bear left 25 yards farther onto the Valley Trail. Go right onto the Grasslands Trail 0.3 mile farther at a saddle and begin climbing.

At 1.7 miles bear right onto the Las Trampas Ridge Trail. It levels in a chaparral thicket and then meets a three-way signed trail junction, where you go left onto the Nordstrom Trail. Hike 0.3 mile past madrone trees, and then bear left onto the Ohlone Trail. After 150 yards the way becomes a gulch that climbs straight toward Vail Peak. Scamper up its knoll for excellent views of Mount Diablo, the San Ramon Valley, San Pablo Bay, and Rocky Ridge.

Continue down the Ohlone Trail to a saddle at 4.3 miles. Bear right there onto the Madrone Trail. Drop past oak woodlands, arc sharply right, gradually climb to the Virgil Williams Trail at 5.2 miles, and bear right again. Admire Mount Diablo on the left, go right at 6.2 miles onto the Springs Trail, and climb to the crest. Head left at 7 miles onto the Summit Trail.

Go right at 7.5 miles onto the Vista Trail and stroll past chamise, sage and artemesia, and ceanothus. Turn left onto the Trapline Trail at 8 miles next to Oak Circle, and then go left again 0.1 mile farther. At 8.6 miles bear left onto the Mahogany Trail and hug a rapidly descending seasonal stream. At 8.8 miles, go left onto the Chamise Trail. Reach Bollinger Canyon Road 0.2 mile farther and turn right for the brief walk to the trailhead.

92 REDWOOD REGIONAL PARK TRAILS

Length: 8.4-mile loop
Hiking time: 5 hours
High point: 1,619 feet
Total elevation gain: 1,100 feet
Difficulty: easy to moderate
Season: year-round
Water: bring your own
Map: USGS 7.5′ Oakland East
Information: East Bay Regional Park District

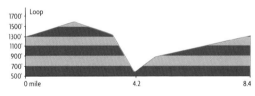

This ridge-top journey travels the outer edges of Redwood Regional Park past huge redwoods and offers numerous views of San Francisco Bay and its surrounding cities and mountains.

From Highway 13 in Oakland, take the 35th Street/Redwood Road exit, travel northeast 1.1 miles, and turn left on Skyline Boulevard. Drive 3.7 miles to the parking area at the corner of Skyline Boulevard and Pine Hills Road.

Begin on the West Ridge Trail, a mostly level dirt road that travels past coast live oak, eucalyptus, coyote brush, and California laurel. Mature Monterey pine and a handful of redwood trees show up at a signed trail junction at 0.4 mile, where you keep right. Obtain views of Mount Diablo and San Francisco Bay as the trail climbs to a tall grove of slender eucalyptus trees at 1.3 miles. Look near an archery range at 1.5 miles for a redwood stump that's 33 feet in diameter. Some botanists think that the magnificent specimen that once stood here was the biggest redwood ever known.

Climb 0.2 mile up 1,619-foot Redwood Peak by bearing left at the signed trail junction at 1.8

miles. You'll pass coast live oaks and redwoods before reaching a cluster of closet-size boulders at the top.

At 2.5 miles, bear left at a trail fork. Descend with views of Mount Diablo and numerous other Bay Area landmarks, and continue on the West Ridge Trail at a trail junction at 3.1 miles. Trek into a gigantic eucalyptus forest, and continue straight past two signed trails on the right. Bear left down the signed Orchard Trail at 3.7 miles, and go right 0.2 mile farther at a group of madrone. At the first of two consecutive trail intersections, make a right and then bear left 20 yards farther to Canyon Meadow. Cross the streambed and head straight to pick up the Canyon Trail. This dirt fire road promptly ascends past dense chaparral and hugs a seasonal stream for a while. Bear left onto the East Ridge Trail at 4.5 miles and climb to a crest at 5.7 miles, where you capture the hike's best southward views from a bench. Enjoy expansive vistas as you remain on the East Ridge Trail past stands of Monterey pine to the trailhead at 8.4 miles.

> The West Ridge Trail travels near a 33-foot-wide redwood stump, the remnant of what may have been the world's largest redwood tree.

Madrone

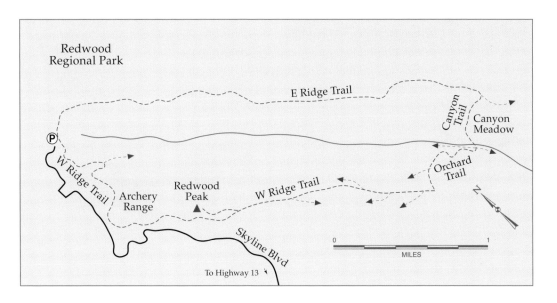

93 GRANT PARK'S PEAK 2987

Length: 9 miles round-trip
Hiking time: 5 hours
High point: 2,987 feet
Total elevation gain: 1,600 feet
Difficulty: moderate
Season: year-round
Water: none; bring your own
Map: USGS 7.5' Lick Observatory
Information: Joseph D. Grant County Park

Oak trees dotting an open landscape can take on unique, sculpted shapes. Such is the case on this hike as you climb through oak woodlands to an oak-ringed meadow and then to Peak 2987 for a 360-degree view of the South Bay, Mount Hamilton, and rolling hills.

From the east side of San Jose on Interstate 680, take the Alum Rock Avenue exit (2 miles

north of the interchange with Highway 101), and drive east 2.2 miles. Turn right onto Mount Hamilton Road and climb 7.7 twisting miles to the Joseph D. Grant County Park kiosk. Go 150 yards farther and park in the paved lot on the left.

Get on the dirt road that skirts the northeast shoreline of scenic, coyote-brush-lined Grant

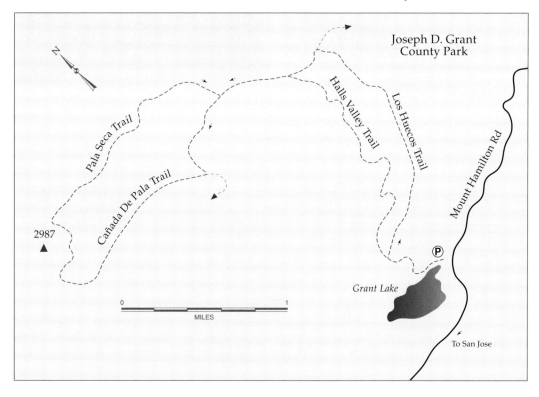

Lake. After 0.2 mile bear right onto the signed Halls Valley Trail. Then cross a willow-lined seasonal stream, climb past a stand of eucalyptus, and bear right 0.2 mile farther onto the signed Los Huecos Trail.

This wide dirt road immediately climbs, rewarding you with views of Grant Lake beyond scattered valley oak and Lick Observatory atop 4,209-foot

> A rare high-ridge wetland patch lies along Cañada De Pala Trail.

Mount Hamilton ahead. When these views vanish, look southward into the broad valley housing San Felipe Creek.

Just before reaching the ridge top, look west at San Jose and the South Bay. Reach the crest at 2.1 miles and bear left onto the Cañada De Pala Trail, noting the nearby twin patriarch valley oaks. A grove of hardy buckeye trees appears 0.2 mile farther at a signed trail junction. Stay straight, but remember that the Halls Valley Trail on the left is the return route. Admire a rare high-ridge wetland patch on the left when you reach a signed trail junction at 2.8 miles. Bear left here, and at 3.1 miles arrive at a large meadow. Bear right 0.2 mile farther at the signed trail junction, and skirt the meadow for the next 0.4 mile along a rush-lined seasonal stream. Climb another 0.8 mile to regain the ridge top, and gain this journey's best panorama by taking the spur trail (signed for Antler Point) left to Peak 2987, highest in the park, which combines all the previously encountered views.

Back on the main path (now called the Pala Seca Trail), a long ridge-top stroll reveals Mount Hamilton and the steep foothills and nearby canyon eastward. At 6.1 miles go left at a previously encountered junction, descend past an old corral, and bear right onto the Halls Valley Trail at

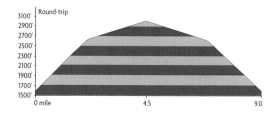

Gray pine, buckeye in bloom, and blue oak

6.4 miles. After 0.1 mile note the huge buckeye on the left and two sycamore trees growing by a seasonal stream on the right. Enjoy the only semi-shaded trail on this hike as you make a long descent under black oak, blue oak, California laurel, and buckeye. At 8.8 miles turn left at the signed trail junction and stroll past Grant Lake to the parking area.

94 HENRY W. COE STATE PARK: COIT LAKE

Length: 26-mile loop
Hiking time: 3 to 5 days
High point: 2,700 feet
Total elevation gain: 4,200 feet
Difficulty: moderate to strenuous
Season: year-round
Water: available at China Hole, Coit Lake, and Los Cruzeros (purify first)
Maps: USGS 7.5′ Mississippi Creek, USGS 7.5′ Mount Sizer, Henry W. Coe
   State Park map
Information: Henry W. Coe State Park

Take a secluded backpack trip in gently sculpted hills past oak savanna to Coit Lake. Along the way you'll have grand views of foothill slopes and canyons. Note that spring and fall are the best times to hike. Backpackers must register at the visitor center. Call ahead to find out about water availability from springs, which can dry up during drought years. You also should purchase the topographical trail map at the visitor center. Many trails wind through the park, and the map will make navigation much easier.

From Highway 101 in Morgan Hill (south of San Jose), take the East Dunne Avenue exit, and climb 12.5 miles to the Henry W. Coe State Park Visitor Center.

To start, take the signed Corral Trail in front of the visitor center. When you reach an open area covered with oat grass, look for a magnificent valley oak decorated with profuse mistletoe growth. Bear right 50 yards farther onto the signed Springs Trail next to another valley oak.

The 1.4-mile-long Springs Trail begins in shade, passes two springs that shrivel up by midsummer, and continues along an open hilltop featuring sweeping vistas of the steep-sided,

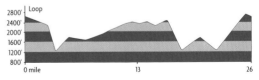

California poppies

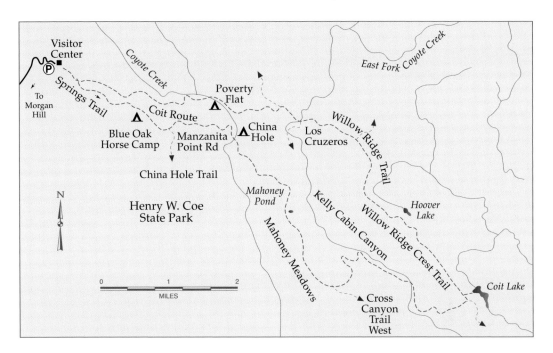

rolling hills that epitomize this large park. As a bonus, this level stretch supports a four-oak-species savanna: valley oak, coast live oak, black oak, and blue oak.

At 1.7 miles pass an attractive third spring lined with native rushes. The trail then leads to a multisigned trail intersection at 1.9 miles, where you go right onto the dirt Manzanita Point Road. Several picnic tables and two outhouses 0.2 mile farther mark Blue Oak Horse Camp. You'll find water at a nearby bass pond, where a spur loop trail leads to one of the Manzanita Point group camps, which are available to backpackers.

At 2.5 miles at the signed trail junction, turn left onto the China Hole Trail opposite the Madrone Soda Springs Trail. Descend past a variety of native flora—including big berry manzanita, ponderosa pine, black oak, chamise chaparral, and eventually blue oak woodland—to popular China Hole, which doubles as a swimming spot and a camp for backpackers.

Continue to Mahoney Meadows and Mahoney Ridge by crossing Coyote Creek, which can be impassable in winter (check with the visitor center ahead of time). The 1.5-mile section from Mahoney Pond to the signed junction of the Cross Canyon Trail West (where you turn left) consists of an oak savanna ridge walk that curves past tall gray pine. Admire views to the right of Coyote Creek Canyon, and turn around to view Blue Ridge, Middle Ridge, and Pine Ridge to the northwest. Your mile-long journey down the Cross Canyon Trail West encompasses a mix of shady and open vegetation. The primary shrub species include ceanothus, ocean spray, and big berry manzanita. Watch for sporadic madrone and black oak closer to the canyon's bottom.

When you get down to Kelly Cabin Canyon, the trail veers abruptly southeast and follows the seasonal creek upstream past laurel, bigleaf maple, sycamore, and coast live oak. After 1 mile the trail departs the creek and then ascends in and out of side canyons to the signed junction with the Willow Ridge Crest Trail, where you turn left.

> Plan this hike for the spring months when three trailside springs are at their best.

After 0.1 mile pick up the 0.2-mile-long trail on your right that leads to Coit Lake, which offers good swimming and camping for backpackers.

Return to the Willow Ridge Crest Trail, and pass shallow Hoover Lake and several sections of chamise chaparral as you appreciate ongoing views of the Pacheco drainage to the east and previously mentioned vistas to the north and west. Turn left onto the signed Willow Ridge Trail 3.5 miles past Coit Lake. You'll spot an unsigned side trail 0.2 mile farther that leads to a spring that usually shrivels up by early summer.

Back on the Willow Ridge Trail, descend 1,000 feet of elevation over 1.3 miles to the East Fork Coyote Creek. Los Cruzeros, another backpack camp, is a short side trip downstream. Cross the creek and continue on the Pacheco Route, now a dirt road. Climb 0.4 mile to a signed trail junction, bear left, and continue left at another signed junction 0.3 mile farther.

Gradually descend for 1 mile to Poverty Flat, another favorite creekside camping spot. From here, briefly follow Coyote Creek to two signed trail junctions, and cross the creek (which may be impassable in winter). Stay straight on the Pacheco Route for a 1.6-mile climb past a variety of oaks, plus gray pine and laurel, to a previously encountered trail junction, where you stay straight on the Pacheco Route. The trail now climbs to a plateau, with splendid views of canyons and rolling hills, and then descends to the trailhead.

Montara State Beach

95 NORTH PEAK MONTARA MOUNTAIN

Length: 6 miles round-trip
Hiking time: 4 hours
High point: 1,898 feet
Total elevation gain: 2,200 feet
Difficulty: strenuous
Season: year-round
Water: none; bring your own
Map: USGS 7.5′ Montara Mountain
Information: Half Moon Bay State Beaches

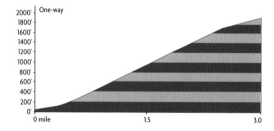

This hike offers an impressive array of wildflowers and chaparral plants, as well as a superb top-of-the-world panorama of the San Francisco Bay area and the Pacific Ocean, including the Farralon Islands.

Watch for a signed entrance gate on the east side of Highway 1 several yards north of the access road to Montara State Beach (10 miles north of Half Moon Bay). If this small lot is packed, you may have to park farther north at the Gray Whale Cove parking area on the east side of the highway or at the Montara State Beach parking lot.

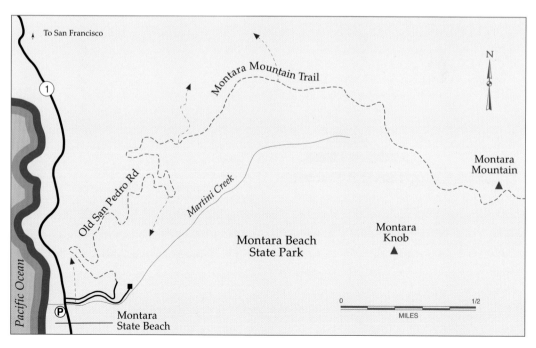

The path initially travels east and parallels a grove of tall cypress trees. Bear sharply left onto Old San Pedro Road at 0.2 mile, just in front of the ranger's residence. Fortunately, this dirt path is wide, because poison oak, identifiable by its three-leafed branchlets, dominates trailside to 0.4 mile.

At 0.5 mile walk past a shady grove of Scotch broom and pampas grass, both hardy, exotic plants. The path now climbs relentlessly, with improving views of the towns of Half Moon Bay behind you and Pacifica northward.

Bear right at 1.4 miles onto the Montara Mountain Trail, a fire road. The steepest climbing occurs from 1.6 to 1.9 miles, accompanied by California poppy and lupine. Blue-blossom California lilac dominates trailside from 2 to 2.5 miles as monumental rock outcrops attract attention in the distance.

You may be tempted to stray off the beaten path to climb a number of small peaks from 2.7 to 2.9 miles, but stay on the main dirt road and reward yourself with a 360-degree view from the microwave/weather station atop 1,898-foot North Peak Montara Mountain at 3 miles. Look for Mount Diablo to the east and Scarpers Peak and the Santa Cruz Mountains to the southeast. Half Moon Bay and its neighboring beaches stretch below to the southwest, and mighty Mount Tamalpais hovers to the north above San Francisco's skyscrapers. To the west, beyond the coastline, stretches the vast blue of the Pacific Ocean, with the Farralon Islands visible on exceptionally clear days.

96 PURISIMA CREEK AND HARKINS RIDGE

Length: 7-mile loop
Hiking time: 4 hours
High point: 1,550 feet
Total elevation gain: 1,200 feet
Difficulty: moderate
Season: year-round
Water: bring your own
Map: USGS 7.5' Woodside
Information: Midpeninsula Regional Open Space District

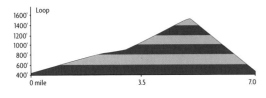

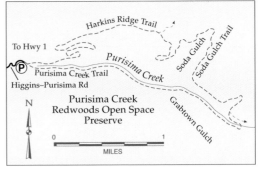

This redwood tree journey parallels cool and peaceful Purisima Creek, passes tranquil, natural herb gardens on the secluded Soda Gulch Trail, and finally travels a view-filled, slender finger of Harkins Ridge.

Turn east on Verde Road 3.5 miles south of the intersection of Highways 1 and 92 at Half Moon Bay. Travel 0.25 mile and go straight onto Purisima Creek Road. Go another 3.7 miles to the reserve and the trailhead.

The first mile along the Purisima Creek Trail,

a dirt road, stays level and shaded, with an equal mix of tall redwood, alder, and bigleaf maple. Come to a large clearing at 1.1 miles, which supports thistle, thimbleberry, poison hemlock, and a few rushes.

The trail ascends noticeably after crossing a bridge roofed by a drooping maple at 1.3 miles. Reach the Grabtown trailhead junction 0.1 mile farther and continue straight. You soon cross another bridge that overlooks a tributary originating from Soda Gulch, higher up to the left. Note the tall redwoods and towering maples that provide shelter for a lady fern community at creekside. Climb gently to the Soda Gulch Trail junction at 2.3 miles, and go left.

The climb moderates as you leave the creek and enter a jungle of redwood and various herbs, including mint, mugwort, and nettle. At 3.5 miles observe two redwoods joined at the trunk, and continue to a sweeping view of the Santa Cruz Mountains at 3.7 miles. The narrow path arcs toward the distant Pacific Ocean at 4 miles and then enters dense chaparral.

> A naturally occurring herb garden includes mint, mugwort, and nettle.

As you approach the top of a knoll, you'll have another view of the Santa Cruz Mountains rolling into Half Moon Bay. California

View from Harkins Ridge

poppy, cow parsnip, and yerba santa then decorate the landscape leading up to the Harkins Ridge Trail junction at 4.9 miles, where you bear left.

The Harkins Ridge Trail, another dirt road, takes you past blue blossom ceanothus and madrone with a background of Purisima Creek's redwood groves as you gradually descend over the next 1.4 miles. Views disappear at 6 miles where the trail bends toward Purisima Creek and descends more rapidly through shaded forest to the trailhead.

97 CASTLE ROCK AND GOAT ROCK

Length: 5.8 miles round-trip
Hiking time: 3 hours
High point: 3,214 feet
Total elevation gain: 800 feet
Difficulty: moderate
Season: year-round
Water: bring your own
Map: USGS 7.5' Castle Rock Ridge
Information: Castle Rock State Park

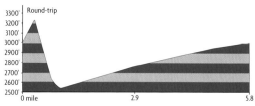

Castle Rock, Douglas fir, and coast live oak

This journey in Castle Rock State Park has many features: sweeping vistas of Monterey Bay, odd-looking sandstone slabs, and groves of black oak and coast live oak.

From the Saratoga Gap vista point at the junction of Highways 9 and 35 (Skyline Boulevard), drive south on Highway 35 for 2.6 miles to the Castle Rock State Park dirt parking lot on the right.

Begin your hike by taking the 0.6-mile-long Castle Rock Trail. (Watch for poison oak growing abundantly on this trail and sporadically on the others.) Douglas fir, tan oak, madrone, black oak, and coast live oak furnish ample shade as you climb the initial 0.2 mile and then bear right onto an old dirt road. At 0.3 mile a cluster of giant coast live oak surrounds 45-foot-high Castle Rock, where you can explore sandstone caves.

From Castle Rock descend the obvious trail to join the Saratoga Gap Trail at 0.6 mile. Serene black oak forest accompanies you down to a creek at 0.8 mile. Hug its bank for 0.1 mile and bear left at a signed junction, staying on the Saratoga Gap Trail.

At 1.1 miles an attractive madrone canopies an observation deck ideal for viewing Castle Rock Falls, which drop about a hundred feet.

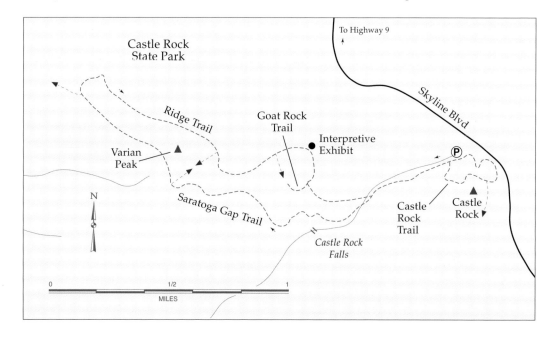

You'll also see a vertical sandstone slab, the Santa Cruz Mountains, Monterey Bay, and the distant Pacific Ocean.

The path now departs the creek and travels along a steep hillside and through chaparral. Peer past eastwood manzanita, buckbrush, chamise, and sticky monkey-flower for more distant ocean and bay views at 1.5 miles. The trail continues its gradual ascent past a few steep, rocky spots. Cross a shaded wooden bridge at 1.8 miles, and stay left 0.2 mile farther at a signed trail junction. The next 0.8 mile stays mostly level along the slope of 2,865-foot Varian Peak. Head right at the signed junction at 2.8 miles into a community of tall madrone. Reach a trail fork at 3.1 miles. Left leads 0.2 mile to Castle Rock Trail Camp (first come, first served). Bear right on the Ridge Trail and climb to a scenic vista point at 3.6 miles. The path levels to a junction at 4.4 miles; stay left.

At 4.7 miles go left at the signed trail fork, and 0.2 mile farther arrive at the interpretive exhibit. Find the signed Goat Rock Trail, and then reach the scenic overlook. From here, explore 80-foot-high Goat Rock's numerous formations; some feature interesting crevices, and others give good views of the Santa Cruz Mountains.

> Explore the recesses of Castle Rock's sandstone caves.

Return to the Ridge Trail and go right. Bear left at 5.4 miles onto the signed Saratoga Gap Trail for the final 0.4 mile back to the trailhead.

98 BUTANO STATE PARK TRAILS

Length: 6.2 miles round-trip
Hiking time: 4 hours
High point: 1,100 feet
Total elevation gain: 1,100 feet
Difficulty: strenuous up the Año Nuevo Trail, otherwise easy
Season: year-round
Water: none; bring your own
Map: USGS 7.5' Franklin Point
Information: Butano State Park

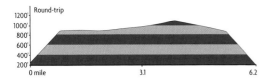

This mostly shaded excursion into whisper-quiet, old-growth redwood forests travels four different trails past a variety of plant habitats.

From Highway 1 near Pescadero Beach (15 miles south of Half Moon Bay), head east for 2 miles on Pescadero Road. Turn right onto Cloverdale Road, drive 4 miles south, and park near the kiosk after you enter the park.

After visiting the nature center and garden next to the kiosk, begin climbing steeply on the Año Nuevo Trail past lush fern gardens and Douglas fir, the latter covered with staghorn lichen. Tree shade coupled with constant

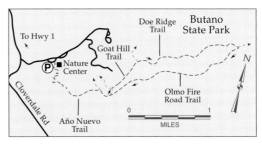

Coast live oak and buckeyes

moisture from the nearby Pacific Ocean nourishes this rich, green jungle.

The path climbs relentlessly until you reach a crest at 0.8 mile, where a bench offers great views on clear days of the vast expanse of the Pacific Ocean. The rare Douglas iris flower grows here beneath a canopy of madrone and Douglas fir.

At 1.1 miles turn right onto the Olmo Fire Road Trail, and go left 0.2 mile farther onto the Goat Hill Trail connector. Bear right 0.1 mile farther on the actual Goat Hill Trail. Travel past level, lush, and shaded scenery for 0.5 mile to the Doe Ridge Trail marker, where you bear right.

For the next 1.4 miles, travel through a huge redwood forest on the serene Doe Ridge Trail. These huge redwoods survived two fires long ago, which explains the charred trunks. Twin redwood stalks sharing a 10-foot-wide trunk catch your attention at 2.9 miles.

Bear right onto the Olmo Fire Road Trail at 3.2 miles. The next 1.8 miles stays level past coast live oak, a few redwoods, and Douglas fir. Enjoy occasional views of the Pacific Ocean when you see parting branches. Reach a crest at 5 miles and walk downhill for 0.1 mile. Turn left onto the previously encountered Año Nuevo Trail to return to the trailhead.

> Keep an eye out for the rare Douglas iris flower along the Año Nuevo Trail.

99 SILVER FALLS AND SKYLINE TO THE SEA TRAIL

Length: 10.2-mile loop
Hiking time: 6 hours or overnight
High point: 1,300 feet
Total elevation gain: 1,600 feet
Difficulty: moderate
Season: year-round
Water: bring your own
Maps: USGS 7.5' Big Basin, USGS 7.5' Franklin Point
Information: Big Basin Redwoods State Park

Walk past tall redwoods to three splendid sets of waterfalls along enchanting Berry Creek. To hike the complete Skyline to the Sea Trail to Waddell Beach, combine the first 4 miles of this hike with the last 6.3 miles of Hike 100 (Berry Creek Falls and Skyline to the Sea Trail). Backpackers must make advance reservations for trailside camping (831-338-8861).

From the interchange of Highways 9 and 236 (6 miles west of Highway 35), drive west on Highway 236 a steep 8.4 miles. From Highway 9 at the town of Boulder Creek (13 miles northeast of Santa Cruz), travel 9 miles on High-

way 236 to the Big Basin Redwoods State Park headquarters.

To start, head west from just behind the fee kiosk, follow signs for the Skyline to the Sea

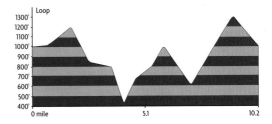

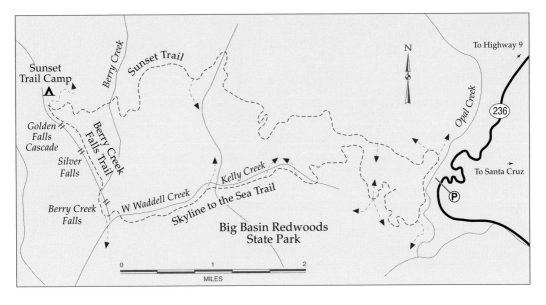

Lightning-charred redwood trunk (Photo by Dionne Soares)

Trail, and turn left at the huge signpost just after crossing a wooden bridge. Bear right at a signed trail junction at 0.2 mile, cross a fire road at 1 mile, and continue on the Skyline to the Sea Trail toward Berry Creek Falls.

> This ramble features three waterfalls: Berry Creek Falls, Silver Falls, and Golden Falls Cascade.

Tall redwoods reach skyward along a moderate descent past a signed trail junction at 1.6 miles, where you continue left. Cross Kelly Creek 0.5 mile farther, and stay left at three signed trail junctions. Reach a series of small pools at around 3 miles, near where Kelly Creek merges with West Waddell Creek.

See magnificent Berry Creek Falls from a wooden bench at 4.1 miles. The trail drops another 0.1 mile to where Berry Creek pours into West Waddell Creek. Backpackers and car-shuttle day hikers can reach Waddell Beach by turning left here (for a description of the rest of the Skyline to the Sea Trail, see Hike 100: Berry Creek Falls and Skyline to the Sea Trail). Bear right for a 0.1-mile climb to Berry Creek Falls, which plunges 70 feet into a sand-bottomed pool. The Berry Creek Falls Trail then escorts you upward for a closer view of the top of the waterfall.

At 4.6 miles reach Silver Falls, which drops 60 feet into a small, oblong pool dammed by a toppled redwood trunk. The trail climbs to a dramatic vista of Silver Falls and then gives striking views of Golden Falls Cascade, a peanut-butter-and-orange-colored series of pools and cascades that decorate the trailside for 200 yards.

After a 0.1-mile climb away from West Berry Creek, reach a signed trail junction at 5 miles, where you bear right onto the Sunset Trail (backpackers can go left 100 yards to Sunset Trail Camp). Break out of the redwood forest shade into a brief section of chaparral consisting of knobcone pine, manzanita, and chamise. You now canyon-hop twice to a signed trail marker at 7.7 miles and turn left.

Smaller redwoods appear over the final 2.5-mile leg. Bear left at the signed trail junction at 9.2 miles. The final mile travels past three signed trail junctions (take a left and two rights), and then alongside attractive Opal Creek under massive redwoods, and finally to park headquarters.

100 BERRY CREEK FALLS AND SKYLINE TO THE SEA TRAIL

Length: 16.3 miles round-trip
Hiking time: 10 hours or overnight
High point: 1,500 feet
Total elevation gain: 1,500 feet
Difficulty: strenuous up McCrary Ridge, otherwise easy
Season: year-round
Water: bring your own
Maps: USGS 7.5' Big Basin, USGS 7.5' Año Nuevo, USGS 7.5' Franklin Point
Information: Big Basin Redwoods State Park

Hike through redwood forest and native chaparral and along quiet creeks, and enjoy views of Waddell Beach, the Pacific Ocean, the Santa Cruz Mountains, and graceful Berry Creek Falls. For a complete Skyline to the Sea journey, combine the last part of this trip with the first 4 miles of Hike 99 (Silver Falls and Skyline to the Sea Trail). Backpackers must make advance reservations for trailside camping (831-338-8861).

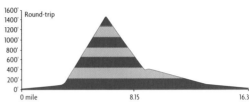

Waddell Creek's marsh

The trailhead, signed for Waddell Beach, is on the west side of Highway 1, 18 miles north of Santa Cruz and 26 miles south of Half Moon Bay.

The Skyline to the Sea Trail begins across Highway 1. Pass Waddell Creek's marsh, followed by Horse Trail Camp, and bear left at 0.3 mile. Climb through a knobcone pine and coast live oak forest, and gain a view of Waddell Beach, its marsh, and the Pacific Ocean as the trail levels at 0.6 mile. Hike past Douglas fir, alder, and redwood, and cross Waddell Creek at 1.4 miles. Reach a signed trail junction 0.1 mile farther and bear left. Backpackers can spend the night 0.2 mile farther at Twin Redwoods Trail Camp.

Over the next 1.5 miles, the riparian habitat along Waddell Creek consists of an impressive array of native trees that grow taller than usual while competing for sunlight; look for alder, bigleaf maple, buckeye, Douglas fir, redwood, and California laurel. Below the trees you'll see redwood sorrel, thimbleberry, fern, horsetail, and periwinkle.

> Follow Waddell Creek from ocean to marsh to redwood grove.

Cross a tributary of Waddell Creek at 3.2 miles. After another 100 yards, leave the Skyline to the Sea Trail and bear right onto the signed McCrary Ridge Trail. This 2.9-mile footpath initially climbs under welcome shade before entering an open area where manzanita and knobcone pine dominate.

At 6 miles the trail ends at a signed trail junction, where you bear right onto a fire road. Watch closely for a signed trail junction 0.2 mile farther and partially concealed by shrubs. Go left onto the Howard King Trail for a shaded 2.5-mile descent through a forest of madrone, California laurel, and Douglas fir.

Reach West Waddell Creek at 8.7 miles, and bear right onto the Skyline to the Sea Trail. At 9 miles turn left onto the Berry Creek Falls Trail. Magnificent Berry Creek Falls, which plunges 70 feet to a small, clear pool, awaits 0.1 mile farther. Allow time to explore the cascades and pools found all along enchanting Berry Creek. Also consider a visit to Silver Falls, only 0.4 mile farther up the trail, and to nearby Sunset Trail

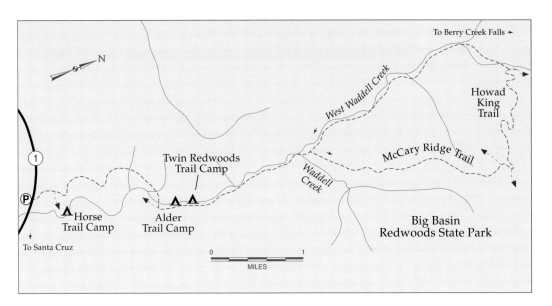

Camp (see Hike 99: Silver Falls and Skyline to the Sea Trail).

To return to Waddell Beach, backtrack to the Skyline to the Sea Trail for the final 6 miles downhill, accompanied the whole time by peacefully meandering Waddell Creek. The same flora encountered along the second and third miles of the hike decorate this scenic section of the wide dirt road. Stay on the road past three junctions.

Almanor Ranger District
Lassen National Forest
P.O. Box 767
Chester, CA 96020
530-258-2141
www.fs.fed.us/r5/lassen

Amador Ranger District
Eldorado National Forest
26820 Silver Drive
Pioneer, CA 95666
209-295-4251
www.fs.fed.us/r5/eldorado
www.fs.fed.us/r5/eldorado/recreation/wild/moke
  (for permits and other information)

Anderson Marsh State Historical Park
5300 Soda Bay Road
Kelseyville, CA 95451
707-994-0688
www.parks.ca.gov

Auburn State Recreation Area
501 El Dorado Street
Auburn, CA 95603
530-885-4527
www.parks.ca.gov

Beckwourth Ranger District
Plumas National Forest
P.O. Box 7
Blairsden, CA 96103
530-836-2575
www.fs.fed.us/r5/plumas

Big Basin Redwoods State Park
21600 Big Basin Way
Boulder Creek, CA 95006
831-338-8860; 831-338-8861
www.parks.ca.gov

Big Bend Visitor Center
Tahoe National Forest
631 Coyote Street
Nevada City, CA 95959
530-426-3609
www.fs.fed.us/r5/tahoe

Bothe–Napa Valley State Park
3801 Saint Helena Highway North
  (Highways 29/128)
Calistoga, CA 94515
707-942-4575
www.parks.ca.gov

Bureau of Land Management / King Range
  National Conservation Area Project Office
P.O. Box 189
Whitethorn, CA 95589
707-986-5400
www.ca.blm.gov/arcata/kingrange

Butano State Park
1500 Cloverdale Drive
Pescadero, CA 94060
650-879-2040
www.parks.ca.gov

Castle Crags State Park
P.O. Box 80
Castella, CA 96017
530-235-2684
www.parks.ca.gov

Castle Rock State Park
15000 Skyline Boulevard
Los Gatos, CA 95033
408-867-2952
www.parks.ca.gov

East Bay Regional Park District
2950 Peralta Oaks Court
P.O. Box 5381
Oakland, CA 94605
1-888-EBPARKS (1-888-327-2757)
www.ebparks.org

Emerald Bay State Park
P.O. Box 266
Tahoma, CA 96142
530-541-3030
www.parks.ca.gov

Feather River Ranger District
Plumas National Forest
875 Mitchell Avenue
Oroville, CA 95965
530-534-6500
www.fs.fed.us/r5/plumas

Golden Gate National Recreation Area
Fort Mason, Building 201
San Francisco, CA 94123
415-561-4700
www.nps.gov/goga

Grindstone Ranger District
Mendocino National Forest
825 North Humboldt Avenue
Willows, CA 95988
530-934-3316
www.fs.fed.us/r5/mendocino

Half Moon Bay State Beach
95 Kelly Avenue
Half Moon Bay, CA 94019
650-726-8819
www.parks.ca.gov

Happy Camp and Oak Knoll Ranger Districts
63822 Highway 96
Happy Camp, CA 96039
530-493-2243
www.fs.fed.us/r5/klamath

Hat Creek Ranger District
Lassen National Forest
P.O. Box 220
Fall River Mills, CA 96028
530-336-5521
www.fs.fed.us/r5/lassen

Henry W. Coe State Park
P.O. Box 846
Morgan Hill, CA 95038
408-779-2728
www.parks.ca.gov

Humboldt Redwoods State Park
P.O. Box 100
Weott, CA 95571
707-946-2409
www.parks.ca.gov

Joseph D. Grant County Park
18405 Mount Hamilton Road
San Jose, CA 95140
408-274-6121
www.parkhere.org
www.sccgov.org/portal/site/parks

Jug Handle State Reserve
c/o Mendocino District Headquarters
P.O. Box 440
Mendocino, CA 95460
707-937-5804
www.parks.ca.gov

Lake Tahoe Basin Management Unit
35 College Drive
South Lake Tahoe, CA 96150
530-543-2694
www.fs.fed.us/r5/ltbmu
www.fs.fed.us/r5/ltbmu/recreation/wilderness
/desowild (for permits and other information)

Lassen Volcanic National Park
P.O. Box 100
Mineral, CA 96063-0100
530-595-4444
www.nps.gov/lavo

Lava Beds National Monument
1 Indian Well Headquarters
Tulelake, CA 96134
530-667-8100
www.nps.gov/labe

McArthur–Burney Falls Memorial State Park
24898 Highway 89
Burney, CA 96013
530-335-2777
www.parks.ca.gov

McCloud Ranger Station
Shasta–Trinity National Forest
P.O. Box 1620
McCloud, CA 96057
530-964-2184
www.r5.fs.fed.us/shastatrinity

Midpeninsula Regional Open Space District
330 Distel Circle
Los Altos, CA 94022
650-691-1200
www.openspace.org

Mount Diablo State Park
96 Mitchell Canyon Road
Clayton, CA 94517
925-837-2525
www.mdia.org
www.parks.ca.gov

Mount Shasta Ranger Station
Shasta–Trinity National Forest
204 West Alma
Mount Shasta, CA 96067
530-926-4511
www.r5.fs.fed.us/shastatrinity

Mount Tamalpais State Park
801 Panoramic Highway
Mill Valley, CA 94941
415-388-2070
www.parks.ca.gov

Muir Woods National Monument
Mill Valley, CA 94941-2696
415-388-2596
www.nps.gov/muwo

Pacific Ranger District
Eldorado National Forest
7887 Highway 50
Pollock Pines, CA 95726
530-647-5415
www.fs.fed.us/r5/eldorado
www.fs.fed.us/r5/eldorado/recreation/wild/deso (for
    permits and other information)

Point Reyes National Seashore
1 Bear Valley Road
Point Reyes, CA 94956
415-464-5100
www.nps.gov/pore

Prairie Creek Redwoods State Park
127011 Newton B. Drury Parkway
Prairie Creek Redwoods State Park
Orick, CA 95555
707-465-7354
www.nps.gov/redw
www.parks.ca.gov

Redwood National and State Parks, Crescent
    City Information Center
1111 2nd Street
Crescent City, CA 95531
707-464-6101
www.nps.gov/redw

Redwood National and State Parks,
    Thomas H. Kuchel Visitor Center
119441 South Highway 101
Orick, CA 95555
707-465-7765
www.nps.gov/redw

Richardson Grove State Park
1600 U.S. Highway 101
Garberville, CA 95542
707-247-3318
www.parks.ca.gov

Salmon/Scott River Ranger District
Klamath National Forest
11263 North Highway 3
Fort Jones, CA 96032
530-468-5351
www.fs.fed.us/r5/klamath

Sinkyone Wilderness State Park
P.O. Box 245
Whitethorn, CA 95589
707-986-7711
www.parks.ca.gov

Sugarloaf Ridge State Park
2605 Adobe Canyon Road
Kenwood, CA 95452
707-833-5712
www.parks.ca.gov

Tahoe National Forest
631 Coyote Street
Nevada City, CA 95959
530-265-4531
www.fs.fed.us/r5/tahoe

Van Damme State Park
c/o Mendocino District Headquarters
P.O. Box 440
Mendocino, CA 95460
707-937-5804
www.parks.ca.gov

Warner Mountain Ranger District
Modoc National Forest
P.O. Box 220
Cedarville, CA 96104
530-279-6116
www.fs.fed.us/r5/modoc

Weaverville Ranger District
Shasta–Trinity National Forest
360 Main Street
P.O. Box 1190
Weaverville, CA 96093
530-623-2121
www.fs.fed.us/r5/shastatrinity

Whiskeytown–Shasta–Trinity National
   Recreation Area
Whiskeytown Unit
P.O. Box 188
14412 Kennedy Memorial Drive (at Highway
   299)
Whiskeytown, CA 96095
530-246-1225
www.nps.gov/whis

Yolla Bolly Ranger District
Shasta–Trinity National Forest
HC01, Box 400
2555 State Highway 36
Platina, CA 96076
530-352-4211
www.fs.fed.us/r5/shastatrinity

Yuba River Ranger District
Tahoe National Forest
15924 Highway 49
Camptonville, CA 95922
530-288-3231
www.fs.fed.us/r5/tahoe

APPENDIX 2: FURTHER READING

Audubon Society Field Guides and *Peterson Field Guides.* (In-depth coverage of plants, animals, and geology)

Bakker, Elna. *An Island Called California: An Ecological Introduction,* 2nd ed. Berkeley: University of California Press, 1985.

Hyndman, Donald W., and David D. Alt. *Roadside Geology of Northern & Central California.* Missoula: Mountain Press, 2000.

Norris, Robert M., and Robert W. Webb. *Geology of California,* 2nd ed. New York: Wiley & Sons, 1990.

San Diego Chapter of the Sierra Club. Jerry Schad and David S. Moser, eds. *Wilderness Basics: The Complete Handbook for Hikers & Backpackers,* 3rd ed. Seattle: The Mountaineers Books, 2004.

Soares, John R. *75 Hikes in California's Mount Shasta and Lassen Volcanic National Park Regions,* rev. ed. Seattle: The Mountaineers Books, 2006.

Stienstra, Tom. *California Camping.* Emeryville, CA: Moon/Avalon Travel Publishing, 2007.

Storer, Tracy I., Robert L. Usinger, and David Lukas. *Sierra Nevada Natural History,* 2nd ed. Berkeley: University of California Press, 2004.

Whitney, Stephen. *A Sierra Club Naturalist's Guide to the Sierra Nevada.* San Francisco: Sierra Club Books, 1982.

APPENDIX 3: WHAT TO TAKE

DAYHIKE ESSENTIALS

day pack
first-aid kit
matches
firestarter (for wet wood)
knife (for kindling)
flashlight, extra bulb, batteries
toilet paper
maps
compass
watch
food
water, water purifier
poncho or space blanket
emergency signaling device
wide-brimmed hat
sunglasses, sunblock
wool cap
extra clothing
adequate footwear

OPTIONAL ITEMS

insect repellent
camera
binoculars
GPS equipment
swimsuit

ADDITIONAL EQUIPMENT FOR OVERNIGHT TRIPS

backpack, waterproof cover
sleeping bag
nylon or plastic ground sheet
air mattress or foam pad
tent
warm jacket or parka
sweater
rain gear
thermal underwear
extra clothing, hiking shorts
gloves
cooking, dishwashing utensils
stove and fuel
small towel
toothbrush
lip protectant
40-foot rope
watch
reading material

INDEX

ABOUT THE AUTHORS

John R. Soares is a writer living in Siskiyou County in far Northern California. He is the author of *75 Hikes in California's Mount Shasta and Lassen Volcanic National Park Regions* (The Mountaineers Books) and numerous newspaper and magazine articles. Visit his websites at *www.gojohnsoares.com* and *www.soaresoutdoors.com*.

Marc J. Soares is a landscape consultant and teaches plant and yoga classes for Shasta College Community Education. He is a professional outdoor photographer and naturalist who writes columns for the *Redding Record Searchlight* newspaper. He also plays guitar and sings in a local jazz band. He has written several hiking guidebooks, including *75 Year-Round Hikes in Northern California* (The Mountaineers Books) and *100 Hikes in Yosemite National Park* (The Mountaineers Books).

THE MOUNTAINEERS, founded in 1906, is a nonprofit outdoor activity and conservation club, whose mission is "to explore, study, preserve, and enjoy the natural beauty of the outdoors…." Based in Seattle, Washington, the club is now the third-largest such organization in the United States, with seven branches throughout Washington State.

The Mountaineers sponsors both classes and year-round outdoor activities in the Pacific Northwest, which include hiking, mountain climbing, ski-touring, snowshoeing, bicycling, camping, kayaking, nature study, sailing, and adventure travel. The club's conservation division supports environmental causes through educational activities, sponsoring legislation, and presenting informational programs.

All club activities are led by skilled, experienced instructors, who are dedicated to promoting safe and responsible enjoyment and preservation of the outdoors.

If you would like to participate in these organized outdoor activities or the club's programs, consider a membership in The Mountaineers. For information and an application, write or call The Mountaineers, Club Headquarters, 300 Third Avenue West, Seattle, WA 98119; 206-284-6310. You can also visit the club's website at www.mountaineers.org or contact The Mountaineers via email at clubmail@mountaineers.org.

The Mountaineers Books, an active, nonprofit publishing program of the club, produces guidebooks, instructional texts, historical works, natural history guides, and works on environmental conservation. All books produced by The Mountaineers Books fulfill the club's mission.

Send or call for our catalog of more than 500 outdoor titles:

The Mountaineers Books
1001 SW Klickitat Way, Suite 201
Seattle, WA 98134
800-553-4453
mbooks@mountaineersbooks.org
www.mountaineersbooks.org

The Mountaineers Books is proud to be a corporate sponsor of The Leave No Trace Center for Outdoor Ethics, whose mission is to promote and inspire responsible outdoor recreation through education, research, and partnerships. The Leave No Trace program is focused specifically on human-powered (nonmotorized) recreation.

Leave No Trace strives to educate visitors about the nature of their recreational impacts, as well as offer techniques to prevent and minimize such impacts. Leave No Trace is best understood as an educational and ethical program, not as a set of rules and regulations.

For more information, visit *www.LNT.org*, or call 800-332-4100.

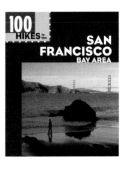
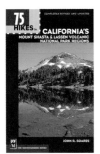
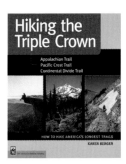

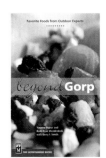